GREAT QUESTIONS IN POLITICS SERIES

The Politics of Bad Ideas

The Great Tax Cut Delusion and the Decline of Good Government in America

BRYAN D. JONES
WALTER WILLIAMS

CENTER FOR AMERICAN POLITICS AND PUBLIC POLICY
UNIVERSITY OF WASHINGTON

GEORGE C. EDWARDS III, SERIES EDITOR
TEXAS A&M UNIVERSITY

New York   San Francisco   Boston
London   Toronto   Sydney   Tokyo   Singapore   Madrid
Mexico City   Munich   Paris   Cape Town   Hong Kong   Montreal

Editor-in-Chief:	Eric Stano
Executive Marketing Manager:	Ann Stypuloski
Production Manager:	Donna DeBenedictis
Project Coordination, Text Design, and Electronic Page Makeup:	Pre-Press PMG
Cover Design Manager:	John Callahan
Cover Designer:	Kay Petronio
Cover Images, Front:	Courtesy of iStockphoto, photographer: LiseGagne
Cover Images, Back:	Courtesy of iStockphoto, photographer: Kativ
Manufacturing Manager:	Mary Fischer
Printer and Binder:	R.R. Donnelley & Sons Company/Harrisonburg
Cover Printer:	Coral Graphic Services, Inc.

Library of Congress Cataloging-in-Publication Data

Jones, Bryan D.

  The politics of bad ideas : the great tax cut delusion and the decline of good government in America / Bryan D. Jones, Walter Williams.

     p. cm.

Includes bibliographical references and index.

  ISBN-10: 0-205-60079-4 (alk. paper)

  ISBN-13: 978-0-205-60079-3 (alk. paper)

  1. Fiscal policy--United States. 2. Taxation--United States. 3. Budget deficits--United States. I. Williams, Walter. II. Title.

  HJ257.3.J66 2008

  336.73--dc22

                                                                      2007031281

Copyright © 2008 by Pearson Education, Inc.

Please visit us at www.ablongman.com

ISBN-13: 978-0-205-60079-3

ISBN-10: 0-205-60079-4

1 2 3 4 5 6 7 8 9 10—DOH—10 09 08 07

Contents

Preface

This book is the result of collaboration between a political scientist (Jones) and an economist turned policy analyst (Williams). Williams' academic education was in economics, and he has been a practicing policy analyst and researcher in the conduct of policy analysis throughout most of his career. The book is an exercise in political economy, because we explore the tight connections between politics and economic ideas. In particular, we examine the interactions between the rise of wrongheaded economic ideas, the decline of policy analysis, and the deterioration of the quality of governance in the United States.

The idea that governments can cut taxes without adjusting future spending and not harm government finance, claimed by some to be justified by certain economic theories, is quite simply claptrap. Indeed, much of what is alleged to be economic theory as currently applied in the "great American tax cut delusion" is not that at all. As we shall see in this book, the assertions made on behalf of "supply-side" economics are really ideology masquerading as serious theory. Supply-side economics does make an important academic contribution, but the so-called supply-side tax policies pushed by political conservatives and put in practice by

Republican presidents and congressional representatives of both parties have discredited the notion as a policy prescription. The policies have not worked as advertised.

Sometimes the claims made by conservative activists and some economists, including two Nobelists, are actually about voters and the incentives of politicians. There is a whole field, generally ignored by the proponents of tax cut theories, that is directed at studying voters and politicians. It is called political science, and it does not support the "starve the beast" theory that has also been popular with conservatives.

Nevertheless, these ideas display an amazing resilience in American politics. No matter how many times they are discredited by analysts or fail to produce in practice, they are resurrected and perform as expected by failing. It is exactly that resilience that we examine in this book.

We appreciate astute comments on various parts of this book from Neil Bruce, Mark Smith, and George Edwards. We are especially indebted to Robert Greenstein, Executive Director of the Center on Budget and Policy Priorities, and members of the center staff for their comments on our use of economic and budget data. Sue Headlee of American University gave the manuscript a very thorough examination, and we benefited greatly from her comments. We also were aided by several other reviewers of the full manuscript for Longman: Bruce Bikle, California State University; Kimberly Johnson, Barnard College; Brian Levey, University of Georgia; and Diane Lowenthal, American University. We alone, of course, are responsible for the results.

BRYAN D. JONES

WALTER WILLIAMS

CHAPTER I

The Politics of Bad Ideas

John Maynard Keynes famously noted that human affairs are more influenced by economic and political ideas than we often realize. Less often noted is that Keynes also opined that these ideas did not have to be correct to be important. Bad ideas can often be as influential in human affairs as good ones.

"The ideas of economists and political philosophers, *both when they are right and when they are wrong,* are more powerful than is commonly understood. Indeed the world is ruled by little else. Practical men, who believe themselves to be quite exempt from any intellectual influence, are usually the slaves of some defunct economist." [Italics added][1]

In this book, we address a serious puzzle: Why over the last quarter century have bad economic ideas become so influential in shaping government policies, and why have they survived so long despite overwhelming evidence that they don't work? Indeed,

[1]John M. Keynes, *The General Theory of Employment, Interest, and Money.* Cambridge: MacMillian Cambridge University Press, 1936.

these wrongheaded notions actually cause serious damage to the federal government's long-term fiscal stability and make it harder for the broad American middle class to maintain its standard of living. Isn't free expression in a democracy supposed to act as a marketplace of ideas, selecting the good ones and eliminating the bad ones? In his dissenting opinion in *Abrams v. United States*, a 1919 case in which the Supreme Court upheld the convictions of five German sympathizers who had published pamphlets critical of the United States during the First World War, Justice Oliver Wendell Holmes first articulated the principle of competition among ideas and their democratic and constitutional basis. He wrote that "the ultimate good desired is better reached by free trade in ideas—that the best test of truth is the power of the thought to get itself accepted in the competition of the market and that truth is the only ground upon which their wishes safely can be carried out. That at any rate is the theory of our Constitution."[2]

Was Justice Holmes wrong? When bad ideas are put into practice in government policy, aren't voters supposed to "throw out the rascals," punishing them for the bad ideas they have implemented? Perhaps the 2006 midterm elections did just that, but there is no evidence that the reason for the Republican losses was their fiscal policies. In any case, these ideas have dominated our thinking about government fiscal policy for a quarter of a century and have already taken their toll. Surely the inefficiency of the alleged "marketplace of ideas" is worth a serious look.

We intend this book to contribute to a general discussion of the issue of the persistence of bad ideas in the face of contradictory

---

[2]*Abrams v. United States*, 230 U.S. 616, 1919.

information. Political scientists in recent years have examined how new ideas and policy proposals come to be taken seriously by policy makers and subsequently are enacted into law, and they have studied the resilience of the beneficiaries of government policies in the face of change.[3] But ours is the first study of the resilience of ideas (as opposed to entrenched political interests) in the face of contrary information. Moreover, we will show the extent to which these resilient bad ideas have contributed directly to a deterioration of our governing institutions as well as our country's future economic well-being. There is a serious practical side to our arguments.

Our specific focus is American fiscal policy since the Second World War. Fiscal policy is intimately interconnected with the well-being of Americans. As a consequence, the state of the economy is one area where electoral stakes are high. Politicians have motive to run productive economies, but they also may be tempted to offer more in tax cuts or government benefits than good economic policy may dictate. This can lead to short-term benefits for the politician, but even in the medium-run it causes the nation difficulty.

In modern American politics, economic theories—some generated by respectable economists, some ginned up by partisan ideologues—have offered "cover" for politicians to do exactly that. In a well-functioning democracy, these theories would be winnowed, and if they were put into practice, they would be eliminated when it became clear that they did not work. In today's

[3]John Kingdon, *Agendas, Alternatives, and Public Policy*, 2nd ed., Boston: Little, Brown 1995; Frank Baumgartner and Bryan Jones, *Agendas and Instability in American Politics*. Chicago: University of Chicago Press, 1993; Bryan Jones and Frank Baumgartner, *The Politics of Attention*. Chicago: University of Chicago Press, 2005.

America, these ideas have become stuck in the public discourse, with politicians repeatedly going back to discredited notions to justify poor fiscal policies.

We argue that bad ideas from a confluence of three separate streams that have produced a torrent of bad public policies. The three sources are bad ideas about economics, bad ideas about the use of information in public policy development, and bad ideas about government and the operation of American institutions. The bad economics that ought to have been eliminated long ago is sustained through the poor use of available information and the partisan operation of our governing institutions.

The three sources are mutually reinforcing. The polarized tenor of our public debate caused our governing institutions, designed to foster a tension between the legislature and executive, to operate more like a parliamentary system. In the period 2001–2007, the Republican governing political party in Congress passively followed the lead of the Republican president. Though divided government has replaced unified Republican rule, the partisan rancor endures. This partisanship is buttressed by a flawed theory of public administration, called "responsive competence," that encourages politicians to interfere with information processing and policy analysis. The president and his legislative party continued to use economic theories that clearly did not comport with the facts to justify their preferred policies, ignoring information provided by analysts. Executive agency directors supervising budget and economic analysts, particularly the director of the Office of Management and Budget and the secretary of the Treasury, ignored the solid analysis coming from their agencies and reiterated the economic party line.

All three sources of bad ideas are intertwined, and in this book we will try to take apart the system both to understand how it operates and to be able to propose better policies. We start at the weakest point, the bad economic ideas, and use this as leverage to examine first the breakdown of sound information-processing in national policy analysis and then the very institutional structure itself.

POLICIES AND FACTS

The disconnect between policies and facts in American fiscal policy is particularly perplexing during this time of great technological gains in the development and dissemination of information. It is clearly possible to bring this power to bear on the analytical capacities of government. Businesses have used the computer revolution to strengthen their organizational structures and their capacities to develop policies and manage operations. These organizational improvements helped restore the nation's techno-logical capacity and return the United States to a high level of economic productivity.

At first, government proceeded along a parallel path to the private sector. After World War II, Republican and Democratic presidents, from Truman to Carter, sought to establish structures that provided sound information and reasoned analysis as a base for their decision making. There were variations in both effort and capability, but all of these presidents sought to be well-informed about the world they faced before making critical decisions.

Since then, however, Presidents Ronald Reagan and George W. Bush shunned this greatly increased information capability, often adopting fiscal policies based on ideology or intuition rather than analysis. Both adopted, in one manifestation or another, the doctrines of "supply-side economics" and "starve-the-beast." Both promised that reductions in the highest income tax rates would increase capital investment sufficiently to bring permanent improvement in the economy and that the tax cuts would materially reduce the size of the federal government. Both continued to follow those ideas in the face of compelling contradictory evidence.

Though we will examine the results of pursuing these flawed policies in detail presently, their deleterious outcomes are obvious for all to see. With the large Bush tax cuts of 2001 and 2003, the federal budget went from a surplus at the end of the Clinton presidency to large deficits that have continued throughout the recovery from the mild recession of 2001. The cuts, which were supposed to spur business investment and jobs creation, have not produced their desired aims, but they have been responsible for the deterioration in the federal government's fiscal situation.

Economists comparing average rates of change for key economic variables during the Bush recovery with the average rates for all of the earlier comparable business-cycle periods occurring during the postwar years found that the economy did reasonably well on growth in the Gross Domestic Product (GDP) and very well on productivity gains. But it fell much below the average on private domestic investment, wages and salaries, and employment. Unlike earlier recoveries from recessions, real median family income failed to grow from the end of the recession in 2001 through 2005. Only the growth rate for corporate profits showed an appreciably stronger increase in the Bush recovery. Real household income showed striking increases only among the top earners, who received income from stocks, bonuses, and "passive" sources in addition to wages.[4]

In this book, we will try to explain both why the bad economic ideas won out when the concepts behind them often were neither logical nor reasonable and why the policies were impervious to hard evidence clearly indicating that the ideas had failed. We will show that bad economic ideas were aided and abetted by bad political ideas that yielded misgovernment and by bad information that the political leaders and their key advisors used to sell the policies and to defend them in defiance of reality. Indeed, the bad economic ideas that flourished in the Bush administration could not be sustained without equally bad ideas about governing that undermine the ability of policy makers to process information and engage in reasoned deliberations.

BAD ECONOMIC IDEAS

We will devote our primary attention to two notions drawn from economic theory that have been used repeatedly to justify cutting taxes: supply-side economics and "starving the beast." These ideas, in one form or another, have become an essential part of Republican Party ideology.

One of the problems of judging these theories is that their proponents continually alter their claims, yet the essential argument is the same: income tax cuts are good for improving economic growth and good for limiting the size of government. We'll focus on

---

[4]Issac Shapiro, Richard Kogan, and Aviva Aron-Dine. "How Does This Recovery Measure Up?" Center on Budget and Policy Priorities, revised April 10, 2006, 2–4.

two different versions of the supply-side thesis that justify tax cuts—the miracle and academic. The basic claim for both of them is that income tax cuts for those in the top brackets will stimulate capital investment enough to greatly increase the level of economic growth.

Proponents of starve-the-beast also call for tax reductions but then argue that the ensuing budget deficits will bring a public outcry that forces Congress to cut federal expenditures. Once the beast (that is, the federal government) has been starved, it will shrink. A smaller national government continues to be a primary objective of the tax cutters under both concepts. That Washington has grown and grown throughout the Bush administration—two huge tax cuts notwithstanding—has not stopped the call for more of the same.

Supply-Side Doctrines

One version of supply-side economics, the "miracle" variety, began life as a bad economic idea while the academic version had credibility with mainstream economists. The "miracle" version that shaped President Ronald Reagan's 1981 tax policy claimed that tax cuts targeting the nation's highest-income citizens will induce so much new capital investment and increased profit that the rise in tax receipts will quickly recover the full cost of the tax cut. No accepted economic concepts nor common sense nor any hard evidence supported this pie-in-the-sky notion that offered a free lunch in bringing lower taxes but no actual program reductions. But as Haynes Johnson observed, "Cut taxes, [the proponents] proclaimed, and miracles would occur. By his [President Reagan's] inauguration day their supply-side doctrine had assumed dimensions of a new economic religion."[5]

The academic version of supply-side economics appealed to many economic theorists because it supplemented the Keynesian approach to economic management, which focused exclusively on short-term demand. In the Keynesian approach, government programs and tax cuts are best targeted toward those with low incomes, who would spend most of them and hence stimulate aggregate demand for goods and services. Academic supply siders argued that there would be greater gain over time for everyone if taxes were cut for those with the highest taxable incomes. Upper income citizens would save their tax benefits and invest them to increase the long-run supply of capital investment. The increased capital investment would cause the economy to grow sufficiently to take the nation to a permanent higher standard of living. Academic supply siders also advocated reducing taxes on investment income, such as that from dividends and capital gains, and ultimately not taxing this income at all. This would make the return on capital more attractive, thereby inducing even greater investment in these productive assets.

The academic version, when put in practice in the 2001/2003 Bush tax cuts, did not produce economic growth that would justify their harmful effects on the federal fiscal situation. The 2001 income tax cut produced massive budget deficits while saving and capital investment declined. Even with the targeting on investment income in a second tax cut program in 2003, the desired changes did not appear. Indeed, aggregate savings plummeted below zero

---

[5]Haynes Johnson, *Sleepwalking Through History*. New York: Norton, 1991, p. 98.

for the first time since the Great Depression, and the proportion of
top income earners who reported saving at least some of their
incomes actually declined between 2001 and 2004.[6]

For a number of technical reasons (centering basically on
whether offsetting factors have undermined the effects of the cuts
and how long it takes for an economy to reach equilibrium), we
cannot say conclusively that the academic version has failed.
Economists can be left to sort out to their satisfaction whether the
academic model had a fair test. This is all academic, if you will. It is
foolhardy for policy makers to continue to do the same thing when
the results to date imply long-run problems for the nation's
economic future. Even if tax cuts operate over the long run (say, 10
to 15 years) to increase savings and investment, the deteriorating
public finances brought about primarily by the tax cuts harm
the economy in the short run. To take one important instance,
according to a recent report from the World Economic Forum, the
deterioration of the United States' public finances has begun to
damage U.S. competitiveness.[7]

Over time the politics surrounding supply-side economics—
morphed into a mantra that justified tax cuts at all costs. This
process started with President Reagan's belief, at the outset of his
administration, that tax rates were too high and had to be cut.
Belief became policy in the first year of his presidency as he pushed

---

[6]Brian K. Bucks, Arthur B. Kinnnickell, and Kevin B. Moore. *Recent Changes in US Family Finances:
Results from the 2001 and 2004 Survey of Consumer Finances.* Washington DC: Board of Governors of
the Federal Reserve System, 2006.
[7]The World Economic Forum, a business research institute in Switzerland, downgraded the competitiveness
of the U.S. economy in its 2006 report because of the poor management of public finances. The United
States experienced the most dramatic drop in rankings of all nations. See World Economic Forum. *Global
Competitiveness Report 2006–2007.* Davos, Switzerland, 2006.

through the largest tax cut in history (slightly larger than Bush's 2001 cut as a percentage of gross domestic product). His success cast in stone President Reagan's image as the foremost opponent of tax increases. The reality was that his administration actually raised taxes several times in his two terms, but the image prevailed.

By the presidency of George W. Bush, conservative Republicans loathed tax increases and fully embraced the view that taxes should never be raised. Neither the soaring costs of war nor the deteriorating fiscal condition of the nation could shake their commitment to tax reductions. Nobel laureate Milton Friedman wrote in a January 2003 *Wall Street Journal* column: "I never met a tax cut I didn't like, and I like President Bush's a lot."[8] Dear to the hearts of true believers in supply-side economics, the most likeable tax cuts both reduced the highest tax rates and provided special benefits to income derived from capital as opposed to that derived from employment. Again, Reagan's image prevailed while his real views were ignored—he actually felt that all income regardless of the sources from which it was derived should be taxed at the same rate. The Tax Reform Act of 1986 (known as Reagan's second tax cut) subjected ordinary income and capital gains to the same tax rate.

In effect, the supply-side doctrine was being used to shift the overall federal tax structure from a moderately progressive system that tended to redistribute income from the wealthy to the less well-off toward one that increasingly benefits the top of the income distribution at the expense of the working and middle

---

[8]Milton Friedman, "The Greedy Hand: What Every American Wants," *Wall Street Journal*, January 19, 2003.

classes. Traditionally, the income tax system included a set of marginal rates—that is, rates on the "next dollar earned"—that increase as income increases. As a separate program, the Social Security system is funded by a payroll tax that is quite regressive, because it charges one rate for wages and salaries below roughly $100,000, and nothing for income above that level. Passive income from stocks, bonds, and real estate, which mainly accrue to the well-off, are not taxed in the Social Security system. So the income tax system was progressive while the payroll tax was regressive.

Reagan and GW Bush both made the system much less progressive. Under Reagan, in 1981 and 1986, top marginal tax rates were lowered, and in 1986 the rate on the lowest category of income was raised (the only time in the history of the income tax that this occurred). In 1983, payroll taxes were increased to fund Social Security, which was headed at the time toward insolvency. Both Presidents GHW Bush and Clinton acted with Congress to raise taxes on the wealthy, but the GW Bush tax cuts heavily favored the wealthy by cutting the top tax rates and treating income earned from capital more favorably than income earned from wages and salaries.

Supply-side economics became the all-purpose justification for tax cuts among conservative Republicans. A critical component of the modern program, and one that will dominate discussions about the state of federal government finances in the next several years, is a result of the "sunset provision" in the 2001 tax cut. The entire legislation was written to expire in 2010 to disguise the full expected costs of the measure and to gain support from Democrats and fiscally conservative Republicans in Congress. Sunsetting occurs when legislation has a specific end date. For example, a special tax increase in 2000 to pay for an extraordinary expense that year might end in 2005, thereby eliminating the special tax. This would be entirely appropriate in that the extraordinary costs would have been paid for by that time.

The administration discovered that the estimated costs of the 2001 tax legislation were so large that they could torpedo the legislation. President Bush supported the sunsetting provision but later demanded an extension of the cuts, claiming that to do otherwise would "raise taxes." This disingenuous argument conceals the reality that the decision to extend a tax cut that has expired is actually a new tax cut.

Often today the term "supply-side" is employed to defend further tax cuts by using whatever argument is immediately at hand. Tax reductions have become disembodied from the theories that justified them in the first place. They are justified on the grounds that they provided short-run stimulation to the economy (which they did, but much less efficiently than the classic bottom-loaded Keynesian cuts), or on the claim that the economy will get worse otherwise, or that they would "pay for themselves," or that legislatively sunsetting tax cut provisions actually raised taxes. Tax reductions have become an essential component of conservative and Republican thought, trumping any serious notion of what effects they have in the real world of public finance. The conservative Republicans' tax mantra is simple: "All tax cuts are good; all tax increases are bad. The ideal form of income tax cuts would reduce the top tax rates overall and totally eliminate taxes on income from capital. Any provision to eliminate a tax cut on a future date (a sunset provision) is a tax increase and hence dangerous."

The miracle version of supply-side economics and starving the beast are pristine examples of bad economic ideas doomed to fail from the get-go. In contrast, the academic thesis, as noted, has credibility among mainstream economists. We defer discussion of this version until Chapter 7, concentrating only on the miracle version in the remainder of this chapter.

Starving-the-Beast

Starving-the-beast, like the miracle supply-side thesis, lacked solid data for the main arguments, yet it too took on religious dimensions. The proponents predicted that an invariable sequence of events would occur. First, big tax reductions—this time without the miracle—would create a large deficit. There was no claim that the tax reductions would pay for themselves.[9] Second, the public would be furious that Congress had put the nation deep in the red and would demand that there be budget cuts sufficient to offset the deficit. Third, fearing that they might be voted out of office, the politicians would move quickly to slash the budget.

Starving-the-beast merges the standard economic notion that tax cuts bring budget deficits with an economist's conception of how the public reacts to deficits and how members of Congress respond to the public's anger. This is not economics. It is a theory of how voters behave. It is political science and very bad political science indeed. There is neither theory nor evidence in political science to support the idea that citizens will revolt over deficit financing of services they are receiving, nor is there evidence that

---

[9]Many proponents of starve-the-beast thought that tax cuts would have positive economic benefits but would not stimulate enough growth to offset their cost.

Congress will respond to any generalized public unhappiness over deficits. The idea survived because it promised the lower taxes and a smaller government that the conservative Republicans so desired.

BAD IDEAS ABOUT GOVERNANCE

Bad ideas and bad information are two of the three components of our study of economic tragedy. Bad economics had been supported by bad information about the effects of tax cuts that the Bush administration continued to champion. But why have seemingly objective government officials, protected by civil service, been so quiet in the face of such untruths? Or have they? To understand this, we need to appreciate the third bad idea in our trilogy—bad political ideas on governance.

Students of public administration depict two fundamentally different governance approaches to federal decision making. The older notion, called *neutral competence,* emphasizes the desirability of a nonpartisan, incorruptible government bureaucracy, selected on the basis of merit and not political considerations.[10] It holds that sound policy data and reasoned analyses are necessary components in the policy making process, and that career civil servant analysts have a duty to present such evidence to their political masters, including the president. Civil service provisions would protect these civil servants against the political retributions of elected politicians.

---

[10]Herbert A. Kaufman, "Emerging Conflicts in the Doctrines of Public Administration," *American Political Science Review*, 50 (4), Dec. 1956, pp. 1057–1073.

The alternate idea, termed *responsive competence,* emphasizes that the federal bureaucracy should be responsive to the president's policy predilections.[11] Responsive competence also stresses strong White House control over agency political executives and all career civil servants, and basically condones punishing civil servants who do not comply with the political demands of the chief executive and his political appointees. It extends to the requirement that policy analysts either tailor their analyses to aid in the accomplishment of these policies, or be excluded from the decision-making process.

The modern notion of responsive competence includes both strong executive leadership and electoral accountability. Proponents argue that responsive competence is required because otherwise the president cannot be held accountable for his actions in subsequent elections, and, moreover, neutral competence can lead to insular public agencies that actually block the policy actions of elected leaders. The bureaucracy comes to operate in its interest rather than the interests of citizens, and elected leaders are powerless to break the stranglehold of the all-powerful bureaucracy. Indeed, in the GW Bush presidency under the intellectual leadership of Vice President Dick Cheney, the idea that presidents are basically unconstrained in their policy actions (at least in foreign affairs) and are accountable only through elections has emerged—a very strong form of responsive competence known as the unitary executive theory.

Clearly both neutral competence and responsive competence have value. But what if the ideas pursued by elected leaders are

---

[11]Terry M. Moe, "The Politicized Presidency," in John E. Chubb and Paul E. Peterson (eds.) *The New Direction in American Politics.* Washington: Brookings Institution, 1985, p. 239.

factually wrong? Even in that case, responsive competence rejects the notion of rigorous neutral policy analysis and requires that the analysis provided meets a president's ideological and political needs.

At the start of his presidency, President Bush was a resolute supply sider; he commented in the summer of 2003 that "The best way to get more revenues in the Treasury is not to raise taxes, slowing down the economy; it's to cut taxes to create more economic growth."[12] But surely the failure of his tax cuts to offset the huge deficits of the first six years of his presidency would chastise his naiveté. Amazingly enough, in the rollout of his 2007 fiscal year budget, President Bush explicitly returned to the old miracle supply side theory: "Tax relief not only has helped our economy, but it's helped the federal budget... You cut taxes and the tax revenues increase."[13] However, the president's own budget analysts in the Office of Management and Budget, in the budget he had just signed, had assumed that tax cuts lead to revenue losses.[14]

Responsive competence provides presidents the institutional means to continue bad policy ideas without the spotlight of sound information and analysis that show the need for correction or elimination. The projections of the Office of Management and Budget (OMB) tax specialists were simply ignored, while OMB's director made the same supply side argument as the president.

---

[12]Jeffrey Frankel, "Ten Defenses for Irresponsible Tax Cuts, and Why They Are Wrong," presented at a panel on budget deficits and the American economy, April 30, 2004.
[13]The White House, "President Discusses 2007 Budget and Deficit Reduction in New Hampshire." The White House, February 8, 2006.
[14]Now one might view this as sleight of hand. Tax cuts always have a simulative effect during part of the business cycle, and this will yield revenue increases. However, these increases overall will be far less than the revenue lost through the cuts. The juxtaposition of the words, however, indicates that the president was being deceptive, or that he was unaware of the analysis on the topic.

Similarly the secretary of the Treasury was making speeches lauding the administration's tax cut program, again in contradiction to analysts in his own department. This is responsive competence at its worst.

The availability of the institutional means to pursue bad ideas that do not comport with sound analysis does not account for their resilience. These ideas continue to guide public policy in a democracy where open debate, at least historically, has been praised and practiced. Neither miracle supply side nor starving-the-beast has any support in the general body of economic theory or in practice. Even though it is easy to show these ideas are wrong, they have great staying power. The touted self-correcting mechanisms in the marketplace of ideas have failed, or at least have been so sluggish that great damage to the nation's fiscal health is occurring. Why these bad economic ideas continue to be so important in today's policy debate goes to the heart of the workings of American democracy.

Federal Decision Making

The United States is in an era in which responsive competence trumps neutral competence. It has not always been thus. We can divide federal government decision making in the six decades after 1945 into two fundamental periods: the analytic revolution that ended with the coming of the Reagan administration and the quarter century that followed, where the mind-set of the "anti-analytic presidency" dominated. Three Republican and four Democratic presidents from Harry Truman through Jimmy Carter all used a reality-based institutional system to provide policy data and analysis to facilitate internal decision making.

On the other hand, Ronald Reagan and George W. Bush embraced an ideologically driven structure in which hard evidence could be rejected when it conflicted with those presidents' worldviews. GHW Bush and Bill Clinton worked with Congress to reestablish a realistic fiscal policy regimen, but Reagan's beliefs dominated political thinking during the period and provided the launching pad for George W. Bush's ideologically driven presidency.

Neutral competence was the pivotal administrative concept of the analytic revolution in the federal government. It embodied the commitment of budget and policy analysts serving presidents and executive branch agency heads to provide sound policy information and analyses without political spin. Given the same circumstances, the same analysis would be produced whether the decision maker was a Republican or a Democrat, a liberal or a conservative. But policy analysts are staff to political leaders. They can fulfill their responsibilities to their political bosses by providing sound data and their implications for the policies under consideration. After that, the decision makers could ignore the analysts' input or use it, but at least sound analysis was available.

The ascendancy of the norm of responsive competence in the federal government is undermining the hard-won governmental capacity to make decisions grounded in sound data and reasoned analysis. Without a reality-based decision-making structure, inept presidential governance is inevitable. Without a reality-based decision-making structure, bad economic theories and other ideologically driven notions are apt to yield flawed choices and failed policies.

POLICY ANALYSIS AND THE ROLE
OF INSTITUTIONS

The miracle version of supply-side economics and starve-the-beast have little or no basis in economics even though they use economic terminology. They are better classified as political ideology, and they involve the actions of politicians and voters. In the coming chapters, we will show in detail that these theories do not work as advertised. But we do not stop with debunking poor ideas. We also put forward a better way, one that emphasizes practical politics and government rather than pie-in-the-sky theorizing. In particular, we rely on the disciplines of policy analysis and political science to illuminate the weaknesses of the theories. Policy analysis is about providing information that enables the evaluation of the successes or failures of government programs. One reason that wrong-headed theories about economic policies have been so pervasive in the modern American political debate is that political leaders have dismissed, again and again, the hard and honest numbers provided by policy analysts, economists, and budget analysts in a number of policy areas.[15]

Modern political science is concerned not just with the sweep of political movements and the choices of voters. It is also about the arrangement of governing institutions. From constitutional analysis to the internal operations of legislatures, political scientists generally accept that institutional arrangements matter fundamentally in public policy choices. This may seem somewhat unsurprising, but think a moment about economic theories, including those that are

[15]Walter Williams, *Honest Numbers and Democracy*. Washington DC: Georgetown University Press, 1998.

our focus here. Neither supply-side economics, nor beast-starving, nor, for that matter, Keynesian economics, has specific roles for government institutions or even business organizations. In the hands of the economic theorist, all but the most bare-bones aspects of government and the economy disappear. The institutional aspects of government vanish; there is no role for legislatures, or presidents, or policy analysts. Similarly, the economics profession has mainly treated the organizational structure of business as a black box without examination of structure or function.

Not so in political science or in the work of many policy analysts, where organizational and institutional facets are seen as fundamental to the course of human affairs. It is true that some political scientists hold a naïve faith that electoral accountability will serve to correct the problems analyzed in this book, and many political scientists support the notion of responsive competence. But electoral accountability is far too blunt an instrument to enforce the kind of institutional responsibility detailed here.

Our positive approach to responsible government requires matching revenue streams to expenditure streams without assuming, as does the starve-the-beast crowd, that this just magically happens. It takes institutional arrangements to enforce this bargain, and a well-developed policy analytic capacity to monitor the bargain. Such arrangements, however, require a consensus between the parties that sound finances are a fundamental bulwark of governance. It is that consensus that has collapsed since Reagan.

Such a program was actually in place for much of the postwar period. Though it has been occasionally stretched seemingly to the breaking point in the United States, a rigorous decision-making process supported by sound policy information and analyses remained the gold standard of policy choice. At least, it was the goal, even when the actual effort may have slipped well below the high standards. In recent years, this standard has been undermined. This deterioration of the capacity of government to analyze relevant policy information has taken its toll in many ways, not the least of which is the elevation of economic speculation to a place of ascendancy in modern American political life.

If you are a libertarian or small-government conservative, wanting a much smaller and less intrusive government, we will show how you are ill-served by bad economics. Paradoxically, following the dictates of right-wing economic theories will almost certainly lead to larger government (but one disproportionately borrowing rather than taxing to pay the piper). If you are a proponent of a larger governmental presence directed at solving social problems, then you too are best served by the responsible government model we lay forth here. Providing big programs without the means to pay for them is as destructive of long-run strong government as making big tax cuts without a way of paying for them. The means we examine are neutral with regard to the size and scope of government. They have served America well in periods of expansion as well as in eras of limited growth. Today, they are being assigned to the ash-heap of history, replaced by bad ideas that yield inept governance.

WHY DO BAD IDEAS PERSIST?

The receptivity of political leaders is the key to any theory of the role of ideas in politics. The tendency of political leaders to put undue faith in bad ideas invariably will undermine the place of sound, factually-based analysis in policy making. Far from disappearing from an onslaught of better theories in the democratic marketplace of ideas, the Republican tax cut ideology has grown and prospered, driving out the better notions of prudent public finance. It reached a fever pitch in the GW Bush administration. Here, a perfect storm of pernicious public policies, supported by bad economic ideas and bad political ideas tied together by bad numbers, have produced misgovernment and failed fiscal policies that have harmed the nation and most of its citizens while benefiting those at the top of the income distribution. How and why this came about and has continued so long is the book's central issue.

Students of presidential decision making are well aware that facts alone are unlikely to be sufficient when making good decisions in complex policy environments. Experienced policy analysts understand that however sound their products, they are a necessary but not sufficient part of good decision making. A critical ingredient is a policy maker who has the skill and intuition to draw on the base of information and analyses and take the needed step beyond the evidence. Even then, there is no guarantee of the right decision, but only a better chance to get it right. At the same time, policy makers who ignore sound numbers that can illuminate difficulties and possible alternatives will generally make wrongheaded policy choices. If they continue to spurn good information—especially if it provides evidence that the policy is not working—needed corrections will not be made. Conversely, policy makers who seek out good data can be rewarded with the opportunity to correct or eliminate mistakes before they fester.

Why would political leaders spurn good data in favor of wrong and misleading theories? At one time, it was common for political scientists to assume that presidents would never rely on bad information when sound data were available. That would risk failure and subsequent electoral sanction or an unfavorable historical legacy at the end of the presidency and thereafter. Why then has President Bush spurned sound data developed by capable analysts in both the international and domestic policy areas in favor of questionable or wrong information that supports bad policy ideas?

Are voters rewarding such decision makers for this irresponsible fiscal behavior? As we show in more detail later, it is more likely that they have simply not connected the poor quality fiscal policy run in Republican presidencies to election choices. Could Republicans have forged an enduring national majority while pursuing sound fiscal policies, limited government, strong defense, and more conservative social issues? We will never know.

WEAKENED INSTITUTIONS

Bad economic ideas, bad political ideas about governing, and bad information in combination have caused system-threatening damage to our governing institutions in recent years. We have touched on the decline of sound decision-making practices and the consequent poor quality of public policies produced in the executive branch, but the problems extend to the legislative branch as well. In their 2006 book *The Broken Branch*, written prior to the electoral victory of the Democrats in November of 2006, the highly respected congressional scholars Thomas Mann and Norman Ornstein spelled out why Congress no longer worked.[16] They leveled most of their criticism at

---

[16]Thomas E. Mann and Norman J. Ornstein, *The Broken Branch*. Oxford: Oxford University Press, 2006.

the Republican-controlled Congress, but they stressed that "the seeds of many of the problems predate the Republicans" and noted that the Democrats contributed to the institutional decline in George W. Bush's first term by their lack of opposition.[17]

The decay of the institutional capacity of Congress so evident during the first six years of the Bush presidency included surrendering independence to the president, particularly in the House; limiting deliberations and oversight with the result of markedly decreasing the availability and use of good numbers; and engaging in excessive partisanship that has swept aside the established rules in both houses of Congress. The Republican leadership kept Democrats out of the decision-making process when legislation was considered and made material changes or added major new provisions in conference committees.

Partisan politics has trumped concern by the Republican leadership for maintaining Congress' institutional strength and independence relative to the presidency. The result has been a breakdown in process, and as Mann and Ornstein argue: "Bad process leads to bad policy."[18] And the process increasingly produced bad information and a failure to obtain the data necessary for sound oversight and lawmaking.

Mann and Ornstein are pessimistic about reform: "President Bush and his congressional leaders found ways . . . [to bend] the rules, precedents, and norms of legislative behavior in ways that left the institution in tatters. . . . The country and its enduring constitutional pact should not and cannot endure a broken branch

---

[17]Mann and Ornstein, p. xii.
[18]Mann and Ornstein, p. 13.

for long."[19] The shift to Democratic control as a result of the 2006 midterm elections opened a window of opportunity to reverse the institutional decay, and early signs on such topics as ethics rules and budgetary procedures have been positive. In particular, Democrats have initiated vigorous oversight of executive branch activities. But there is no guarantee. The Republicans under Newt Gingrich instituted a powerful set of reforms in 1995, only to discard them in the increasingly partisan atmosphere of the late 1990s. Electoral change alone does not magically repair the institutional decline. That will take extraordinary efforts, as discussed in a later chapter.

The Broken Branch implies only a single broken institution among the three established by the Constitution. But the executive branch is broken too. Readers may question whether his presidency can be called broken when President Bush dominated Congress and had great success in pushing through his policies during his first six years in office. But broken can imply "not working at all," as with a dead battery in an automobile, or "not working properly," as illustrated by a faulty gas pedal that can become stuck at a high speed, with the latter fitting the Bush presidency. In the American constitutional structure that derives its strength from balance, the framers feared an all-powerful president who could push aside the cherished checks and balances that protected the desired equality among the branches.

Just as is the case with Congress, the breakdown of the presidency started before the Republicans gained control of both branches in 2001. But like the legislative branch, institutional

---

[19]Mann and Ornstein, pp. 13, 213.

deterioration has accelerated in the 21st century. Key changes include the increased centralization and polarization that concentrated power in a small inner circle around the president, the abandonment of a reality-based decision-making process buttressed by hard numbers and reasoned analyses, and the sophisticated use of propaganda as a weapon to sell and defend the administration's flawed policies.

Our upcoming assessment will show that the United States is facing the worst long-term threats to its fiscal solvency and to the standard of living of most Americans in the postwar era. The current fiscal policies keep making the problems worse, but they go unattended by a dysfunctional political system. The triumvirate of bad economic and political ideas and bad information has propelled the nation into a downward spiral that must be arrested.

Of course electoral accountability lives in America, despite complaints about partisan redistricting and voting irregularities. Unfortunately, we do not think that elections alone can restore sound policy making, economic or otherwise. Elections are blunt instruments, and economic issues are complex. The prevailing view is that the 2006 midterm elections centered on the Iraq War and institutional corruption, not economic theories and policy analysis. The system-threatening problems are too dangerous for us to view them as treatable by elections alone.

Some conservatives, such as William Niskanen, have argued that divided government is the solution to our policy ills.[20] The extreme parties in modern America have abandoned the moderate center

---

[20]William Niskanen, "Give Divided Government a Chance," *Washington Monthly,* October 2006.

where most Americans reside and where public policy making is most successful. We need to balance these extremes by refusing to allow either political party to control all branches, say the proponents of divided government. This is a strong point, one on which Americans delivered in the midterm election of 2006, but it is at best only part of the answer.

We will argue that the institutional failures, not just political failures, must also be addressed. Blocking bad policy is not enough; good policy must also be forged. The nation's most threatening fiscal problems will continue to fester in the polarized political environment until viable institutions provide the base for sounder policy analysis. The answer is not in replacing Republican rule with Democratic rule, although Democrats could hardly do worse. It rather lies in restoring the postwar agreement between the parties that people of good intentions can come to an agreement about the facts even when they differed on the solutions.[21]

---

[21]John Dean has very recently provided a stinging analysis of broken governmental processes in which he lays blame on the very nature of the modern Republican party. See John W. Dean, Broken Government. New York: Viking, 2007.

CHAPTER 2

The Tax Cut Theories

Underlying swirling theories about the effects of taxes on the size and scope of government is a philosophy of limited government, a normative stance about the relative sizes of the public and private spheres. That philosophy has a rich tradition in the United States; indeed, liberty and its twin, limited government, were key in the minds of the authors of the Constitution in Philadelphia.

Some conservative analysts and university and think-tank economists have developed claims that make limited government easy. Simply cut taxes, something everybody likes, and—presto!—you get limited, responsible government. We enter the enterprise of examining the arguments of the conservative supply siders and starve-the-beasters with a great deal of skepticism. Bad government is evident enough worldwide, its effects clearly devastating to economies, to social structures, and even to the health and well-being of citizens. To assume, as some conservative economists do, that politicians will respond to the "incentive" of lower taxes by responsibly cutting spending seems questionable at best.

In any case, the most obvious claims of the conservative economists are not difficult to test. This book offers some simple data that easily refute the claims of the right—so simple that it is very surprising that these types of observations are so lacking in the public debate over the last quarter of a century. The facts are hiding in plain sight, and they are not supportive of the supply side, starve-the-beast proponents. Rather the available evidence overwhelmingly refutes their economic ideas. Perhaps complex models can tease out subtle effects of tax cuts on the growth of government revenue (as some supply siders claim) or on the restraint of spending (that the beast-starvers assert), but they are not evident. If they are not evident, then they are not practical solutions to the goal of limited government. And we will have to search elsewhere for that sorcerer's stone.

There is no secret where to find that key—it is in the hard work and good will of tough and fair-minded politicians, aided by institutional arrangements that reward responsibility rather than undermine it. Politicians are in the unenviable position of knowing exactly what their constituents want—more benefits from government and less taxation to provide it. There is no equilibrium here; and as a consequence, political judgment, compromise, good information from responsible civil servants, and wisdom matter. How our elected leaders navigate between the Chabrydis of low taxes and the Scylla of high benefits determines what kind of government citizens get.

THE THEORIES AND THEIR
POLITICAL INCARNATIONS

Most Americans saw the national government as a crucial factor in the economic success story during the first quarter century after

World War II, but they came to view government less positively as the economy soured in the 1970s. Starve-the-beast and the earlier, closely related concept of supply-side economics, came to epitomize the curb-the-federal-government, antitax ideology that shaped the presidencies of Ronald Reagan and George W. Bush. The new thinking took hold after socioeconomic and political problems profoundly disturbed citizens and wore away their trust in the federal government to treat these problems successfully.

The United States emerged from World War II as the economic colossus—by far the largest producer of goods and services, and the world's banker. It had no challengers. Not since the heyday of the Roman Empire had there been such economic power.[1] Strong economic growth and successful federal government policies—particularly the GI Bill that helped millions of veterans gain more work skills and buy a house—created a burgeoning, optimistic middle class. Americans accepted the national government as a necessary good that had demonstrated its worth in the Great Depression and World War II and was still doing the job after the war. The economic and political environment during the 1950s and well into the 1960s could not have been more different than the early years of the 21st century.

Today much has changed. The United States imports goods and services at such a rate that it has a record trade deficit and is by far the biggest debtor in the world. Many see government as the problem—a necessary evil to be constrained. That change began in the later years of the 1960s amid social and political unrest that brought destructive riots in some major cities and

---

[1]Paul Kennedy, *The Rise and Fall of the Great Powers*. New York: Random House, 1987, p. 358.

widespread protests against the Vietnam War. The American economy slowed visibly after the first major oil price increase engineered by oil-producing nations in 1973 and suffered double-digit inflation with the second oil price hike in 1979. President Jimmy Carter's disastrous efforts to rescue Iranian hostages made the national government look feebler yet.

From this base of problems and the resulting public dissatisfaction, Ronald Reagan successfully launched a full-scale attack on the federal government as the main source of America's predicament and promised to restore the nation to its earlier dominance. The country turned from the active, pragmatic governance and egalitarianism of Franklin Roosevelt's New Deal that had prevailed for nearly 50 years to Reaganism, with its antigovernmentalism and free market fundamentalism.

As is well documented by Jacob Hacker and Paul Pierson, this turn in public philosophy has not been based on the kind of consensus that underlay the Roosevelt coalition. Rather it has been the result of strong policies enacted using narrow yet very cohesive majorities.[2] But it has been remarkably successful none the less.

ECONOMIC POLICY AS RELIGION?

In 1981, President Reagan engineered a massive income tax cut that is still the largest as a percentage of GDP in American history. It became the first and perhaps the most important battle in the antigovernment war. A handful of advocates who believed in the

[2]Jacob Hacker and Paul Pierson, *Off Center*. New Haven: Yale University Press, 2005.

power of large income tax reductions to induce saving and investment apparently convinced Reagan on the miracle version of the
supply-side thesis. Led by economist Arthur Laffer (the theorist)
and former *Wall Street Journal* editor Jude Wanniski (the propagandist) the idea never generated any enthusiasm among most
professional economists. That did not appear to matter to Reagan
who Wanniski claimed " 'knew instantly that it [supply-side eco-
nomics] was true.' "[3]

Macroeconomics is the study of the total (aggregate) economy
and hence focuses on the broadest measure of national product.
Macroeconomic policy is about using government to manage the
broad national economy. During the Great Depression, the British
economist John Maynard Keynes developed a conceptual framework that dominated both theoretical and practical thinking
about macroeconomics from then until the presidency of Ronald
Reagan. In Keynesian economics, aggregate demand for goods
and services took center stage in the formulation of public policy,
whereas aggregate supply received limited attention. If a government needed to address problems of inadequate or excessive (and
hence inflationary) economic growth, its fiscal policies would aim
to increase or decrease aggregate demand. Such a strategy contained the assumption that businesses would be able to respond
directly and seamlessly with the needed increases or decreases in
the supply of goods and services. Supply was assumed to match
demand, but Keynesianism did not study how this happened.

Supply siders rejected the notion that demand would necessarily call forth supply in a seamless manner. They advocated policies

---

[3]Quoted in Haynes Johnson, *Sleepwalking Through History*. New York: Norton, 1991, p. 105.

directed at increasing the amount and quality of goods and services, proposing tax cuts at the top of the income scale to stimulate greater work and saving. They reasoned that the money people saved from the tax cuts would be used to increase the supply of capital investment. In turn, this larger base of productive goods such as plant and equipment would induce higher economic growth over time.

This was a reasonable line of thought, but it was corrupted in practice by the arguments of the miracle supply siders. They postulated that income tax cuts would quickly induce such massive increases in work and investment that the additional tax revenue would wipe away the initial revenue decline from a tax cut. Tax cuts for those in the highest income brackets were particularly important, because these people would invest a larger proportion of their benefits from the tax cut. These investments would flow to productive capital investments and make free-market capitalism flourish again. Keynesianism also advocated tax cuts, but because the idea was to increase aggregate demand, the cuts would be more efficient if they went disproportionately to lower income citizens, who would spend a larger proportion of the cut. So Keynesian demand-stimulating tax cuts worked best when targeted on the poor, whereas supply-side theory generally favored targeting the wealthy.

Enter Reagan. He believed that Washington was always the problem, never the solution. The dead hand of the national government must be severed so that the unfettered free market could bring forth the economic growth needed to restore America to its early postwar preeminence. For the miracle supply-side advocates, deep cuts for those in the highest income tax brackets became a magic fix and painless to boot. No wonder the ever-optimistic Reagan found the supply-side doctrine so appealing.

Keynesian theory indicated that tax reductions, as well as increased government spending, were the right fiscal policies for stimulating growth during periods of economic stagnation. Such cuts would serve to stimulate aggregate economic demand, which would in turn stimulate the production of more goods and services. President John Kennedy's tax cut that helped the United States recover from a recession in the early 1960s became part of the supply siders' mantra of justification for Reagan's 1981 tax reduction policy. Keynesian theory, however, never postulated the supply siders' miracle of rapid economic growth sufficient to wipe out budget deficits.

Though President Reagan enthusiastically adopted the miracle supply-side notion as his own, Reagan's budget director, David Stockman, claims he never bought it literally. Stockman hoped to cut government the old-fashioned way, by cutting spending: "[Senator Phil Gramm of Texas] and I thought of ourselves as the complete supply siders. We wanted to shrink both sides of the budget equation."[4] Stockman basically thought of supply-side doctrine as a positive spin on old-fashioned Republican fiscal conservatism. Limited government didn't just result in more liberty; it freed the creative impulses of capitalism and generated more economic growth. Unfortunately, Republican politicians began to parrot the Wanniski version; Stockman began to refer to the "dreamers in the White House" who would not support the necessary cuts to bring down the size of government. Again we

---

[4]David Stockman, *The Triumph of Politics*. New York: Harper and Row, 1986, p. 52.

recall Lord Keynes, who in the last paragraph of his *General Theory* noted that "Madmen in authority, when they hear voices in the air, are distilling their frenzy from some academic scribbler of a few years back."[5]

As the Reagan deficits swelled, critics contended that the supply-side thesis had been, in the words of David Stockman, a "Trojan Horse."[6] That is, those proposing the tax cuts recognized that there would be large deficits and expected them to block any increases in discretionary social programs and possibly to reduce their size. President Reagan and the true believers who initially proposed the extreme version of supply-side economics likely were surprised by the deficits. Others in the administration may simply have seen the opportunity to block future growth in the federal budget.

NO HORSE NEEDED:
STARVE-THE-BEAST

The Trojan Horse features of the supply-side thesis fell by the wayside as conservatives became increasingly emboldened. Enter a new notion: starving the beast. No need to pretend: the real objective was small government. "Starve-the-beast" is associated with the antigovernment crusader Grover Norquist, who said that his goal is to shrink government: "I don't want to abolish government, I simply want to reduce it to the size where I can drag it into

---

[5]J. M. Keynes, *The General Theory of Employment, Interest, and Money*. London: McMillan, 1973.
[6]Johnson, *Sleepwalking Through History*, p. 110.

the bathroom and drown it in the bathtub."[7] Norquist advocated
cutting taxes as a lever to limit government.

Starving-the-beast has been elevated to the exalted status of
economic theory by some very serious academic economists, two
of them Nobel laureates. Many other economists have spoken out
against these ideas, and some have produced analyses.[8] Indeed,
some 450 economists, including ten Nobelists, decried the Bush
tax cut strategy in a *New York Times* advertisement appearing
February 11, 2003. They stated that "passing these tax cuts will
worsen the long-term budget outlook, adding to the nation's projected chronic deficit." Unfortunately, they had the misfortune of
not offering politicians something for nothing, and the plea fell on
deaf ears.

Starving the beast implies that lower tax rates will deny government revenues and subsequently force politicians to cut back
spending. Economists Gary Becker (a Nobelist), Edward Lazear,
and Kevin Murphy claim that government is like a household in
being constrained by its revenue. They assert that "Tax cuts make
sense for two reasons. First, government spending responds to tax
revenues so that lower revenues imply lower government spending. Second, economic growth depends on both human capital
and physical capital, and investment in human capital, as well as
physical capital, is responsive to tax rates."[9]

---

[7] This quote (and a similar one indicating that he wanted to cut government in half in 25 years) have reached
the level of legend. Norquist denied saying it to Bill Moyers on the PBS program *NOW* (October 1, 2003).
But you can hear him say it in a profile on NPR by Mara Liasson in May 2001: http://www. thenation-
aldebate. com/blog/archives/2005/02/norquist_sidest. html.
[8] William Gale and Peter Orszag, "Bush Administration Tax Policy: Starving the Beast?" *Tax Notes*,
November 15, 2004, pp. 999–1002.
[9] Gary S. Becker, Edward P. Lazear, and Kevin M. Murphy, "The Double Benefits of Tax Cuts," *Wall
Street Journal*, October 12, 2003.

The mechanism through which spending restraint is accomplished is the deficit. Supposedly a large deficit will not be tolerated by the public, and this will put pressure on politicians to rein in spending. In an op-ed piece in the *Washington Times*, Veronique de Rugy, then a scholar at the American Enterprise Institute, wrote, "Economic theory suggests that government spending eventually adjusts to available tax revenues because politicians are unwilling to let deficits rise above some unspecified level. Deficits are an effective weapon against the political temptation to engage in spending binges because the public's unhappiness with deficits forces spending restraint."[10]

Nobel laureate Milton Freidman wrote in a *Wall Street Journal* editorial that the only way to control the size of government is "the way parents control spendthrift children, cutting their allowance." Cutting taxes will cause resulting deficits that "will be an effective—I would say the only effective—restraint on the spending propensities of the executive branch and the legislature." What will stop them? Why, public opinion, of course: "The public reaction will make them effective."[11]

What if parents cut the allowance of spendthrift children, but allow them to keep their credit cards? Modern U.S. experience suggests that this is more like what happened. The massive 1981 income tax reductions produced huge deficits, but they did not stimulate enough economic growth to resupply government coffers, nor did they restrain spending enough to staunch the red ink. Prior to this tax cut, no postwar yearly budget deficit had exceeded $74 billion. Thereafter, the United States had a string of large federal budget

---

[10]Veronique de Rugy, "Keep Starving the Beast," *Washington Times*, June 1, 2003.
[11]Milton Friedman, "What Every American Wants," *Wall Street Journal*, January 19, 2003.

deficits under both Ronald Reagan and George H. W. Bush. The yearly deficit in 1983 rose to $207.8 billion, nearly three times as great as the highest pre-Reagan deficit, and set a record at that time of slightly over $290 billion in 1992, almost four times the $73.8 billion under Carter. Such huge increases in the yearly budget deficits surely represented a fair test of the political argument underlying starve-the-beast, the public's fury at the mounting deficits, but there simply were no sustained outcries from the public.[12]

The latter Reagan years and the GHW Bush and Clinton presidencies were consumed with pursuing fiscal balance. These policies were forged from a combination of tax increases and expenditure limitations, which were difficult to achieve politically. Both sides had to give in a classic running battle. The new fiscal prudence was not caused by public ire at the deficit, but by the dictates of federal law. The Omnibus Budget Reconciliation Act of 1990 required budget cuts, called sequesters, if deficit reduction targets were not achieved. In effect, the political parties had agreed to tie their hands and put a shotgun behind the door to enforce the bargain into the future. We show in later chapters that this approach—basically creating institutional mechanisms for forcing political leaders to do what is right—worked and continued to work until Republicans in Congress, supported by President GW Bush, destroyed the system by refusing to renew the sequestration procedures in 2002.

George W. Bush outdid Reagan with two massive individual income tax cuts in 2001 and 2003 that yielded even higher deficits. Still, the people did not rise up in anger or even seem all

---

[12] The deficits have not been adjusted for inflation because given the starve-the-beast argument, it is more likely that citizens would react to and be angrier at the larger nominal figure.

that concerned with the deficits. When pollsters ask people to list the most important problems facing the nation, the budget deficit is usually mentioned by a tiny fraction, and when it is included within a list, it ranks consistently low.[13] That has not deterred proponents from continuing to praise tax cuts as the best way to drive down federal expenditures.

TWO POINTS DO NOT DETERMINE
A CURVE

Both theories used to justify tax cuts have a certain logical plausibility when extrapolated to the extremes, which can account for part of the appeal. In the case of supply-side economics, it is clear that if a government that relies solely on an income tax taxes at 0 percent, then it will receive no revenue. If it taxes at 100 percent, it will confiscate all income, and no citizen will earn any (at least on the books, available to be taxed).

In a 1974 meeting with Jude Wanniski and Dick Cheney, Arthur Laffer drew something like Figure 2.1 on the back of a napkin in the Two Continents restaurant in Washington DC.[14] Laffer claimed that government tax policy was to the right of Point A. If so, then it must be true that cutting back taxes will generate more government revenue. Haynes Johnson wrote:

The seductive supply side myth took tangible form, its acolytes claimed, in Washington early in December 1974 . . . when three

---

[13]When given the option of several important priorities, however, reducing the budget deficit does gain considerable support.

[14]Arthur Laffer, "The Laffer Curve: Past, Present, and Future," The Heritage Foundation. n.d. Laffer is quoting Wanniski's version because he said that he didn't remember the details of the evening.

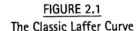

FIGURE 2.1
The Classic Laffer Curve

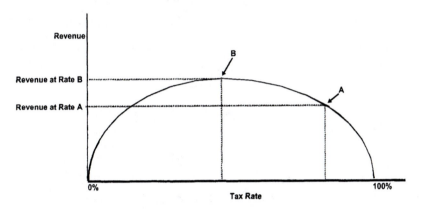

men met for cocktails at the Two Continents restaurant, a block from the White House. There, in a moment of frustration over his inability to explain to Richard Cheney, [President Jerry] Ford's chief-of-staff, the benefits that would ensue if his tax-cutting theories were adopted, a bubbly young economist named Arthur B. Laffer seized a cocktail napkin and drew on it what became known as the Laffer Curve.[15]

In our depiction of the Laffer curve in Figure 2.1, the tax rate on income is graphed on the x-axis, and the government revenue that will be derived from that rate is on the y-axis. The tax rate is set through the political process. Laffer argued, according to Wanniski, that in actuality there was an optimum tax rate shown at point B on the graph. If government tried to tax beyond this optimum rate, then people would reduce their work effort, in effect valuing leisure more than working at high tax rates.

[15]Johnson, *Sleepwalking Through History*. p. 99.

For example, let us assume that government is taxing income at Rate A, a high rate. If government lowered the tax rate to Rate B, then government revenue would not fall, as traditional wisdom suggested, but would actually rise as people worked harder and increased their investments in response to the lower rate that allowed them to keep more of their income. Moving the rate from A to B actually would yield a bonanza of tax revenues at least sufficient to replace the decline in federal revenues from the tax cut. It offered a free lunch solution.

The curve is trivially true—that is, it must be correct at the endpoints (0% and 100%). But that does not help in real fiscal policy making, because no one really knows the shape of the curve or the point at which revenue production is optimum. Laffer implied that the tax rate at which government revenue would begin to decline was low, but it need not be, and his claim lacked any evidence whatsoever. That is the point: neither Laffer nor anyone else knew or now knows where the curve peaks, nor is there any evidence about the actual shape of the curve.

It is actually possible that government can raise taxes and still raise revenue at very high rates of taxation, albeit at less efficiency than at low levels of taxation. Wealthy individuals turn to politics to try to manipulate the tax code to avoid taxation at high tax rates. But high rates at lower income levels could actually work to sustain government revenues. People work even harder as tax rates rise in an attempt to maximize after-tax income rather than opting for more leisure by not working. Surely that would be the response of those with dependents to support.

Supply siders had no idea where government policy might be on the curve, or how much revenue might be replaced through growth when taxes are cut. Nor did they even know the basic shape of the curve. There is no "theory" or systematic hypothesis, in the sense of a rigorous formulation supported by evidence. It is basically a bad economic idea, really quite unbridled speculation about how economies and governments are related, a complex topic that defies reduction to a simple curve. Such speculation should never have been the basis for our nation's economic policies.

Starve-the-beast is similarly deceptive. It claims, plausibly, that over the long run, government revenue streams and spending streams must be in balance. Or so it seems logically. As economists Becker, Lazear, and Murphy note, "The sum of present and future public spending, discounted by the rate of interest on government bonds, must equal the sum of present and discounted future tax revenues."[16]

The problem is not the logic in the extremes—the statement is trivially true. Rather the problem is knowing what mechanisms are supposed to enforce the balance, and when they are supposed to operate. We noted previously that the typical starve-the-beaster assumes that public opinion will push for the balance. We have found nothing in the empirical or theoretical public opinion litera-ture, which is both vigorous and robust, that would support the "economic theory" that the public will not tolerate deficits as a general matter. In some situations—war and recessions—they can be quite supportive of deficits, and in others, they can be quite oblivious to them. They may not like deficits in the abstract and can even list priorities for cutting deficits. Most people most of the time want more for less. But they can be reminded of the collective

---

[16]Becker, Lazear, and Murphy.

good and instructed—if that is the right word—on the desirability of raising taxes and cutting services.

To be a viable theory of political action, as well as to fulfill the dictates of scientific testability, starve-the-beasters would need to specify a threshold beyond which deficits will not be tolerated by the public. We invite the reader to ponder whether a social movement based on deficit reduction has emerged in the United States or elsewhere. Such a social movement would be necessary to make deficits the cornerstone of a theory merging tax cutting and limited government. Moreover, the theories assume that services will be cut and taxes will not be raised. None of this is supported by even a cursory reading of the historical record. The selective reading of the record of Reagan-Bush-Clinton by Becker, Lazear, and Murphy is that spending was restrained because of the Reagan tax cuts. The problem with this is that Reagan, Bush, and Clinton all raised taxes, and did so briskly, while simultaneously attempting to restrain spending. This points to hard work by governmental leaders to lower the deficit by building consensus and cutting deals.

Starving the beast rests on assumptions of a great public outcry over rising deficits and of frightened politicians lowering expenditures. But no such outcry that might panic politicians is to be found. At some point, one supposes, investors in government bonds will deny government access to the credit markets, as is sometimes postulated as the restraining force that will ultimately rein in the fiscal irresponsibility of cutting taxes with no plans to limit spending. But another future is possible. Politicians may punt on the hard choices when faced with spending demands from concrete constituents, purchasers may continue to buy U.S. Treasuries pretty much regardless of the fiscal picture at least in the short run, and economic theories assure politicians that things will work out fine in the end. To the extent that this happens, the logical mechanism that can enforce the bargain is economic ruin. In any case, there is no evidence so far that politicians are anticipating a dire economic future despite excessive spending and borrowing.

One reason for the serene demeanor of politicians is that obliging Japanese and Chinese governments, already heavily invested in U.S. Treasuries, keep buying them, seemingly without much regard for America's fiscal deterioration. These governments, and citizens from abroad, are actually financing two deficits: the government deficit and the trade deficit. The United States is currently buying more from foreigners than we sell them, and the difference is huge. Although at a strikingly high level of $618 billion in 2004, the trade deficit rose more than 27 percent in 2005 and then, to a record $764 billion in 2006. Apparently China and Japan continue to buy U.S. bonds to prop up the federal government and the consuming American public with credit so that they can continue to export their goods to the American marketplace. Deficits can be financed with an international credit card, and the nation moves deeper and deeper into debt.

A BETTER THEORY

Strangely enough, a perfectly sound theory about the relationship between public opinion and tax rates is in plain view, and it is simpler than the preceding contortions. It's just this: people roughly compare the level of benefits they are receiving with how much they pay in taxes, and then they decide whether to support more or less government. If the ratio of benefits received to taxes paid gets too low, then they support less government. So the op-ed crowd demanding limited government ought to support tax increases to stimulate revulsion toward spending.

The availability of better theory and the emerging facts of tax cuts have caused one conservative economist to change sides. William Niskanen, once a vigorous defender of Reaganomics,[17] now claims that "starve the beast won't work."[18] The reason he cites for changing his mind is the evidence. An analysis that he and a collaborator did showed a strong inverse relationship between the tax burden and federal spending between 1981 and 2003.[19] The data led to this observation: "A tax increase may be the best policy to reduce the relative level of federal spending."[20] As taxes are raised, people are likely to become more resistant to government spending. This is called the price theory of government.

Here is the way this works. Assume first that the benefits of government spending to citizens are constant for each new dollar spent. That is, older, established programs are worth the same on a per dollar basis to citizens as programs that might be added today or in the future. This is naturally very simplified; actually benefits differ among groups and the nature of the current challenges facing government. In tracing this logic out, assume next that the value placed by citizens on the income they earn is

---

[17] William Niskanen and Stephen Moore, "Supply Tax Cuts and the Truth about the Reagan Economic Record," *Policy Analysis* #261. Washington DC: Cato Institute, 1996.
[18] William Niskanen, "Starve the Beast Does Not Work," *Cato Policy Report* March/April. Washington DC: Cato Institute, 2004.
[19] Niskanen and Peter Van Doren, "Some Intriguing Findings About Federal Spending," paper presented at the Public Choice Society, Baltimore, MD, March 11–14, 2004; Niskanen and Van Doren, "Some Intriguing Findings About Federal Spending," in Jeffrey A. Frankel and Peter R. Orszag, eds., *American Economic Policy in the 1990s.* Cambridge, MA: MIT Press, 2004.
[20] Niskanen, "Starve the Beast," p. 1.

inversely proportional to after-tax income. That is, the smaller the income left after taxation, the more valuable it is to the citizen. This just incorporates the well-established economic principle of declining marginal utility—the first (after-tax) dollar earned is worth more than the next dollar earned, and so on. As the tax rate increases, the "pain" associated with taxation increases, because the citizen has less and less income to enjoy on his or her own.

If these two simple assumptions are incorporated into a theory of citizen tax resistance, then we get a curve like the one in Figure 2.2. We depict on the y-axis the benefits derived from government programs by the citizen divided by the costs experienced by him or her through the pain of taxation. On the x-axis we depict the rate of taxation. As the tax rate increases, the benefit/cost ratio must decline, because each new program added is

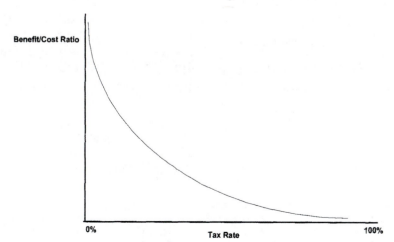

FIGURE 2.2
The Benefits from Government Programs and the Tax Rate

constant in its per-dollar benefits while each additional dollar of taxation brings increases in tax-pains.

If this curve is anywhere close to correct, and we think it is at least a pretty good approximation, then government benefits relative to the level of taxation decline as the tax rate rises for the typical citizen. As these benefits decline, surely the conditions for resistance to further taxation (and hence government expenditures) improve. Of course no one can say when resistance might break out, and it is clear that different societies have different levels of tolerance for taxation. But the implications are culture-free: in any society, as taxes increase, resistance is encouraged. Similarly, as tax rates decline, then people are likely to become more accepting of government.

Only one more element is necessary here: that people are more sensitive in their politics to taxation than to levels of the public deficit. Taxes are close, and deficits are remote, so this makes considerable sense. Moreover, economists are fond of pointing to what they call the fiscal illusion, which occurs when the system for raising revenue is obscure and lulls people into thinking that government is cheaper than it actually is.[21] Shifting the burden for raising revenue from direct taxation to deficit financing can be seen as an exercise in the fiscal illusion. We won't rely solely on this argument, but we will also examine the proposition that people are more sensitive to taxes than to debt in detail later in this book.

[21]James Buchanan, *Public Finance in Democratic Process: Fiscal Institutions and Individual Choice.* Chapel Hill: The University of North Carolina Press, 1987, Chapter 10. Available electronically through The Collected Works of James Buchanan, The Library of Economics and Liberty. Indianapolis, IN: The Liberty Fund, 2001.

LESS TAXES, MORE GOVERNMENT

What is the implication of this? We can state it baldly: cut taxes and you set the conditions to get more government. Logic implies that the public will encourage politicians to produce more public programs when tax rates are lowered, and as we shall show shortly, the data support it. The only question is what kind of big government you get. It can be liberal or conservative; it can center on increased social programs, welfare benefits, and health care; or it can center on more prisons, police, and military. Low taxes encourage people to press for more government, whereas higher taxes make them resistant to more government. Paradoxically, the starve-the-beasters have it backwards. They have provided cover for huge, albeit conservative, government. It may also be true that increases in taxes lead to less government, although that is less clear from the historical data that we will examine shortly.

Political scientist Ted Lowi years ago argued that the parties could not really be distinguished by their ideologies; rather they were different because the coalitions of interest groups that supported them were different.[22] Perhaps that remains true in the modern ideological age. Starve-the-beasters are perhaps not interested in limited government; rather they simply prefer whatever business prefers. Business generally prefers low taxes and plenty of government contracts. Although the motives of the purveyors of this radical ideology that masquerades as economics are not known, the validity of the specific claims will be assessed in upcoming chapters and found wanting.

---

[22] Theodore Lowi, *The End of Liberalism*, 2nd Ed. New York: Norton, 1979.

CHAPTER 3

Evaluating the Claims

In Chapter 1, we raised the issue of why bad ideas are sometimes so persistent, even where they are subject to the democratic marketplace of ideas.[1] We particularly pointed to questionable economic ideas. In Chapter 2, we showed how political ideology and partisanship undergird the popularity of the miracle version of supply-side economics and the starve-the-beast approach. Now we turn to a full examination of the validity of these notions when they are held up in the harsh light of facts.

Both the miracle supply-side and starve-the-beast theories claim to justify tax cuts without the need to adjust revenue flows accordingly. Because taxes have been cut repeatedly in the United States since the Second World War, we can study the correspondence between tax reductions and subsequent government revenues.

Though both of the theories focus on tax cuts, they postulate different causal mechanisms about how they operate. Miracle

[1]We appreciate comments from Neil Bruce and Mark Smith on the material in this chapter.

supply-side theory says that tax reductions raise more revenue because of their "supply-side" stimulative effects on the economy. According to these supply-siders, tax cuts have an immediate Keynesian-type effect via the "demand side"—that is, tax cuts, by putting more money in people's hands, increase the demand for goods and services. But they also have a supply-side effect by which they provide the incentives for people to work and invest more because they keep a higher proportion of what they earn. As a consequence, the supply-side effects, in the miracle version, offset the tax losses and actually pay for themselves. This effect would not be as rapid, because it could take a little while to work themselves through the economy, but they should be observable within a couple of years. Otherwise, the rising deficit could have negative economic effects (by exerting an upward pressure on interest rates, hence causing a decline in investment) that would offset any benefits from the supply-side effects.

The starve-the-beast mechanism suggests a different causal chain. It holds true to the old economic maxim "there is no such thing as a free lunch."[2] In this theory, tax cuts cause revenue declines; supply-side effects are not powerful enough to offset revenue losses. As a consequence, they increase the deficit. However, then the deficit does work miracles: voters get upset about them and demand that politicians restore fiscal balance.[3] They do so by reducing the size of government programs.

[2]This is the title of Milton Friedman's collection of essays from his *Newsweek* column; Friedman, *No Such Thing as a Free Lunch*. La Salle, IL: Open Court Publishing, 1975.
[3]At least in Friedman's version. See Friedman, "What Every American Wants," *Wall Street Journal*, January 19, 2003. The version promoted by Gary Becker and his colleagues contains no explicit mechanism. Gary S. Becker, Edward P. Lazear, and Kevin M. Murphy, "The Double Benefits of Tax Cuts," *Wall Street Journal*, October 12, 2003.

TABLE 3.1
Claims of the Tax Cut Theories

	QUESTION	MIRACLE SUPPLY-SIDE	STARVE-THE-BEAST
1A	How do tax cuts affect *government revenue?*	Increase revenue	Decrease revenue
1B	If revenue is cut, how does that affect *spending?*	No prediction	Decrease spending
2	How do income tax cuts affect the *deficit?*	Decrease deficit	Increase then decrease deficit
3	How do tax cuts affect *spending?*	No prediction	Reduce spending
4	How do deficits influence *voter ideology?*	No prediction	Become more conservative
5	How do tax cuts affect *government size?*	No effect	Shrink government

At base, both theories make factual claims about how tax cuts affect government. We can set up these claims as a set of questions, and Table 3.1 summarizes five separate questions that arise from the claims made by the two theories. These questions involve the role of tax cuts on government revenues, government spending, public deficits, voter ideology, and the size of government.

1. How do income tax cuts affect government revenue and spending patterns? Supply-side theory predicts that, at least over time, tax cuts will increase revenues, but starving-the-beast assumes that tax revenues will fall. For spending, supply-side makes no predictions, but starve-the-beast claims that, over time, spending will fall.

2. The theories also differ in their predictions about the consequences of tax rate reductions on the federal deficit, with

supply-side theories asserting that the deficit should fall, whereas starve-the-beasters claim that deficits will rise.

3. Supply siders make no predictions about changes in government spending, but starve-the-beasters make a strong claim here, namely that spending should go down.

4. The reason for the starve-the-beast claim that spending should go down is due to changes in voter ideology. Voters become more conservative as a direct consequence of the rise in the deficit. Supply-side theory makes no claims about changes in voter ideology..

5. The size of government should decrease after income tax cuts, if we are to believe the starve-the-beast argument. Again, supply side makes no prediction here.

So these theories make different claims about the effects of tax cuts. Of the two, starve-the-beast accepts standard economic theory about government finance (tax increases raise revenue; tax cuts decrease revenue), while supply-side theory makes new claims about how strongly the effect of tax cuts will influence economic growth, thereby offsetting the tax losses caused (only temporarily) by cuts in the tax rates. On the other hand, starve-the-beast makes some very strong claims about the role of voters, which supply theory avoids. The idea that income tax cuts can have supply-side effects is not denied by economists pursuing the starve-the-beast theme; they just think these effects are not strong enough to replenish the national treasury. Indeed, today many economists accept the supply-side notion that cuts in taxes will cause individuals and businesses to invest more; because the wealthy receive the largest tax cuts, they will save the most and use that to invest.

Since the Second World War, tax rates have been cut several times and raised twice, but reductions, in both the individual tax rate schedule and in taxes on business and capital gains, have predominated. This enables us to examine the impact that changes in tax rates have on revenues, on spending, on the preferences of voters, and on the size of government relative to the size of the economy.

Our analysis shows the following:

- Income tax cuts decrease revenue, both in the short run and the longer run. The key assumption of the miracle supply-side thesis is wrong.
- Income tax cuts increase the deficit. The lost revenue from tax cuts is made up by borrowing.
- Income tax cuts have no influence on the path of government spending.
- Deficits are associated with more liberal public opinion; rather than turn against government and its programs when deficits rise, people want more of them.
- Income tax cuts do not automatically limit the growth of government.

THE TAX CODE

The U.S. tax code is a marvel of complexity, with both general provisions directed at large classes of individuals and corporations as well as a myriad of special provisions for particular industries and relatively narrow instruments designed to achieve goals through specific tax incentives. All sorts of tax deductions and tax credits are employed to protect particular classes; for example, investment tax credits for industry are designed to promote the purchase of equipment that is necessary to economic growth.

All of this may not be surprising given that tax provisions are written by legislators responding to particular demands from more-or-less organized interests, but it invariably leads to calls for "tax reform," "tax simplification," and so forth. These calls for tax reform—or so-called "revenue-neutral tax reform"—should be distinguished from the tax cutting theories of conservatives, where the aim is definitely not revenue neutrality.

The theories of supply-siders and starve-the-beasters mostly relate to the overall tax burden or to taxpayers in the upper brackets of income and wealth. There are two reasons for this. First, in supply-side theories, a critical underlying notion is that economic growth generally is limited by the supply of capital for investment. If tax rates are lowered on those who have accumulated capital—that is, the well-off—then they will be in a position to invest the money that would otherwise have been taken in taxes by government. This investment bonanza, in supply-side theories, will "pay for itself" by generating enough income to offset the losses generated by the tax cut, even taking into account the lower tax rate. Supply-side theories place a real premium on cutting taxes on income generated from wealth, because cutting these taxes will generate higher real returns for investors and encourage them to invest rather than consume more of their assets. For starve-the-beasters, the manner in which taxes are lowered is less important than the necessity of denying revenue to government. The most effective way, however, to deny revenue to government is to cut taxes on those who have the most income, whether that is individuals or corporations.

In the analysis that follows, we will concentrate on the top marginal income tax rate for individual taxpayers. Some analysts have focused on effective tax rates instead of the top marginal rate; the effective rate is the rate that taxpayers in a given bracket can expect to pay in a given year (that is, after credits and deductions). Similarly, corporate rates or rates on capital are worthy of examination. Or tax burdens could be examined.

Indeed, starve-the-beasters could argue that it is the federal tax take, the amount of taxes relative to the size of the economy, that is most relevant. Remember, however, that the theories we are examining here are theories about fiscal policies. Congress has no direct control over the federal tax take, because it responds both to tax rates and to ups and downs in the economy. And, in any case, we'll show later on that tax cuts do indeed cause revenue declines, as they are supposed to do in the starve-the-beast theory.

The top marginal rate captures much of what conservatives object to—the taxation of those who could use their income to invest. Moreover, across time there has been a tendency for income tax rates to ebb and flow in impressive unison. For example:

- When taxes are lowered on top income earners, they tend to be lowered on lower income earners as well. The correlation between the top bracket tax rate and the bottom bracket rate since 1946 is 0.70.
- When taxes are lowered on individual incomes, they also tend to be lowered for corporations and for capital. The post–World war II correlation between the top marginal tax rate for married individuals filing jointly and the top marginal rate for corporations is 0.84, whereas the

correlation between the top marginal rate for married individuals filing jointly and the effective tax rate on capital for corporations and individuals (1953–2003) is a robust 0.75.

- When tax brackets are altered, the effective tax rate tends to change as a direct consequence. The correlation between the top tax bracket rate and the effective tax rate for the middle income quintile (1979–2001, when data are available) is 0.75.[4]

Figure 3.1 plots three selective but important tax rates over time: the top marginal rates for individuals and corporations, and the effective tax rate for individuals. After the income tax was ruled constitutional, initial rates were low, but they were increased during World War I and then steadily raised beginning in the early 1930s through the early 1950s. After that, tax rates in the United States have moved steadily downward, except the two rate increases in the early 1990s. This period is a critical one in U.S. public finances, the only period associated with a trend toward smaller deficits, and we shall explore the reasons for this later.

The most dramatic decline in tax rates for individuals occurred in two steps between 1981 and 1986. In 1981, the Economic Recovery Tax Act enacted the Kemp-Roth tax cut measures premised on supply-side economic principles. It dropped the top tax rate to 50 percent. The Tax Reform Act of 1986 lowered that rate to 28 percent.

---

[4]Interestingly, the correlation between the top tax bracket and the effective tax rate for the top income quintile drops to 0.25, indicating that higher income earners can avoid the full brunt of taxes better than can middle income earners. Also, the effective income tax rate differs from the effective total federal tax rate, because of payroll (that is, Social Security) taxes.

FIGURE 3.1
Tax Rates, 1913–2004

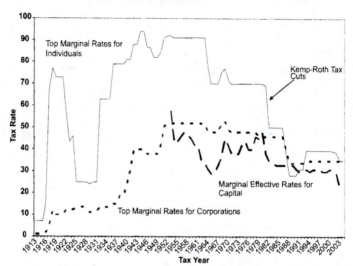

Sources: TruthandPolitics.org [http://www.truthandpolitics.org]; "Tax Facts," Urban Institute, Brookings Tax Policy Center [http://taxpolicycenter.org].

The prospect of large budget deficits led President GHW Bush to call a budget summit in 1990, resulting both in a tax increase for the top individual rate to 31 percent and a retreat from Bush's infamous "no new taxes" pledge. In the 1993 Omnibus Budget Reconciliation Act, President Clinton prevailed in a very close congressional vote in a series of provisions that, among other tax increase and budget reduction measures, raised the top income tax rate on individuals to 39.6 percent.

In the spring of 2001, in the face of what seemed to be large budget surpluses, President GW Bush prevailed on Congress to lower taxes, including a drop of the top individual rate to 35 percent in stages in what was termed The Economic Growth and Tax Relief Reconciliation Act. (If you are getting the feeling that all tax and budget acts have really great sounding names, you'd be right. Nobody ever named one of these things The Hard Times Fiscal Stringency Act.)

The 2001 tax cut, and Bush's subsequent tax reduction in 2003 (termed The Jobs and Growth Tax Reconciliation Act) were far more sweeping than a simple reduction in top tax rates. They contained other provisions for well-off individuals (including the reduction and eventual elimination of the estate tax) and provisions for the treatment of investment income that, taken together, caused a large reduction in federal tax receipts.

EVALUATING THE CLAIMS

We now turn to examining the claims that underlie the two theories. The failures of these theories can mostly be illustrated by reasonably simple graphs, but in an appendix we provide more extensive analysis.

■ Question 1a: How Do Tax Cuts Affect Government Revenue?

Our first questions involve the relationship between tax cuts and government finances—revenues and expenditures. For modern conservative starve-the-beasters, the engine for limiting government is denying revenue to government through cutting tax rates. For supply-siders, rate cuts will deny revenues only in the short run. What has actually happened in the long run is that the year-to-year percentage change in government revenues—the sum of revenues from all sources of revenue—has declined. As taxes are

cut, government revenue growth slackens. There are lots of variations, especially associated with recessions and recoveries, but the
trend is downward. This downward trend is slight, but it cumu-
lates from an expected revenue growth of 4.7 percent a year (in
the late 1940s) to around 3 percent per year today.

In a growing economy, it is possible to cut taxes and keep
revenue growth at a constant percentage—one of the great benefits
of a robust economy. That did not seem to happen; as the United
States cut income tax rates, revenue growth declined. Starve-the-
beasters claim that this is to be expected, and that the lowered
revenue from taxes will lead to deficits. But the facts belie the claims
of the miracle supply-siders—over the long run, tax cuts are associated with revenue losses.[5] Of course there are lots of reasons for
revenue losses and gains, including the general state of the economy.
But certainly if tax rate reductions were as good for revenue streams
as the supply-siders claim, we could not observe the generally negative association between cutting tax rates and decreases in revenues.

■ Question 1b: How Do Revenue Reductions Brought About by Tax Cuts Affect Government Expenditures?

It seems completely sensible to think that revenue reductions bring
about spending reductions, and it is fundamental to starving the
beast. At first look, the claim seems valid: the correlation between
year-to-year changes in receipts coming to the federal government
and changes in outlays (or expenditures) the following year is
0.49, and this is statistically significant. A correlation coefficient can

---

[5]A more complete analysis presented in the appendix indicates that recessions cause declines in government revenues (and, of course, expansions cause increases in revenues), and tax rate increases impact
revenue changes positively. Tax decreases cause revenue declines.

go between –1.0 (a perfect inverse relationship) and +1.0 (a perfect positive relationship). The correlation coefficient of 0.49 indicates that if revenues increase one year, the next year it is likely but not certain that expenditures will increase. Additionally, if revenues decrease, then it seems that the next year it is likely that revenues will decrease, as the starve-the-beasters claim.

A closer look raises lots of doubts, however. Figure 3.2 is a graph, known as a scatterplot, on which we look at how two variables affect one another. The figure is a picture of changes in receipts from taxes (on the horizontal x-axis) and outlay or

FIGURE 3.2
Percentage Change in Revenues, Lagged One Year, and Changes in Expenditure, Constant (2000) $

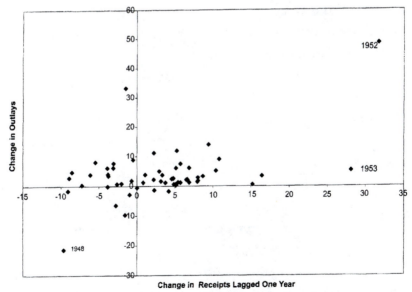

Change in Receipts Lagged One Year

Source: Calculated from Table 1.3, Historical Statistics, U.S. Office of Management and Budget (http://www.whitehouse.gov/omb/budget/fy2008/).

expenditure changes in the subsequent year (on the vertical y-axis). We want to know what happens to expenditures when receipts or revenue increased or decreased the year before. The correlation coefficient of 0.49 indicates that the two variables go together, and Figure 3.2 is the "picture" that goes with that number.

The correlation is due almost entirely to two extreme values: 1952, when taxes were raised to pay for Social Security increases and the Korean War, and 1948, when a recession reduced receipts during the reduction in spending associated with the demobilization after the Second World War. In effect, the relatively high correlation coefficient is a result of how it is computed, which involves estimating a line from (in this particular case) the values for 1948 to those in 1952.

The high correlation is mostly based on these two extreme values. And it is never a good idea to conclude the validity of a relationship conditioned on one or two values. Dropping these two years causes the correlation to drop to 0.004, statistically indistinguishable from 0. In addition, it seems as if whatever relationship there might be in the data is because revenue increases lead to expenditure increases. This occurs primarily because policy makers anticipate the need for new sources of revenue to cover new programs or wars.

In any case, it is not evident that revenue declines are associated with expenditure cuts. Looking only at the period after 1970, when the largest tax cuts occurred, the correlation is similarly indistinguishable from 0. During the period in which the politics of tax cuts were pursued most vigorously, a period that spans 35 years, there is no association between tax cuts and expenditure decreases. Giving the system time to adjust by examining whether expenditures are affected by revenues two and three years before yields the same result: there is no discernable relationship between changes in revenues and subsequent spending.

In a similar study, Niskanen reports a strong *negative* relationship between year-to-year changes in federal revenues as a percentage of GDP and changes in federal spending for the period 1981–2005. When the tax cut fever was strongest, the resulting cut in the revenue stream resulted in large increases in federal spending.[6]

As sensible as the revenue-expenditure connection might seem, there is no evidence that revenue reductions cause expenditures to be cut. It is more likely that the determinants of expenditures are entirely separate from the determinants of revenue flows. They march to different drummers. Borrowing and raising taxes to cover expenditure demands makes up the difference.[7]

So tax cuts affect revenue flows adversely, but revenue limits do not cause spending cuts. If that is so, then tax cuts should exert upward pressure on the deficit, which is completely contrary to the claims of conservatives.

■ Question 2: How Does Cutting Taxes Affect the Federal Deficit?

Both miracle supply siders and starve-the-beasters claimed that tax cuts would reduce the deficit, but the mechanisms were different.

---

[6]William A. Niskanen, "'Starve the Beast' Does Not Work," Washington, DC: The Cato Institute, May 2006. Niskanen controlled for the unemployment rate and the size of the deficit in his regression equation, and both exerted upward pressure on federal spending.

[7]This does not happen generally in state governments, because most constitutions prohibit running deficits in the operating budget. But national governments can avoid this limit by running deficits. The starve-the-beast crowd thinks they can enforce expenditure cuts by enacting tax cuts, but they don't specify how or when this will happen.

In the supply-side variant, the deficit caused by tax cuts is quickly erased as economic productivity soars. Starve-the-beasters, however, require some intermediate steps: voters put pressure on politicians because of high deficits, and politicians respond by limiting spending. Both, however, lead to the same long-term prediction: if a government cuts tax rates systematically over a long period of time, deficits will decline or even disappear.

Well, government *has* cut tax rates over a long period of time, but, contrary to the claims of the conservative economists, the deficit has increased. A strong inverse relationship exists between the top marginal tax rate charged on personal income and the size of the federal deficit. As Figure 3.3 shows, the top marginal tax rate (for families filing joint returns) has declined throughout most of the postwar period. Corresponding to that decline is an increase in the federal deficit, or what is the same thing, a decline in the federal surplus (with a few minor fluctuations around the trend line) throughout most of that period.[8] There is no apparent decrease in the deficit that is associated with tax cuts.

The other side of the coin is that deficits can be decreased by increasing taxes, something that most people understand intuitively when not confused by pseudo-economic dogma. And, indeed, the only substantial deviation in the trend toward increased deficits since the 1950s was associated with the increases in tax rates in the early 1990s. Federal surpluses of the late 1990s were built from tax increases earlier in the decade—along with powerful

---

[8]Tax rates from TruthandPolitics.org [http:/ /www. truthandpolitics.org]; "Tax Facts," Urban Institute-Brookings Tax Policy Center [http:/ /taxpolicycenter.org]; Surplus/Deficits from the U.S. Office of Management and Budget, Historical Statistics (http://www.whitehouse.gov/omb/budget/fy2008/).

FIGURE 3.3
Tax Rates and the Federal Deficit, 1948–2006

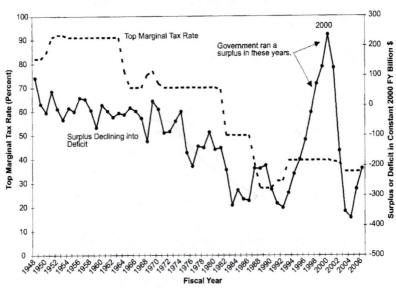

Sources: Tax rates from TruthandPolitics.org [http://www.truthandpolitics.org]; "Tax Facts"; Urban Institute Brookings Tax Policy Center [http://taxpolicycenter.org] Surplus/deficit from the U.S. Office of Management and Budget, Historical Statistics, Table 1.3 (http://www.whitehouse.gov/omb/budget/fy2008/).

budgetary controls that dampened the rate of growth of yearly expenditures and strong economic growth.

Of course the eye can be fooled when we just look at a graph across time. That is a major reason that social scientists do more complex statistical analyses. However, more detailed analysis fails to offer any support for the notion that tax cuts decrease deficits. Indeed, the analysis supports the opposite: decreases in the top marginal tax rate tend to increase the deficit. Details are in the book's appendix.

One might speculate that the association between lower tax rates and increased budget deficits is simply due to a growing economy that enables government to run higher absolute deficits without increasing its share of the national economy. This is not the case; the trend holds whether we calculate the deficit in constant dollars or as a percentage of GDP.

The figure, incidentally, shows how easy it is to pick anecdotes to support particular theories. Look at the late 1980s, when tax cuts were followed by revenue growth and deficit declines. That is the story that supply-siders are fond of recounting. Unfortunately, the effects are more likely due to rebounds from the severe recession of the early 1980s. Moreover, even the vaunted Kennedy tax cuts of the 1960s did not increase revenues enough to improve the deficit (either in real dollar terms or relative to the economy). Neither did the lauded tax cuts of the early 1980s have such an effect. Finally, politicians who raised taxes in the early 1990s seem to have been rewarded by rapid growth in government revenues, growth robust enough to push the fiscal balance sheet into the black.

The preceding analyses rest on the assumption that politicians would expect to feel the (alleged) wrath of voters and cut spending quickly after cutting taxes; indeed, that is clearly what Reagan budget director David Stockman anticipated. Conservative economists might argue, however, that it takes time for tax cuts to work through the system. So one might not expect deficits to be brought under control immediately. That is, politicians are not rational expectationists—somehow they must feel and respond to the actual deficit.

A two-year lag, however, yields similar results as does the one year lag; two years after the tax cut, the government's deficit is larger than it would have been without the cut. Similarly, three years after the tax rate reduction, it is still putting upward pressure on the deficit, clearly not lowering it. At some point, one has the right to expect a positive effect on the balance sheet, if the theory has any validity at all. But we are running out of data (or what statisticians call degrees of freedom) to test the theory (because we lose one every time we lag a year). It is easier to conclude the obvious: tax cuts, along with recessions, cause government deficits.

Borrowing from the Trust Funds

In the above analysis, we've looked at the federal government's unified budget. The unified budget has two components: the general budget and the trust funds. The general budget is what people normally think of when government spending is at issue: agriculture, defense, education, and so forth. But the budget also consists of trust funds, which collect taxes and spend money independently. There are several of these funds, such as the highway trust fund and the superfund for cleaning up toxic sites, but far and away the biggest of these is the Social Security trust fund. The reason for using these trusts is to allow them to build up surpluses to pay for future obligations or to link expenditures to specific sources of revenue.[9]

Until 1983, Social Security was a pay-as-you-go system in which the payroll taxes that were collected immediately went to pay the retirement benefits of older Americans. But at that time, Social Security actuaries projected that the Social Security trust

---

[9] The most thorough analysis of the politics and public policy of trust funds is provided by Erik Patashnik, *Putting Trust in the U.S. Budget: Federal Trust Funds and the Politics of Commitment.* Cambridge: Cambridge University Press, 2000.

fund would be unable to pay its obligation within two years. President Reagan appointed the National Commission on Social Security Reform, headed by Alan Greenspan. The commission's recommendations led to the 1983 Social Security Amendments that increased the retirement age and raised payroll taxes enough to solve the short-term financial crisis and to set aside enough funds to pay for the coming increases in the number of retired Americans—today known as the baby boom bulge.

The Social Security trust fund began to run larger and larger surpluses, and the difference was invested in U.S. treasury bonds. That meant that the unified budget was masking increasingly large deficits in the general budget. In effect, the government was borrowing from the Social Security retirement funds set aside by working Americans through payroll taxation to pay for current programs. In 1999 and 2000, the general budget ran a surplus for the first time since 1960. For those two years, government did not need to borrow from the trust funds to pay for the general fund deficit. In the 2000 election, both candidates pledged to balance the general government budget, not just the unified budget, in the famous "lock box" pledges. Bush immediately violated this pledge with his 2001 tax cuts.

So the deficit is actually much worse in fact than the unified budget indicates. If one wants to estimate the effect of government deficit financing on economic activity, then the unified budget is the right number. But if one is concerned with the present and future obligations of government, then the two components must be separated. These trust funds are real, in the sense that government must repay the treasury bonds issued to the funds, just as it must repay citizens or foreign governments who hold them.

Figure 3.4 shows the two components separately. The hatched area is the amount that the federal government borrows from the Social Security trust fund and other similar trust funds to pay for current programs. The graph suggests that the Reagan tax cuts led to increases in borrowing from the trust fund, until the GHW Bush and Clinton tax increases reduced the need for borrowing. The GW Bush tax reductions led to the massive trust fund borrowing taking place today.

Better models of the effects of tax rates on federal deficits could be constructed, and all sorts of counterfactuals can be envisioned (for example, the deficit would have been worse if we had not cut taxes). But the claims of the starve-the-beasters are not subtle, and simple diagrams like those presented in Figures 3.3 and 3.4 do great damage to the notion that tax cuts lead to

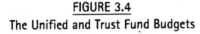

FIGURE 3.4
The Unified and Trust Fund Budgets

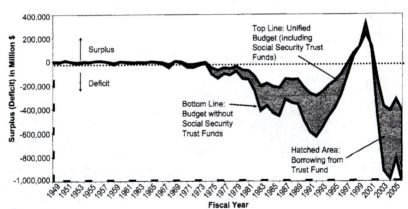

Source: U.S. Office of Management and Budget, Historical Statistics, Table 1.1 (http://www.whitehouse.gov/omb/budget/fy2008/).

responsible financing and undermine its claim to be a guide for pragmatic public policy action.

■ Question 3: Do Tax Rate Cuts Force Politicians to Limit Spending?

Perhaps the deficit is not of such dire consequence after all. What conservatives want is less government, and the keystone to that is restraint in spending. Some conservatives do not appear to care how big the deficit is, because they believe that it does not affect the economy adversely. Vice President Dick Cheney allegedly told Treasury Secretary Paul O'Neill that "Reagan proved that deficits don't matter."[10] So maybe we want to examine the effects of tax cuts on changes in spending and drop the notion that the deficit somehow intervenes between tax cuts and spending restraints.

Figure 3.5, in which the median percentage change in federal government outlays and the top marginal tax rate are plotted, speaks to this issue. The most important thing to note about that graph is that over the period of the graph (1953–2004), there have been lots of increases and decreases in the annual percentage change in spending, but in the end the trend has led nowhere. The regression trend line has a negligible slope (clear enough from the graph). Year in and year out, the typical (median) change in inflation-adjusted outlays is 2.17 percent. There are important medium-term trends here, particularly a growth period in the 1970s and a period of restraint in the 1990s, but these are obviously not associated with changes in tax rates. (The correlation between tax

---

[10]Ronald Suskind, *The Price of Loyalty*. New York: Simon and Schuster, 2004.

FIGURE 3.5
Tax Rates and Spending, 1953–2004

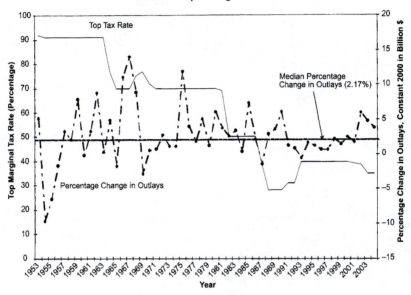

Sources: Tax rates from TruthandPolitics.org; "Tax Facts." Outlays from the U.S. Office of Management and Budget, Historical Statistics.

rates and the percentage annual change in outlays is a statistically insignificant 0.058.)

Whatever drives spending is not connected to tax cuts. This might seem surprising at first, but many elements of government spending are not particularly sensitive to tax cuts. These include defense spending, spending to counter the effects of recessions, agriculture subsidies, and Social Security and Medicare (which have dedicated taxes, but which are real expenditures).

Figures 3.2 to 3.5 taken together indicate that tax cuts do not limit spending, but they do increase the deficit. The deficit does not in itself or in combination with tax cuts cause subsequent restraint in spending. Trust fund borrowing actually masks the severity of the deficit problem; tax cuts are having a more dire effect on the nation's fiscal balance sheet than the unified budget deficit suggests.

■ Question 4: Does Public Opinion Force Limited Government After Tax Cuts?

We now turn to the politics of taxes and deficits. The starve-the-beasters, claim that the public will rise up and pressure politicians to cut programs is central to the argument. The claim has nothing to do with economics and everything to do with politics, as at least some op-ed economists realize. Will Wilkerson of the Cato Institute notes that "'Starve-the-beast' is really a conjecture about the psychology of voters and legislators".[11]

It is strange that Nobel economists Friedman, Becker, and the starve-the-beast crew argued that deficits, which after all finance current benefits out of future tax revenues, would be more of a limitation on the size of government than the current tax burden. The starve-the-beasters seem to have ignored economic theory and replaced it with a theory of public opinion—that people are more sensitive to the size of deficits than to the current tax burden. But that is not good political theory, either, and has no serious support in the political science literature.[12]

And, indeed, this claim is perhaps the easiest to refute of all the bogus claims put forward by the op-ed economists. Because of

---

[11]Will Wilkerson, "Political Discipline, Not Just Less Pork." *Philadelphia Inquirer*, December 26, 2004.
[12]Though this exact version has not been previously tested, certain associated hypotheses have been. Most importantly, liberal public opinion is negatively associated with the size of government. We discuss this below.

advances in the measurement of public opinion, we can examine the relationship between the top marginal tax rate and the public's general mood about the desirability of government. The starve-the-beast theory states that if tax rates go down, the deficit will go up (so far, so good); the public reacts negatively to the deficit, and this forces politicians to cut spending. The implications are that public opinion should be influenced in a conservative direction by the deficit, and in a conservative direction by reductions in the tax rate.

There are several approaches to the measurement of public opinion over long periods of time, but the best for our purposes is Jim Stimson's measure of public mood.[13] Stimson, of the University of North Carolina, developed a computer algorithm for combining numerous independent polls of American public opinion relevant to the approval of government programs. His approach assures a high degree of comparability across time so that we can say whether liberalism is higher or lower today than it was, say, 20 years ago.

Figure 3.6 graphs Stimson's public mood measure (higher values indicate liberalism) versus the top marginal tax rate from 1970 to the present. On the face of it, this does not look good at all for the op-ed economists. As tax rates have declined over the period, the public has become more liberal. In the brief period when they rose, the public became more conservative (those exceptional 1990s, once again).[14]

---

[13]James Stimson, *Public Opinion in America*, 2nd ed. Boulder, CO: Westview Press, 1999.

[14]For the full period, 1953, when Stimson's measure starts, through 2004, the revenue variable is significant, but the tax rate variable is not. This could be a function of top tax rates being somewhat less meaningful before the Kennedy-Johnson era tax cuts, because they could be effectively lowered by particular tax provisions.

FIGURE 3.6
Public Mood and the Top Marginal Tax Rate, 1970–2004

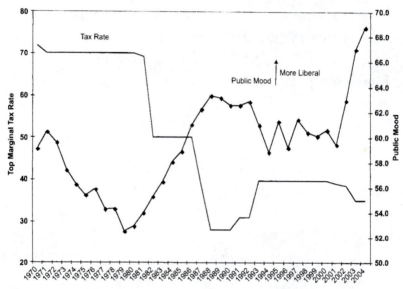

Sources: Tax rates from TruthandPolitics.org; "Tax Facts." Public mood updated from Stimson, 1999 using data from his personal website (http://www.unc.edu/~jstimson/).

This is a powerful picture, probably the most important graph in the book. It shows that as tax rates decrease, in general, liberalism increases. And it looks as if when taxes are increased, the public becomes more conservative. Because Stimson's measure is based on how much people approve of particular government programs, it directly assesses how much government they want at any given time.

Of course liberalism is not caused by tax reductions alone; many other causal factors are likely to be involved. But Figure 3.6 suggests an important association between the two. Moreover, modern public opinion research has shown that the public reacts with more conservatism when government spending goes up, and with more liberalism when spending goes down.[15] When government gets big, people respond by becoming more conservative. We've added something important here—it may be the case that people react not so much to the size of government as to the taxes they have to pay to support it.

Figure 3.7 is a simple scatterplot concerning public mood and the tax rate. That is, it takes the information plotted across time for the two variables in Figure 3.6 and plots them against one another, with tax rates on the horizontal axis and liberalism on the vertical axis. The result is a strong negative relationship, which

FIGURE 3.7

Scatterplot of Public Mood and the Top Marginal Tax Rate, 1970–2004

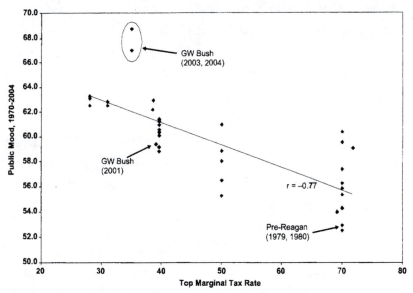

Sources: Tax rates from TruthandPolitics.org; "Tax Facts." Public mood updated from Stimson, 1999.

[15]Stimson, *Public Opinion in America*, 1999; Christopher Wlezien, "Patterns of Representation: Dynamics of Public Preferences and Policy," *Journal of Politics* 66, 2004, pp. 1–24.

we already suspected from Figure 3.6, but the power of this association is surprising: a correlation coefficient of -0.77 is very impressive. Note that various values of liberalism (on the y-axis) are associated with any given tax rate (the x-axis), which indicates that liberalism is driven not only by tax rates, but by other factors as well. Also note that, unlike the association between revenues and expenditures depicted in Figure 3.3, a few extreme values cannot account for the relationship.

Marked on the graph are a few important dates. Note that the high water mark of public conservatism (that is, low liberalism) is in the 1979–1980 period, right before the election of Reagan. Tax rates were high then, and many new government programs had been initiated in the previous 15 years. Note also the 35-year highs in liberalism in 2003 and 2004, and the much more moderate public mood in 2001, before the massive Bush tax cuts. It is likely that the increase in liberal public opinion is caused by more than tax rate cuts, because the level of liberalism is far above the prediction line. But it is likely that at least part of the move toward more liberalism is the lower Bush tax rates.

Higher tax rates are associated with more conservative public opinion; low taxes and tax cuts are associated with more liberal public opinion. That is enough alone to refute the starve-the-beast contention that tax cuts will provoke voter outrage toward government. But what about the deficit? Do voters react negatively toward large deficits by becoming more conservative? The answer is no; there is no relationship between the absolute or the relative size to GDP of the deficit and public mood. The correlation between the size of the deficit (in constant dollars) and liberal public mood (1952–2005) is 0.08. As the deficit increases, the public actually demands more government, but the relationship is not strong.

Maybe people respond not to the size of the deficit but to whether it is going up or down. That is, maybe if deficits are growing, people become politically more conservative. That starve-the-beast prediction does not hold either: the correlation between the percentage change in the deficit and political liberalism is 0.21. This relationship is positive; as deficits grow, citizens become more liberal—presumably because they are being offered government services at bargain-basement tax prices, financed by borrowing.

The findings reported here open up several important questions. First is the issue of why there is such a strong relationship between opinion and income tax rates, particularly the top marginal rates. Maybe voters react to total taxes rather than singling out the income tax. Since 1979, the percentage of households where payroll taxes exceeded income taxes has risen from 26 percent to over 38 percent, according to calculations made by the Tax Policy Center. It turns out, however, that there is absolutely no relationship between the level of the payroll tax and Stimson's measure of public mood. No matter what the payroll tax rate has been, it is irrelevant to the extent of liberal or conservative mass public opinion.[16]

Second, though we can be sure that liberal public opinion and tax rates are inversely related, we can't be sure of the particular mechanism that links the two. We've used top individual rates as a surrogate for the entire tax structure, but we can't say how the relationship works. Why would people be so sensitive to income

---

[16]The correlation is 0.06—even in the wrong direction.

tax rates rather than payroll taxes, given that more people pay payroll taxes than income taxes? And the vast majority of taxpayers never pay a cent at the top rate, although we showed at the beginning of this chapter that when the top rates are cut (or raised), the lower rates are also cut (or raised).

One possibility is that the extensive debate on tax policy—especially since 1980—has sensitized people to that aspect of the tax rate. Republicans have continuously attacked taxes in general, and especially the unfairness of taxes on the most well-off (recently including the federal estate tax). Simultaneously, most understand that payroll taxes go to support Social Security, an overwhelmingly popular program that has traditionally been justified as an insurance program rather than a government benefit financed out of taxes. Clearly more work is needed in specifying this relationship.

Finally, it is possible that factors other than tax policies account for variations in public opinion. However, given the findings here and those by other scholars that liberal policy activities are inversely related to liberal public opinion, it is almost certain that public policy actions are the source of changes in public opinion, and that the mechanisms are generally consistent with those we describe here.[17]

A more complete analysis, presented in the appendix to the book, shows that both increases in tax rates and increases in the revenue collected by the federal government are (separately) associated with increases in conservative public opinion, controlling

---

[17]Robert Erikson, Michael MacKuen, and James Stimson, *The Macro Polity*. Cambridge: Cambridge University Press, 2002.

for recessionary years. It seems that lowering taxes and shrinking government (assessed by revenues) result in increases in liberalism and increased demands for government programs. Raising taxes and increasing the size of government result in more conservative opinion and reduced demands for government programs. Taxes and government revenues exist in dynamic balance with public opinion, much the way the temperature in your home is in balance with how much your furnace runs, governed by the setting you enter on your thermostat.[18]

■ Question 5: Do Tax Cuts Limit the Size of Government?

Now let's examine more directly the size of government itself. It is not easy to measure the complete size of government, and there is considerable debate about how to do it. Fiscal policies alone are not enough, because regulations, court decisions, and assorted mandates on other levels of government that result in more spending and regulations at these other levels all should be taken into account. What Niskanen reminds his fellow libertarians about, however, is a good approach: "Above all, keep in mind that the size of government is best measured by the level of federal spending and regulation."[19] Reducing taxes and revenues only shifts burdens to future generations.

Figure 3.8 plots federal outlays as a percentage of gross domestic product. From the end of the Second World War through 1983, the size of government, measured as the ratio of government spending to the total size of the economy, increased in a steady

---

[18] This analogy is due to Chris Wlezien.
[19] Niskanen, " 'Starve the Beast Does Not Work,' " Cato Policy Report March/April. Washington DC: Cato Institute, 2004.

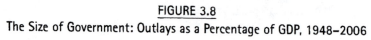

FIGURE 3.8
The Size of Government: Outlays as a Percentage of GDP, 1948–2006

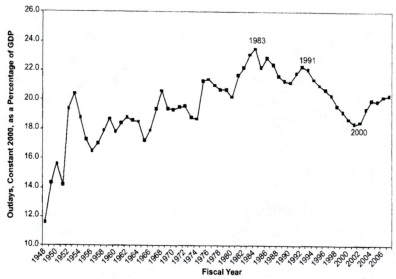

Source: U.S. Office of Management and Budget, Historical Statistics, Table 1.3
(http://www.whitehouse.gov/omb/budget/fy2008/).

fashion. The year 1983 initiated a period of contraction of the relative size of government that, save for a couple of years in the early 1990s, continued until GW Bush assumed the presidency. Since then, a sharp increase in the size of government has occurred, much to the dismay of at least some conservatives.[20]

And, indeed, as we have come to expect, the conservative op-ed economists' predictions fail. Over the 1948–2004 period, there is an inverse relationship between the top marginal tax rate and the size of government. The lower the tax rate, the greater the size of government relative to GDP; the correlation is −0.53.

[20]Veronique de Rugy, *The Republican Spending Explosion*. Cato Institute Briefing Paper #84, 2004.

In an analysis of federal spending from 1981 through the early Bush years, William Niskanen and Peter Van Doren report a negative relationship between the relative level of spending and the federal tax burden, controlling for the unemployment rate. Niskanen and Van Doren suggest that spending demand decreases as the tax burden increases.[21] Their finding has strong support here: as tax rates increase, demand for more government falls.

But does spending actually react to public pressure? A statistical analysis indeed shows that spending is responsive to changes in public mood. If the public moves in a conservative direction, then government spending (as a percentage of GDP) falls. Details are in the appendix.

THE LIKELY CAUSAL MECHANISM

We may state very simply what we have learned from examining the role of public opinion in responding to taxes:

- First, as tax rates fall, public opinion becomes more liberal. There are of course other sources of liberalism than just the taxes people pay, but one source certainly seems to be the tax rates people are charged by government. Conversely, if the benefits people feel they are receiving from government relative to the taxes they pay seem low, then they react by becoming more negative toward government.

---

[21]Niskanen and Van Doren, "Some Intriguing Findings About Federal Spending," paper presented at the Public Choice Society, Baltimore, MD. March 11–14, 2004; Niskanen and Van Doren, "Some Intriguing Findings About Federal Spending," in Jeffrey A. Frankel and Peter R. Orszag, eds., *American Economic Policy in the 1990s.* Cambridge, MA: MIT Press, 2004.

- Second, as public opinion becomes more liberal, the size
  of government grows. Again, there are many more reasons government adds programs, and the mechanisms by
  which this occurs are complex. But the general finding is
  clear: liberal public opinion equals more government.

It seems to be this simple:

Tax Cuts ———➤ Liberal Public Mood ———➤ More Government

And, for conservatives, the implication is that if you want to
use an indirect method operating through public opinion to get
less government, you need to raise taxes, not cut them.

Tax Increases ——➤ Conservative Public Mood —➤ Less Government

SUMMING UP

The period since the Second World War has seen a long-term
decline in the top marginal tax rates on income for individuals, for
corporations, and for capital gains. What has been the effect of
this change? First, this decline has been associated with increases
in the federal deficit, whether measured in inflation-adjusted dollars or as a percentage of the economy. The only exception to the
postwar tendency of U.S. policy makers to reduce taxes took place
in the period between 1991 and 2000. Then, when taxes were
raised, the federal deficit declined. This is true even when taking
into account the recession of 1990–1991.

Second, as tax rates declined, the size of government *increased.*
On the other hand, when taxes were raised in the 1990s, the size of
government (measured as a ratio of expenditures to the size of the

overall economy) decreased. There was a sharp difference between the Reagan years and the administrations of GHW Bush and Clinton. The downside of the Reagan tax cuts was an unprecedented increase in the federal deficit. In contrast, *the tax increases of GHW Bush and Clinton led not only to declines in the deficit but eventually to a federal surplus and, at the very same time, ushered in the longest period of shrinkage in the size of government in the modern era.*

In dramatic fashion, all of this was reversed in a micromoment—the election of GW Bush. Tax rates were lowered, the deficit ballooned, and the size of government rose briskly. This is not a function of the very mild 2001 recession, nor is it due only to increased military and homeland security expenses after the terrorist attacks on the U.S. in 2001, as Republicans have argued. Clearly military and homeland security were a large part of the total increase, but spending increased across the board, in virtually all categories, in a general big government orgy.

Third, public opinion becomes more conservative when taxes are raised, more liberal when they are cut, and does not respond to the size of the deficit. It is hard to avoid the conclusion that people very roughly compare benefits to tax costs: they respond positively to more government when they are paying low taxes, and negatively when they are paying high taxes. If government offers low taxes through a borrowing program, people will not demand lower benefits (because public opinion is not very sensitive to the size of the deficit). They will actually demand more benefits. As a consequence, the size of government grows when tax rates are cut, and government shrinks when taxes are raised. Borrowing from the future encourages present consumption.

The starve-the-beast argument is exactly backwards: limited government is facilitated when taxes are raised to pay for government programs out of current revenues. Big government is facilitated when part of the cost of current programs is shifted to future generations through borrowing. It would seem that paying present benefits from current taxes is what would encourage smaller government.

Tax cuts have harmed the nation's future fiscal health by implementing these cuts without imposing immediate spending restraints. William Gale and Peter Orszag of the Brookings Institution argue that deficits during the next decade will reduce national savings as much as 2–3 percent of GDP. Essentially, deficits shift resources from investment to consumption, because up to 80 percent of tax cuts are mostly spent rather than saved by households.[22]

But there is a second consumption component to tax cuts. They stimulate citizen demand for more government services. When tax rates fall, public opinion becomes more liberal, essentially putting more pressure on government to provide public programs. When tax rates rise, the public becomes more conservative, reducing demand for public programs. This works fine in a pay-as-you-go system, which enables people to decide roughly how much in taxes they want to pay for programs.

Borrowing to finance tax cuts under the notion that future spending restraints will result because of public distaste for deficits, however, has the opposite effect. It causes more demand, because people are more sensitive to changes in the tax rate than to the deficit. So tax cuts without simultaneous spending restraint

---

[22]William G. Gale and Peter Orszag, "Bush Administration Tax Policy: Starving the Beast?" *Tax Notes*, November 15, 2004.

have a dual negative effect on the nation's balance sheet: they increase private consumption, and they increase political demands for more government programs.

All of this does not mean that government spending will not be cut in the future but it surely will be difficult. Public opinion is but one source of policy change, and in recent years Republicans have been adept at enacting policies that generate little public support while simultaneously refusing to act on matters important to the public.[23] However, Republicans in power have shown a distinct taste for big government themselves. Not content to cut taxes and maintain the existing path of public expenditures, they have greatly expanded government—the greatest expansion since Lyndon Johnson's Great Society, a point that we examine in more detail later.

The miracle supply-side and starving-the-beast theories underscore how bad ideas can take on lives of their own and survive the hard fact that the ideas are not only wrong but cause results diametrically opposite to what the advocates predicted. To date, we have only explored the miracle version of the supply-side economics, but evidence is now accumulating that the GW Bush tax cuts probably did not result in the benefits claimed by academic supply-side theorists. First we turn to an examination of how the two clearly wrong theories, the miracle supply-side and starve-the-beast theories, have worked to undermine the kind of sound financial management that does work.

---

[23]Jacob Hacker and Paul Pierson, *Off Center*. New Haven: Yale University Press, 2005.

CHAPTER 4

Budgetary Politics and the Spending Mind-Set

Have the pseudo–economic theories justifying tax cuts become ideological systems for undermining fiscal responsibility? Economists William Gale and Peter Orszag think that "The 'starve-the-beast' strategy may simply not work as a means of achieving political equilibrium."[1] Destabilizing one side of the revenue–budget equation does not imply that the other side will come into equilibrium as a consequence. If they are right, and in this chapter we show that they are, starve-the-beast is unmasked as nothing but a justification to spend now and let someone else pay later.

Starve-the-beast is not an economic theory; it is a political one. As a consequence, the place to look for the key to budgetary dynamics is not economics, but politics. Harvard political scientist V. O. Key noted in 1940 that political scientists had never really

---

[1]William Gale and Peter Orszag, "Bush Administration Tax Policy: Starving the Beast?" *Tax Notes*, November 15, 2004, pp. 999–1002. Orszag left the Brookings Institution to become director of the Congressional Budget Office in January 2007.

developed a theory of budgeting.[2] In a narrow sense, that is still the case, because no theory of budgets can be produced without a full appreciation of politics.

In this chapter, we take a look at the interplay between politics and public budgets, showing how political settlements (or lack of them) have influenced the course of public finance in post–World War II America. In particular, we show how the evolving position of the Republican Party emphasizing tax cuts without consideration of the implications for budgetary deficits has undermined the ability of the U.S. government to run a sound financial system. This position has been enabled by the muddled economic thinking we analyzed in earlier chapters—both supply-side economics and starve-the-beast theories justify tax cuts without the need to match programs to the resulting revenue flow.

We are used to thinking of public budgeting as a dry and essentially boring topic, run by professional accountants and budget specialists with green eyeshades. But budgeting is not left to professionals, because public budgeting is profoundly political. A public budget puts numbers to public priorities, and public priorities are determined through the interplay of political actors. So public budgeting is a profoundly political activity.

IF AN ECONOMIST SAYS IT, IS IT ECONOMICS?

Because public budgeting is political, economic theories may be of limited utility in the setting of budgetary priorities. That does not mean, however, that we are free to ignore good economic advice

---

[2]V. O. Key, Jr., "The Lack of a Budgetary Theory," *American Political Science Review*, 34, pp. 1137–1144.

in the budgetary process. When former Federal Reserve chairman Alan Greenspan told Congress of his concerns that the budget deficit will hurt the economy, as he has told Congress repeatedly in recent years, he was offering sound economic analysis. Here is what Greenspan said before the Senate Budget Committee in April 2005 (Bold added for emphasis.):

> *Indeed, under existing tax rates and reasonable assumptions about other spending, these projections make clear that **the federal budget is on an unsustainable path**, in which large deficits result in rising interest rates and ever-growing interest payments that augment deficits in future years. But most important, **deficits as a percentage of GDP in these simulations rise without limit.** Unless that trend is reversed, at some point these deficits would cause the economy to stagnate or worse.*[3]

When Greenspan argued that budgetary limits ought to be imposed by spending limits rather than tax increases, as he did in January 2001 in testimony before the Senate Budget Committee and again in February 2004 before the House Budget Committee, he crossed the line. He shifted from being a highly regarded economist to acting as a political advocate. An analysis by Jason Furman and Orszag concluded that there is "little evidence to justify an automatic preference for tax cuts on other than ideological grounds."[4] Both small limited governments and large welfare states can run vibrant economies. This is a point regularly made by Peter G. Peterson of the Concord Coalition, an organization that

[3]"Testimony of Chairman Alan Greeenspan, Budget Process Reforms, Before the Senate Budget Committee, April 21, 2005. Board of Governors of the Federal Reserve Board web page, News and Events. http://www.federalreserve.gov/
[4]Jason Furman and Peter Orszag, *Tax Cuts vs. Spending Increases: Is There a Basis for Chairman Greenspan's Preference for Tax Cuts?* Washington DC: Center on Budget and Policy Priorities, 2001.

advocates sound public finances. One may wish for smaller government, but that is a political preference, not an economic dictate.

Economists, even highly respectable ones, sometimes make statements about the economy that are not based on sound economics, but rather are based on political preferences. Greenspan's pronouncement prescribing spending limits rather than tax increases may appear to be sound economics applied to public budgeting because the speaker at the time was a highly respected economist holding a prestigious formal position. But it is an ideological assertion about tax hikes that came from Greenspan's political beliefs rather than his economic analysis. His failure to make this distinction likely gave unwarranted credibility to his assertion. The same judgment applies to similar statements in op-ed columns by Nobel laureate economists unless they explicitly cast off their mantle of expertise.

BUDGET POLITICS AND CONGRESSIONAL PROCEDURES

Politics does not smoothly translate into budget figures. For example, one might think that political party positions on the desirability of government programs would be reflected in budgets. That is, traditionally in the United States the Republicans stood for limited government and the Democrats opted for expanded government. As we shall see shortly, this is not the case in modern America; party positions have evolved on the issue of government financing to the point that the vice president of the United States, Dick Cheney, could comment that "deficits don't matter."[5]

---

[5]Ronald Suskind, *The Price of Loyalty*. New York: Simon and Schuster, 2004.

We simply cannot understand the interplay of politics and public finances without grappling with the institutional procedures that govern the process of public budgeting. The set of procedures that have evolved to enact the federal budget are complex and offer plenty of venues for the interplay of budget politics.[6] Table 4.1 defines some of the most important budget terms and indicates where the action takes place, both in the executive branch—where budgeting begins—and in Congress—where the final document is assembled.

These different procedures can lead to surprising outbreaks of politics that move in ways that nobody really anticipated. Both the deliberate actions of Congress and the entrepreneurial activities of politicians have caused budgetary politics to morph through the years. In the 1950s and 1960s, budgets were dominated by the chairs of the various subcommittees of the appropriations committees; they were termed "the College of Cardinals" as a tribute to their power. Today, however, the budget process has become far more complex, involving not only appropriations committees but also substantive authorizing committees and budget committees, as well as the party leaders and the Congressional Budget Office.

Two examples show how politics, budgets, and congressional procedures are intertwined. In 1981, President Reagan and his congressional allies used the budget reconciliation process, established to regularize the congressional budget process, to enact The Economic Recovery Tax Act, a vast law that cut both taxes and

---

[6]For a full history and political analysis of the modern era, see Lance T. LeLoup, *Parties, Rules and the Evolution of Congressional Budgeting*. Columbus, OH: Ohio State University Press, 2005.

TABLE 4.1
Budget Terms

BUDGET TERM	DEFINITION	MAJOR ACTOR
Budget outlays	Actual expenditures in a fiscal year	Federal agencies
Budget authority	Legal authority granted to government agencies to spend funds	Congress
Appropriations	Legislation that provides budget authority	Appropriations committees
Authorization	Legislation that establishes or continues a federal program or agency	Substantive committees
Budget resolution	Concurrent resolution that lays out budget plans	Budget committees
Budget reconciliation	Resolution that reconciles budget resolution with actual appropriations recommendations	Congress
Mandatory spending	Spending determined by permanent law, not by annual appropriations	Substantive committees
Discretionary spending	Spending determined by annual appropriations	Appropriations committees
Continuing budget resolution	Authorization to agencies to continue funding at present levels; used when appropriations process unfinished	Congress

Sources: OMB Watch, Glossary of Important Budget Terms web page (http://www
.ombwatch.org); The Budget Process: Glossary of Terms, House of Budget Committee
web page (http://budgethouse.gov/glossary.htm).

expenditures in a manner that would have been difficult if not impossible through normal processes. This legislation is the centerpiece of Reagan's presidency, and one of the most important pieces of legislation enacted in the 20th century.

In November 1995, the federal government closed its doors, sending home all employees deemed nonessential. This almost complete government shutdown was repeated in a partial shutdown in

December 1995 and January 1996. The impasse was reached when President Clinton threatened to veto some appropriations bills because he deemed them inadequate. Republican leaders in Congress, who were aggressively trying to cut government programs at the time, pointed out that they would need to pass a continuing resolution, and that would carry forward "big government" at current levels. So they refused to pass the continuing resolution that would have allowed the government to operate. Indeed, there is some evidence that some Republicans had built this brinkmanship into their strategy, assuming that Clinton would refuse to go along with the large budget cuts they had in mind at the time.[7] In the fiery exchanges that followed, Clinton was able to define his position to the public as the moral high ground, essentially blaming Congress for an impasse that both branches of government had created. Congress relented and passed the resolutions.

BUDGETARY ERAS AND THE CULTURE OF SPENDING

All of this political activity occurs within broad mind-sets, or cultures of budgetary behavior. The most astute student of budgetary politics in recent times, the late Aaron Wildavsky, concluded that a "culture of spending" (or, on the other side of the coin, of fiscal prudence) characterized governments. In effect, mind-sets can grip Washington officials, leading them to support bursts of spending with little regard for where financing for the new initiatives will

---

[7]Skip Porteus, "'We'll Let the Government Shut Down,'" *The Albion Monitor.* February 18, 1996.

come from or to advocate for the imposition of fiscal discipline. These mind-sets lead to general eras of budgetary behavior, longer-run periods that are characterized by either a positive or a negative orientation toward spending public money. It is not the case, of course, that everybody within a big-spending era wants more government, but it is true that the proponents of limited government have a much harder time making their case during these periods.

Orgies of spending irresponsibility interspersed with periods of calm fiscal sanity seem to be common in human societies. Carolyn Webber and Wildavsky carefully document different spending regimes in a variety of societies throughout history, and the story is repeated from Babylon to modern America.[8] Not infrequently the lack of spending restraint, oftentimes when powerful leaders decide to embark on major wars, is a major cause of the decline of societies.

Politicians often talk of balanced budgets and fiscal restraint as a matter of course, but budget numbers can undermine their statements. If there is deviation from the fiscal regime they claim to be running, it is some necessity—such as war or natural disaster—that caused the spending increases, not their good intentions. This can confuse the observer, which of course it is designed to do, and often it takes a few years of history to isolate these regimes.

During the budget shutdown battles of the 1990s, politicians often spoke of fiscal restraint. "The House Republican leadership," Congressman Mark Souder of Indiana said in 1995, "has said that

---

[8]Carolyn Webber and Aaron Wildavsky, *A History of Taxation and Expenditure in the Western World.* New York: Simon and Schuster. 1986.

the minimum goals are to balance the budget in seven years, reform welfare, save Medicare, and have tax cuts. The freshmen have communicated to the leadership that that is not enough."[9] President Clinton, in his speech to the American public about the shutdown, touted his deficit reduction accomplishments and promised a balanced budget.

The statements of Souder and Clinton were not mere rhetoric. Congress and the president did indeed balance the budget and present the American public with four years of budgetary surpluses. Interestingly, too, the vitriol spewing forth from Washington and the truly bad blood between the Republican Congress and Democratic president Bill Clinton masked a very important underlying agreement: whatever government did, finances must remain in balance.

Fast-forward ten years. On September 13, 2005, House Majority Leader Tom Delay declared an "ongoing victory" for fiscal responsibility and said that there was simply no more fat to be cut from the federal budget. "After 11 years of Republican majority we've pared it down pretty good."[10] But this was rhetoric with no substance; budgets had soared during the previous four years, and deficits had ballooned. The same kind of empty rhetoric was coming from the White House as it promised to cut the deficit in half by 2011 in the budget it presented Congress in February 2006. To hear the White House and the congressional leadership talk, an amazing fiscal regime of responsibility was in place, and the vitriol characteristic of congressional–presidential interchanges in the

---

[9]Quoted in Porteus. "'We'll Let the Government Shut Down.'"
[10]Amy Fagan and Stephen Dinan, "DeLay Declares 'Victory' in War on Budget Fat," *Washington Times*, September 14, 2005.

1990s was gone, replaced by a virtual love-fest. Yet Congress and the president had conspired to borrow money at a furious pace, raising the national debt by almost 50 percent in five years.

Budget talk is not a good indicator of spending regimes, but we can study these regimes by using real budgetary data. In this chapter, we will isolate fiscal regimes that have characterized the U.S. federal government since the Second World War. Though the general outlines of these regimes—and this analysis suggests that there have been four of them—are clear, there is lots of year-to-year variability in spending patterns, and one can easily miss changes from one regime to another without a careful examination of the actual numbers.

Isolating these regimes is important in telling the story of the increase in the size of the U.S. government that has occurred since World War II. But there is a second reason for this exercise: it will enable us to examine the *causes* of shifts from one regime to another. We'll have a look at several different kinds of information as we're defining U.S. fiscal eras, but they will all lead to a similar general conclusion.

FOUR FISCAL ERAS: THE FIRST LOOK

Budgetary politics occur within broad basic understandings among government officials about taxing and spending. These understandings can operate formally, when they incorporate rules of balanced budgeting and careful expenditure estimates. Or they can operate informally, when major players agree, often implicitly, that governmental spending ought to be controlled or increased.

In any case, we may roughly categorize these understandings as falling in two bands: either fiscally restrained or fiscally aggressive.

A research team of political scientists, including Jones, has developed a method for assessing broad-based changes in spending mind-sets in Washington.[11] First, they examined a given year's budgetary commitments, formally known as *budgetary authority*, rather than actual expenditures, which are called outlays. Outlays include spending that could have been authorized in past years, such as when Congress approves the construction of a new fighter plane or a public housing complex. Budget authority is a better measure of current decision making in Congress and hence provides better insight into the current mind-set or culture that prevails at any particular time.

To estimate budgetary eras, the research team used Office of Management and Budget subfunctions, because changes in these categories of spending will be more sensitive to changes in budget behavior in Washington than total budget figures. It is the infamous supertanker problem: the ship won't turn immediately when the pilot steers to port or starboard. Similarly for categories of spending; major changes can be detected before they are seen in the overall budget totals. OMB classifies government activity according to broad functional categories, such as military affairs or education. These functional categories relate to actual government goals, not to the agencies they are assigned to or to object categories (such as personnel, supplies, and so on.) The subfunctions are subcategories of these functions. For example, education

---

[11]Bryan D. Jones, Frank R. Baumgartner, and James L. True, "Policy Punctuations: U.S. Budget Authority, 1947–95," *Journal of Politics*, 60, 1998, pp. 1–30.

is divided into elementary and secondary, higher education, research, training activities, and other. The researchers studied only the functions related to actual government programs, ignoring those that are used to account only for financial transactions.

The research team took the average inflation-adjusted percentage change for the Office of Management and Budget's subfunctions. The bigger the percentage increase for a particular program, the greater the congressional commitment to that program. To take one very important example, Figure 4.1 shows the annual inflation-adjusted percentage increases for the OMB subfunction for health. This included Medicaid, but Medicare is classified

FIGURE 4.1
Percentage Change in Budget Authority for Health, 1948–2006

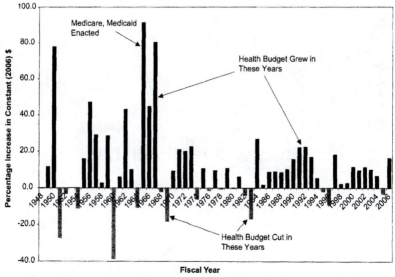

Source: Calculated from Policy Agendas Project, Center for American Politics and Public Policy, University of Washington (policyagendas.org).

separately.[12] Note the large percentage increases in health budgets right after the Medicare and Medicaid programs were enacted in 1965 as budgets grew robustly. In most years, the federal health budget grew, but in a few years (1982 and 1983, for example), it shrunk, at least in real dollar terms.

For comparison purposes, Figure 4.2 presents the actual totals for health care. Relatively large percentage increases add lots of money when the program budget is big. Large percentage increases

FIGURE 4.2
Actual Budget Authority for Health Care

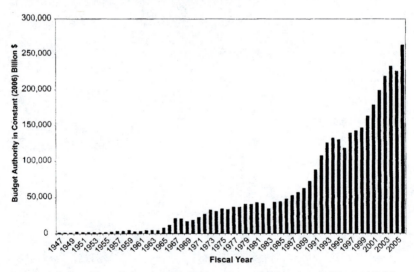

Source: Calculated from Policy Agendas Project, Center for American Politics and Public Policy, University of Washington (policyagendas.org).

---

[12]The data are available from the Policy Agendas Project at the University of Washington (policyagen-das.org). Users can make graphs directly from the web.

in large programs cause the overall health care budget to grow more than do similarly large percentage increases in smaller programs. Finally, as the budget grows very large, the absolute amounts added by smaller percentage gains can be very large. One of the big problems facing policy makers today is that cutting relatively small percentages from the big ticket items, such as health care, can involve truly monumental absolute cuts.

Even if Congress made lots of cuts in many programs, it is possible that the overall federal budget could increase, because the large programs would continue to grow. It is also possible that Congress and the president could prioritize programs, cutting some and adding to others. Though that does happen, we are more interested here in situations where Congress tends to increase the budgets for most programs briskly, or to limit most of them to modest growth (or actually cut them). That captures what we mean by "budgetary eras."

Given this focus, it would be misleading to examine only one or a few of the many programs government runs. Hence, we use the median, or the middle value for a set of numbers, to prevent the results from being too affected by very large or small values, rather than the mean (which people sometimes call the average). The idea behind this is simple: if the typical government function (regardless of the size or importance of the function) is growing more quickly than in earlier years, then it is likely that a culture of spending is in place.

So we trace the value of the median subfunction across time. This method enables us to isolate three broad epochs of spending, two of which are epochs of restraint, and one of which involved explosive growth in the typical subfunction.[13] Jim True subsequently isolated a fourth period of growth, beginning in 2001.[14]

The results are presented in Figure 4.3. The chart looks a little complicated, but the pay-off for taking the time to understand

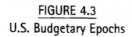

FIGURE 4.3
U.S. Budgetary Epochs

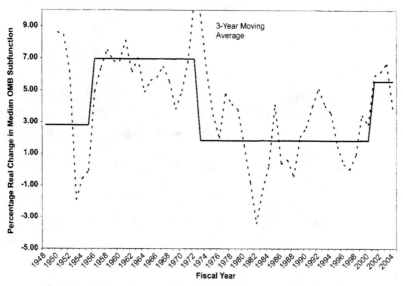

Source: Updated from Jones, Baumgartner, and True, 1998, and True, 2003 using data from the Policy Agendas Project, Center for American Politics and Public Policy, University of Washington (policyagendas.org).

---

[13]We did careful statistical tests of the epoch approach. See Jones, Baumgartner, and True 1998, for details. We used *Congressional Budget Authority*, which reports the spending that Congress has authorized in a given year, rather than outlays, which are the actual expenditures. *Budget Authority* is closer to the actual budget decisions; outlays can be affected by spending over several years for capital projects and hence do not directly reflect congressional decision making. The data are from the Policy Agendas Project, which presents reliable figures from 1947–2004; OMB tabulations are reliable only after 1976. In this analysis, we focus on OMB programmatic subfunctions (those not dealing with transfers or administration of the government branches; the 800 code subfunctions.

[14]James L. True, "Has the National Government Begun a New Era of Robust Growth?" presented at the Midwest Political Science Association Meetings, Chicago, IL, 2004.

it is worth the effort. The dotted line traces the annual percentage change in budget authority for the median subfunction. The
solid line is the average percentage change during each of the
four fiscal eras. The median change for the entire period is
3.2 percent per year, which means that the typical government
function grew at more than 3 percent a year during the whole
postwar period.

There are very clear differences between the eras—each is
characterized by distinct budgetary behavior. The first of the four
eras, 1948–1955, is one of considerable experimentation but general fiscal restraint; the typical government subfunction grew at a
rate of 2.8 percent a year. Fiscal year 1956, however, initiated
a period of sustained growth. This era came to an end in the mid-
1970s, and the next quarter of a century was a period of relative
budgetary restraint. Indeed, the two years with the greatest
growth in the median subfunction during the later era, 1977 and
1983, did not ever reach the overall average for the 1956–1973
period of growth. The period of restraint ended in 2001, and a
period of much more robust spending ensued.

It is obvious that these budgetary eras do not correspond to
what we normally think of as political eras in post–World War II
America. What is the middle of the Eisenhower administration
doing as a starting point for growth? And didn't Reagan initiate
the period of conservative, limited government? The picture using
real budget data is quite a bit different. Though the picture certainly involves politics, it also involves the very nature of
American fiscal institutions—how Congress and the president go
about making critically important decisions both about government programs and how they are to be funded.

Before turning to this storyline, we will first show that these eras carry clout in the overall fiscal balance sheet of the nation. The epochs of budgetary politics have strong impact on the course of total government spending, and hence the very size of government. Figure 4.4 shows the total growth in budget authority since the Second World War. We can clearly see the accelerated growth associated with the era of vibrant government beginning in 1956. We can even more clearly see the pay-off of the era of restraint. Government, in real terms, does not grow during the later years of that era.

As we noted previously, budget talk can be happy talk when things are going poorly (as today), and great debates can occur when an underlying consensus about balanced finances is in place (as in the 1990s). So now we're going to take one final look at

FIGURE 4.4
Total Budgetary Authority, Adjusted for Inflation

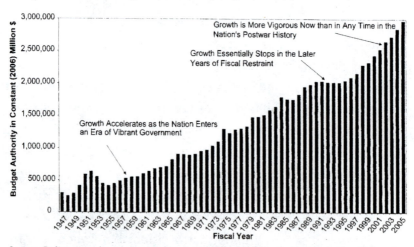

Source: Policy Agendas Project, Center for American Politics and Public Policy, University of Washington (policyagendas.org).

these budgetary eras, this time to show that general spending restraint or profligacy in budgetary behavior can be detected by examining real budget data. Figure 4.5 plots the budgetary eras by using the percentage changes in the total budgetary authority for each era. It is clear that a rising budgetary tide lifts all boats: when the average government program receives an inflation-adjusted increase, the total budget for the federal government grows. Though Congress and the president do set priorities among programs, there is a strong tendency to establish more-or-less lenient rules for spending and to apply them more-or-less across the board.

FIGURE 4.5
Eras of Budget Behavior for Total Budget Authority

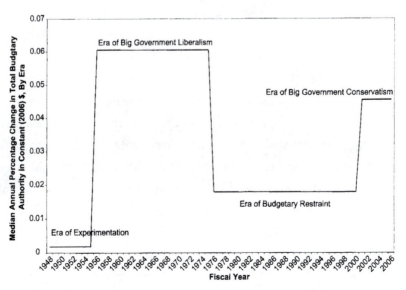

Source: Calculated from Policy Agendas Project Center for American Politics and Public Policy, University of Washington (policyagendas.org).

To make this figure more useful, we have labeled the budget eras according to their basic characteristics. The first period, *the era of experimentation*, is characterized by low growth in budget authority but a great deal of year-to-year variability. During the *era of big government liberalism*, dominated by large Democratic legislative majorities, laws were passed that empowered minorities and the poor, added many government programs that had major budgetary impacts, and regulated industry with consumer and environmental measures. The *era of budgetary restraint* reigned in the expansionist impulses of the 1960s and 1970s and closed with a period of no-growth government.

Until the Democrats won control of Congress in the November 2006 midterm election, the *era of big government conservatism* was carried forward by disciplined Republican control of the presidency and Congress, rather than by the large legislative majorities that the Democrats fielded in the earlier big government era. These conservative years were characterized by just as much activism as the previous liberal big government period and is different more for its penchant for using the private sector rather than government to run programs through incentives and contracting, and by its aggressive moves to limit consumer and environmental regulations on business. The programs funded are not so different from the earlier era. Republicans funded both the war in Iraq as Democrats did in Vietnam, and huge new initiatives in education (No Child Left Behind) and in health (Medicare Reform, including adding drug benefits, a major new entitlement).

What was different is that Republicans funded increases from borrowing where Democrats funded their expansion from taxes. Borrowing was necessary because Bush and the Congressional

Republicans aggressively cut taxes while increasing expenditures, leading to large deficits.

EXPLAINING THE PATTERNS

The eras isolated by our approach look odd, especially the cutpoints between the eras. The first period of big government growth was initiated in 1956, predating the Kennedy–Johnson activist period by five years. The end of the period of great budgetary growth occurred in the mid-1970s, five years before Reagan captured the presidency and initiated a program of tax cuts and expenditure restraint. What is going on here?

Headline-capturing events may not reflect changes in actual policy or budget commitments. In the case of budgetary eras, events were conspiring early in President Dwight Eisenhower's second term to push the nation into a new period of spending unlike any that had occurred previously. Similarly, the era of budgetary limits had been initiated not by Reagan but by President Nixon's refusal to spend congressionally appropriated funds, and Congress' reaction to what amounted to a severe constitutional crisis.

To gain a better understanding of the politics behind budgetary eras, we will need to examine recent political history from the new vantage point we have gained from our analysis of budgetary eras.

THE SPENDING EXPLOSION

The first years of the era of big government liberalism linked together General Eisenhower, the Republican president, and a solidly Democratic Congress, who together added new programs and increased funding for old ones in highways, education, science, housing and urban renewal, and Social Security.

It may surprise many to find this burst of government activity in the 1950s, but on reflection it makes sense. The Soviet *Sputnik* success generated a vigorous response in not only science and education (the National Defense Education Act, for example) but in highways (the Interstate Highway System was partly justified in defense terms) and other areas. Big increases in housing and urban development and Social Security also occurred during the mid-1950s. Vigorous lawmaking buttressed this spending. Among the ten most important laws enacted since 1955, as chosen by a panel of political scientists and policy practitioners convened by *Roll Call* magazine, two were enacted in this period—the Federal-Aid Highway Act of 1956 that established the Interstate Highway System, and the National Defense Education Act of 1958. The latter law passed in response to the Soviet launching of the first space satellite, *Sputnik*, and boosted the nation's educational infrastructure in science and math.[15]

Democrats Propel Government Growth

This era of rising budgets was pushed along strongly by the big Democratic majorities in 1964, after the assassination of President Kennedy. If we look only at important statutes passed, 1965 stands out as the most critical legislative session in the postwar period.

It is important to look at lawmaking as well as budgets because statutes generally increase governmental involvement in civil society. Figure 4.6 graphs those laws that were most discussed

---

[15]Louis Jacobson, "Ten Bills That Really Mattered," *Roll Call*, May 3, 2005.

in the *Congressional Quarterly*. After some necessary adjustments for changes in the *CQ* structure, we isolated 576 important, extensively discussed laws passed between 1948 and 1998. After 1998, changes in the *CQ* made it impossible for us to continue the series.[16]

Figure 4.6 isolates a period of particularly intense lawmaking beginning in 1964 and extending through 1978. The vertical lines on the graph demarcate a period of almost frenetic lawmaking. The huge Democratic majorities that flooded Congress in 1965

FIGURE 4.6
Count of Most Important Laws, 1948–1998

Source: Policy Agendas Project, Center for American Politics and Public Policy, University of Washington (policyagendas.org). Laws ranked by coverage of the topic by the *Congressional Quarterly*.

---

[16]Details may be found at the Policy Agendas Project website, policyagendas.org.

after conservative Barry Goldwater's defeat passed the Voting Rights Act as well as Medicare and Medicaid. They also created the Housing and Urban Development Department. Three of *Roll Call* magazine's ten most important laws were passed in 1965—the Voting Rights Act, Medicare and Medicaid enacted in the Social Security Amendment Act of 1965, and the Immigration and Naturalization Act. Two others were passed in 1964—the Civil Rights Act and the Gulf of Tonkin Resolution, meaning that half the acts on the list were passed in a two-year period.[17]

Large numbers of important laws were also passed in 1970, 1976, and 1978, but in none of those years did the particular statutes have the far-reaching social and budgetary implications of 1965. Five of an expanded list of 17 laws from the *Roll Call* magazine study were passed in these three years, and included major initiatives in environmental quality, criminal justice, and Social Security benefits.[18] All of these laws fell in the second half of the list and paled in comparison to the high water mark of Lyndon Johnson's Great Society.

The period of most vigorous lawmaking occurred from 1964 to 1978, whereas the era of large budgetary increases fell between 1956 and 1976. Budgets rose smartly for years before lawmaking exploded in the mid-1960s, but increased spending and vigorous statute-making ended around the same time.

Budgetary politics are critical, however, in increasing the scope of government when programs are in place (as many were following the New Deal legislation of the 1930s), or when one piece of

[17]Jacobson, "Ten Bills."
[18]Jacobson, "Ten Bills."

legislation can be augmented through discretionary budgetary allocations over the years (as in the case of the Federal-Aid Highway Act of 1956, which established the Interstate Highway System). Laws are necessary to establish the legal basis for future interventions via spending and rule making. Indeed, the laws passed in the 1965–1978 period reached broadly into society, redefining race relations in the South through forcing open accommodations and voting rights, regulating consumer products and the environment, instituting community development and housing programs, and initiating vast new government spending in health care and retirement benefits.

The End of the Road

The culture of unrestrained spending came to a halt in the 1974–1976 period, with President Nixon's impoundments of congressional funds and the enactment of the Congressional Budget and Impoundment Control Act of 1974. A burst of lawmaking occurred in 1976–1978; in hindsight this was the last gasp of vigorous, aggressive government of the liberal variety.

It was replaced by an era of budgetary restraint beginning in late 1970s and continuing for a quarter of a century, through the Reagan, GHW Bush, and Clinton presidencies. This may seem counterintuitive, because there was so much heat over budget control and deficits during the 1980s and early 1990s, but, in fact, it was this dialogue that enforced the period of expenditure limits. Debates about economics, taxes, and spending dominated the Reagan years, with important policy consequences. But they took place in a framework that had been set in the earlier period. We examine this in more detail in the next chapter.

Reagan's presidency looks unproductive by one major measure—the number of important laws passed. In 1978, 24 important pieces of legislation (by the measure used in Figure 4.6) were passed, but in 1981 only 11 were. Were Congress and Reagan half as productive in 1981 as Carter and Congress were in 1978? A central aim of Republicans was to limit future growth of government. Their diagnosis was that the growth of government was propelled by the notion that government is the best instrument for solving social problems, and many argued that a reduction in activity levels by the federal government was highly desirable. As a consequence, the decline is best regarded as a major accomplishment from the perspective of President Reagan's objectives.

Even more remarkably, the topics of lawmaking shifted from a panoply of topics to two: fiscal policy and defense. Reagan focused congressional attention on an intense but limited agenda. Many of the fiscal policies enacted during the period were accomplished through the budgetary processes, and the most controversial laws passed during his tenure as president were budget reconciliation and appropriations bills. The Reagan years provided a special lesson that budgets cannot be divorced from politics.

Figure 4.7 categorizes the most important laws passed by five major topics: (1) defense and foreign affairs, (2) economics and budgets, (3) human services and law, (4) commerce and infrastructure, and (5) agriculture and public lands. The figure shows the relative proportion of each category for each year. Note the increase in legislation on human services and law (including crime, justice, and civil rights) during the 1960s and 1970s, and the abrupt decline of lawmaking on these topics beginning in 1981. The major subjects for lawmaking in the Reagan years were budgets and the

FIGURE 4.7
Most Important Legislation Categorized by Topic

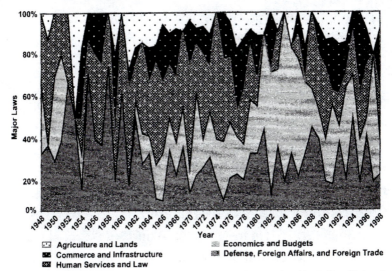

Agriculture and Lands
Commerce and Infrastructure
Human Services and Law

Economics and Budgets
Defense, Foreign Affairs, and Foreign Trade

Source: Policy Agendas Project, Center for American Politics and Public Policy, University of Washington (policyagendas.org).

economy—indeed, in domestic affairs, these were virtually the only topics that major legislation addressed. If productivity is measured as the ability to focus the agenda, then Reagan was very productive indeed.

THE ERA OF BUDGETARY RESTRAINT

Success by President Reagan in restraining his budget, however, did not bring an era of presidential fiscal prudence. Fiscal prudence leads to reasonable budgetary balance, and as a consequence requires sensible tax policies as well as budgetary restraint. Reagan's mix of limited budget growth and large tax reductions produced a quantum increase in the dollar amount of yearly budget deficits and the ratio of those deficits to GDP. Though Reagan successfully practiced budget restraint, which is an aspect of fiscal prudence, he was fiscally imprudent in pursuing the policy of massive tax cuts.

Fiscal prudence involves an explicit presidential policy strategy to constrain or reduce overall spending and/or to increase federal receipts through taxation in order to maintain or restore fiscal balance. The latter is defined as an average deficit/GDP ratio less than one percent per year over an entire presidency. Budgetary restraint is best accomplished when a president works with Congress to establish and self-enforce rules to restrict spending when budgets threaten to get out of balance. Presidential prudence involves pursuing fiscal policies that (1) are intended to maintain or restore a rough parity between federal tax receipts and budget expenditures, and (2) incorporate an adequate base of realistic assumptions and available sound data indicating a reasonable chance of achieving the desired balance.

The restrictive definition of fiscal prudence means that the actual existence of fiscal balance does not necessarily signify prudence. Strong economic growth can raise tax receipts sufficiently to maintain or restore parity without any direct fiscal policies aimed at doing so. It is not enough to "luck out"; sensible policies that are actually aimed at fiscal prudence are required.

We will briefly consider the deficit/GDP ratios of all the postwar presidents, except George W. Bush, in spelling out the importance of this concept and the closely related one of the ratio of the federal debt to GDP. During the first two decades of the postwar period, the deficit/GDP ratio stayed in rough balance, ranging between an average surplus of 1 percent of GDP per year in the Truman presidency and an average deficit of 0.9 percent for both Kennedy and Johnson. In the postwar era, only Truman had an overall surplus/GDP ratio over his entire presidency, but Eisenhower came close with an average deficit/GDP ratio of 0.5 percent per year.

John Kennedy's tax cut and Johnson's greater expenditures for the newly passed poverty program and the far more costly Vietnam War widened the gap between revenue and expenditures. But they did not move it as high as a 1 percent deficit/GDP ratio per year over their entire presidencies. Though these presidents pursued aggressive policies that expanded government, the favorable GDP growth rate enabled this to occur without upsetting fiscal balance.

Although presidents ballyhoo their role in strong economic growth, and voters tend to reward or punish them in elections based on the economy's performance, changes in economic growth are likely to be brought about by forces outside a president's control. With the exception of Eisenhower, who explicitly tried to balance the budget, strong economic growth, not any direct fiscal policies, kept the fiscal balance that marked the period of more than two decades, from the end of demobilization after World War II through the 1960s.

In the next period, running approximately through the Nixon/Ford and Carter presidencies, the many economic problems brought an average deficit/GDP ratio of 1.9 percent. Faced with strong adverse economic forces, none of these presidents undertook major fiscal policies intended to move the deficit/GDP ratio toward parity.

President Reagan experienced a 4.2 percent deficit/GDP ratio over the course of his presidency. This deterioration from the earlier period came in part from exogenous factors but also from the shortfall in federal revenues from the 1981 tax cut. A clear sea change occurred, as shown by the sharp upward turn of the federal debt/GDP ratio.

With massive borrowing during World War II and demobilization, the ratio had exceeded 120 percent but then steadily declined to under 33 percent by 1981 with only small increases in a handful of years. Although President Reagan did keep budget expenditures under control, his massive 1981 tax cut was an important factor in raising the debt/GDP ratio to nearly 52 percent by 1988.

The presidencies of both GHW Bush and Bill Clinton included new budget controls on spending and major tax increases. These acts of fiscal prudence, however, do not necessarily imply bold presidential leadership. GHW Bush was bedeviled by his "no new taxes" pledge made during his campaign for the presidency. Although he realized that the fiscal problems he faced almost certainly demanded a tax increase if fiscal balance was to be restored, he feared the political consequences of breaking his pledge and left it to Congress to take the lead.

President Bush may have backed into a policy of fiscal prudence, but he recognized the necessity of such policies. Unfortunately, Bush's prudent fiscal policies were not enough to restore rough parity between revenue and spending or turn around the rising debt/GDP ratio. Clinton acted more boldly and built on Bush's fiscal policies with a strict budget regimen and another tax increase. The continuing effort at fiscal prudence combined with the extraordinary economic growth that began in 1995 finally restored a reasonable balance between revenues and expenditures.

President Clinton's initial budget surplus came after nearly three decades of deficits, starting in 1970. It also halted the unbroken string of large yearly budget deficits that ensued after Reagan's 1981 tax cut. Further, the debt/GDP ratio started to decline again after rising to more than 67 percent. The 1990s can be labeled the era of presidential fiscal prudence in combining tax hikes with stringent budget controls—a unique period in the postwar era.

The high water mark of the era of fiscal prudence was initiated by GHW Bush's tax increase and spending limits enacted in 1991 and was cemented in place by Clinton's similar action in 1993. The strong economic growth in 1995–2000 came after the extraordinary presidential fiscal prudence during the 1990s; this is probably no accident. In addition, this period shows that the trace of public policy is not always tedious, incremental adjustment; strong trends apparently can be reversed by presidential policies.[19]

The era of fiscal prudence came to a dramatic close with the election of GW Bush in 2000 (although cracks were appearing by 1998). The mild recession of 2001 alone cannot account for this reversal; imprudent tax cuts and a Republican spending orgy were much bigger culprits. We examine this reversal in detail in Chapter 6. The tax and budget policies pursued by Bush and Congress were responsible for the return of red ink in the yearly budget and the quick turn upward of the debt/GDP ratio after its brief decline in the last years of the Clinton presidency.

---

[19]The point is not that tax increases cause economic growth, but that a consistent policy of budget controls and tax hikes, after long years of budget deficits, can encourage economic growth by convincing investors that the government is serious about fighting these deficits.

A CLOSER LOOK AT HIGHWAYS

Politicians love highway and mass transit spending, at least when it's done in their districts. The outlays bring concrete projects, ribbon-cutting, construction contracts, and jobs, all of which House and Senate members can take credit for. Moreover, federal highway money comes as a grant-in-aid to states, allowing governors and mayors to take credit as well. As a consequence, highway bills have always been the mother lode of pork. But they have just as often aggravated presidents, who see highway bills as oftentimes wasteful, sapping public funds from what they see as more needed projects. The story of highway spending in the United States mimics spending eras in a remarkable way. Indeed, they may be the signature program for the dynamic politics of the federal budget. Figure 4.8 traces budget authority for ground transportation since WW II.

Federal highway spending had increased modestly during the early 1950s, but it shifted markedly upward after the Federal Aid Highway Act of 1956, which established the Interstate Highway System. The program grew robustly throughout the Period of Liberal Big Government; then President Nixon impounded, or refused to spend, appropriated funds for highway construction. Transportation was one among many programs that he refused to fund, provoking a constitutional crisis that was shoved off the agenda only with the emergence of Watergate.

Note, however, how subsequent to that period, highway funding, in real dollars, did not grow for almost all of the Period of Fiscal Restraint. When Republicans took both branches of Congress in 1994, they struggled with what to do when lucrative pork projects ran smack into their announced platform of limited government.

FIGURE 4.8
Budget Authority for Ground Transportation

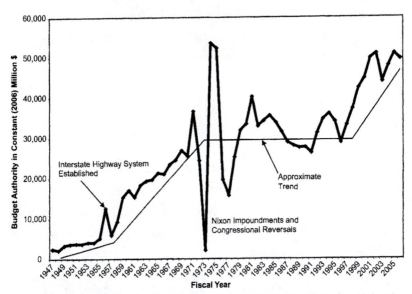

Source: Policy Agendas Project, Center for American Politics and Public Policy, University of Washington (policyagendas.org).

It is easy to see that pork won, and since 1997 ground transportation has experienced its greatest period of growth ever. The House Transportation and Infrastructure Committee enjoyed able leadership first under Representative Bud Schuster of Pennsylvania, and then under Don Young of Alaska. Both worked tirelessly to build transportation funding; their levels of effectiveness can be judged by looking at Figure 4.7. After several continuing resolutions that funded transportation at current levels, Congress passed a reauthorization of transportation funding in the summer of 2005, ensuring continued robust growth in highway and mass transit funding.

DOES PARTY MATTER?

One might speculate that partisan control of Congress is what makes the difference in budget mind-sets. Supposedly Republicans promote limited government and Democrats want to enact more programs. That should lead to an aggressive spending mind-set when Democrats are in control and a restraint mind-set when Republicans are in control.

The partisan control thesis is not borne out. The correlation between the percentage of Republicans in Congress (both houses together) and the real percentage change in spending for the median subfunction is actually a modestly positive (but statistically significant) 0.28. That is, the greater the Republican control of the legislative branch, the higher the spending growth—completely opposite of what the thesis suggests. Democratic control of Congress was exceptionally strong from 1959 to 1981 and continued with fewer congressional seats until 1995. So one could say that the first big-spending era was associated with Democratic control of the legislative branch. But the first era of big spending ended when Democrats had one of the biggest partisan majorities in both houses of Congress in history, primarily because of the post-Watergate rejection of Republican candidates. The subsequent era of controlled spending continued throughout the Reagan presidency and ended in 2001, which began a period of Republican ascendancy. As a consequence of this, the modest association between Republican congressional membership and spending is probably spurious, driven by other factors. The simple idea that party control causes budgetary mind-sets is almost certainly not true.

A second possibility is that unified government, in which one party holds both houses of Congress and the presidency, is what matters. Perhaps unified governments can't resist using government to build support though the allocation of funds. Certainly there is evidence during the most recent period of unified government that this happened, and we explore this in detail in Chapter 9. Divided government, on the other hand, could cause gridlock as the parties are able to veto each other's spending excesses. Between 1995 and 2001, when a Republican Congress faced the Democratic president Bill Clinton, the United States experienced a period of budgetary restraint. Today, many conservative intellectuals, viewing the experiences of the GHW Bush and Clinton administrations, are lauding divided government as a tool for enforcing fiscal discipline. But what is the story if we examine the entire U.S. postwar experience?

Figure 4.9 graphs our budget eras, the solid line, against the periods of unified government (the hatched regions of the graph) since the Second World War. There are problems with the idea that unified governments spend more. The first era of big government began with the Eisenhower presidency in a period of divided control. It was well underway when Kennedy captured the presidency and began eight years of unified Democratic control. The growth era came to a halt in a period of divided rule but was not restored in the period of unified Democratic control under President Jimmy Carter. Moreover, in the two-year period of unified rule following the election of Bill Clinton, budgetary restraint was the order of the day. The era of restraint survived until the period of unified control under the Republicans, when the era of big-government conservatism began.

FIGURE 4.9
Unified Government and Budgetary Eras

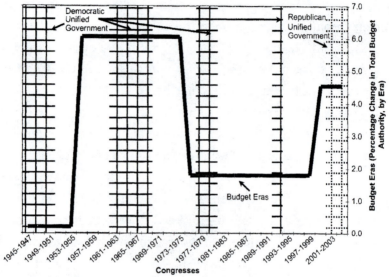

Source: Calculated by the authors.

If fiscal prudence is our standard rather than just budgetary restraint, the record is even less favorable to the divided government argument. Indeed, the last two years of the GHW Bush administration and the first two years of the Clinton administration look very similar in their extraordinary fiscal prudence—budgets were controlled and taxes were adjusted to meet program demands. Yet Bush experienced a divided government while Clinton enjoyed a unified one. Something else was at work.

It is hard to believe that party positions don't have anything to do with budgetary control. Part of the answer to this conundrum is that Republicans shifted philosophy during the period, especially after 1980. Instead of emphasizing fiscal conservatism and budgetary stringency, Republicans began to tout tax cuts as the critical element of their fiscal strategy. GHW Bush agreed to a tax increase (while the Democratic Congress made heavier cuts than they were inclined to do) in 1991, but Republican activists mounted a vicious campaign against Bush on the grounds that he violated the "no new taxes" pledge he made at the 1988 Republican National Convention. President Clinton, facing a Republican Congress after 1994, held down expenditures.

GW Bush, said to be fearful that the Republican right would attack him in the manner that it did his father, fully bought the tax-cut mantra of his party's most extreme members. In the process, he was able to prove definitively that neither the supply side nor the starve-the-beast theories held any water whatsoever (see Chapter 3).

That would suggest that parties matter, but they matter in a complex and evolutionary manner. Looking at the fiscal history of the United States since the Second World War, it is hard to make any firm generalizations about parties and finances. If we step back, however, and think of parties as evolving to fit the needs of building electoral coalitions and satisfying the party faithful, then the patterns make sense. But as long as this evolution occurs, and it always will, it is fruitless to dream of fiscal prudence as being achievable either by party control or by divided government.

FISCAL ERAS IN AMERICA

Putting the specifics of public financing in the U.S. national government into a broader perspective is not difficult, because the eras of budgetary restraint and profligacy demark themselves in a straightforward manner. Our analysis confirms the suggestion by Gale and Orszag that starve-the-beast does not provide a political equilibrium. The first period of budgetary exuberance began after a long period of relatively high tax rates, and of course neither supply side nor starve-the-beast theories say anything about this. The two periods of budgetary exuberance are associated with increasing deficits and tax cuts—that is, when we have exuberance, we tend to have it on both sides of the equation. Periods of fiscal restraint on the budget side of the equation are more complex, however. Budgets were essentially under control when the Reagan tax cuts were implemented in 1981. These tax cuts were clearly destabilizing and instituted a period of political struggle over the budget.

We now know why starve-the-beast fails to provide a political equilibrium. Cutting taxes and borrowing to fund them has the effect of lowering the tax costs of government programs in the present. This causes voters to support more government, not less, because they are comparing something they are getting in the present (government programs) with something that abstractly will have to be paid in the future (the government's debt).

Similarly supply-side economics, by advocating tax rate cuts without regard for the spending side of the budget equation, leads to borrowing. It also lowers the tax cost for citizens, leading them to demand more government services. The results of both supply side and starve-the-beast tax cuts are the same: they destabilize both the revenue side (by reducing revenues) and the expenditure side (by uncovering more demand for government programs).

CHAPTER 5

Institutions, Rules, and Politics

In 1972, President Richard Nixon scored a landslide reelection victory over Democrat George McGovern. Democrats, however, continued to hold sizable majorities in both the House and the Senate, actually gaining two Senate seats. In the midst of a great expansion of the federal government, with northern liberal Democrats replacing more conservative southern Democrats, Nixon wanted to stem the big government tide he and other Republicans saw as engulfing the nation. But he had few allies in Congress; even the old system in which the appropriations committees served as "guardians of the treasury" had sharply eroded.

In the past, presidents had occasionally refused to spend money that Congress had appropriated, generally when it was clear to everybody that the spending was wasteful or otherwise harmful and usually in consultation with congressional leaders.[1] Nixon now moved to expand vastly this process, impounding funds

---

[1] Rudolph G. Penner, *Repairing the Congressional Budget Process.* Washington DC: The Urban Institute, 2002.

for subsidized housing, suspending community development, curtailing transportation funds, ending several farm programs, and refusing to allow spending under the Clean Water Act. In essence, the president employed an obscure budget procedure to re-order national domestic priorities.[2]

To say that Congress was alarmed would be an understatement. Years later, a former staffer for Speaker of the House Carl Albert later referred to Nixon's actions as "one of the boldest assaults on legislative prerogatives in the history of the country."[3] Congress responded by attempts to restore funding for specific programs with tighter guidelines on the spending process, but members of Congress also challenged Nixon in court. In *Train v. City of New York* (1975), the Supreme Court decided in favor of Congress, but on relatively narrow grounds.[4] The legislative branch had won the constitutional showdown, but the president had the best of the substantive argument.

Nixon argued, correctly, that Congress had no mechanism for controlling spending. There was no way for Congress to compare revenues with expenditures, and at the time, no congressional budget at all was prepared. The several separate appropriations bills were simply passed, and, in essence, sent to the Treasury Department to pay the bills. In the past, congressional appropriations committees had acted as "guardians of the purse,"[5] but in the early 1970s this system had broken down, for a number of

---

[2]Virginia A. McMurtry, *Item Veto and Expanded Impoundment Proposals*. Washington DC: Congressional Research Service Issue Brief for Congress, 2001.

[3]Joe Foote, "A Man of the House," *Extensions*. Norman, OK: Carl Albert Center, University of Oklahoma, 2000 (http://www.ou.edu/special/albertctr/cachome.html).

[4]McMurtry, *Item Veto*.

[5]Richard Fenno, *The Power of the Purse: Appropriations Politics in Congress*. Boston: Little, Brown, 1966.

reasons. The appropriations committees, dominated by southern conservative Democrats and Republicans, faced more northern Democrats interested in expanding government programs. Authorizing committees had found ways to circumvent the limits imposed by the appropriations committees, primarily through entitlements and indexing benefits, a process budget scholar Kent Weaver termed "automatic government."[6] The authorizing committees—the committees that write legislation establishing programs—began to write programs that entitled individuals to benefits if they met certain predetermined criteria. Appropriations took place by formula—just calculate the number of people that met the criteria and write the check. Indexing keyed benefit growth to a benchmark that generally would itself increase—such as inflation or changes in wages. The old relatively informal system of budgetary controls had collapsed by the mid-1970s, taking with it the only institutional mechanism for enforcing fiscal prudence.

The executive branch, on the other hand, had been preparing a unified budget since the Budget and Accounting Act of 1921, which established the Bureau of the Budget in the Treasury Department. The Bureau was moved to the White House in 1939, and had been reorganized by Nixon into the Office of Management and Budget in 1970. The executive branch had the organizational capability to do the budget math.

The severity of the impoundment battles is reflected in Figure 5.1. That figure shows the average yearly increase in budgetary subfunction, adjusted for inflation.[7] After 1974, the percentage

---

[6]Kent Weaver, *Automatic Government: The Politics of Indexation.* Washington DC: Brookings Institution, 1988.

[7]Budget Authority was granted by Congress but not spent by the president, so subsequently the totals for several fiscal years during the impoundment wars had to be adjusted.

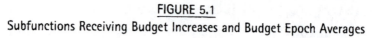

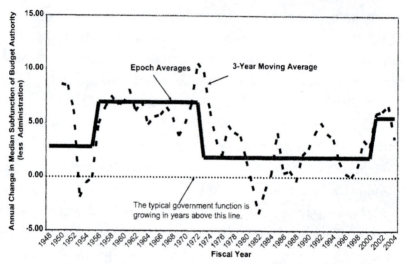

Source: Calculated by the authors from Policy Agendas Project, Center for American Politics and Public Policy, University of Washington. (policyagendas.org).

increase in subfunctions went down by an impressive amount. Moreover, more subfunctions received cuts than received increases in 1974, for the first time since 1954. The average government program had received hefty increases for 20 years before Nixon took unilateral action, and government had grown robustly as a consequence. The Nixon impoundments brought that era to an end.

Nixon's impoundments not only reordered national domestic priorities, they hit Congress members right where it hurt most. This group is generally very happy to announce projects in their home districts, and many of Nixon's impoundments impinged on credit-claiming. Figure 5.2 shows two programs affected, ground transportation and community development. Spending for highways

FIGURE 5.2

Budget Authority for Ground Transportation and Community Development

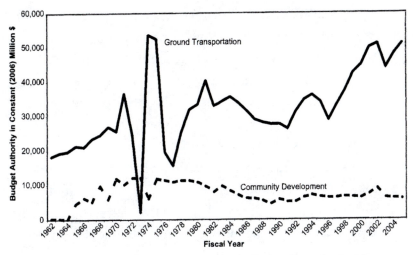

Source: Calculated by the authors from Policy Agendas Project, Center for American Politics and Public Policy, University of Washington.

and mass transit declined from more than $50 billion in 1972 to under $2 billion in 1973 (in 2004 dollars). Community development dropped by half a year later (impoundment wars lasted sporadically until 1975).

THE END OF AN ERA

In 1974 in an acknowledgement that Nixon was right when he accused Congress of lacking the ability to monitor its own spending, Congress passed and the president signed the Congressional Budget and Impoundment Control Act. That act set forth procedures for temporary and permanent budget recessions, distinguishing between temporary impoundments and permanent budget reductions. More importantly, it set forth a set of procedures that would produce a legislative budget that would be similar in form to what the executive branch had produced for half a century. Each house of Congress would have a budget committee that produced a general budget resolution and a process for reconciling this budget resolution with the appropriations bills that would emerge from the appropriations committees later in the year.

Certainly this complicated legislative procedures considerably. Congress now had a process of authorization by which laws are passed to establish and continue programs; a budget process that established budget rules; and an appropriations process that allocated money to particular programs. The act also established the nonpartisan Congressional Budget Office (CBO) to produce budget estimates and an independent analysis of the executive budget. Over the years CBO projections have proved more accurate than those produced by the President's Office of Management and Budget. The nonpartisan structure of CBO doubtless has much to do with this.

During the first years of the act, many observers, in and out of Congress, held the opinion that the process had failed. First, the growth in entitlement programs seemed to be impervious to the new budgetary process. For years liberals had been frustrated by the refusal of the appropriations committees, which remained in the hands of southern conservatives, to appropriate enough funds to support the programs they had legislated in the authorizations process. They began to enact statutes that required expenditures, leading to the increase in entitlement programs noted previously. Social Security already required that spending be keyed to the eligible elderly, and benefit levels had been indexed to wage increases. This "automatic government" was expanded through more mandatory spending programs.

The automatic government problem particularly affects services that are mandated through eligibility requirements. For example, Medicare provides particular health care services for elderly Americans. If the price for services goes up, then appropriations must go up. To deal with this, Congress has delegated rule-making authority to the Department of Health and Human Services to develop schedules of payment for particular procedures. In the case of Social Security, the procedure is much simplified and easier to project over long periods of time through established actuarial means.

Figure 5.3 shows the growth in mandatory programs in comparison to discretionary domestic and defense expenditures. Note the rapid growth in mandatory programs during the early 1970s. Today mandatory programs such as Social Security, Medicare, and means-tested entitlements (for example, Supplemental Security Income) dwarf both domestic and defense discretionary spending, which is appropriated annually in the budgetary process.

The second reason the congressional budget process had at first been deemed to have failed was the highly conflictual nature of budget politics, oftentimes not yielding the required formal legislative budget. "Governing by continuing resolution" became a derogatory phrase for the need to pass congressional resolutions that continued to fund government functions when formal appropriations bills were not passed. In 1995 and 1996, President Clinton's vetoes of appropriations bills and the subsequent refusal

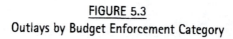

FIGURE 5.3
Outlays by Budget Enforcement Category

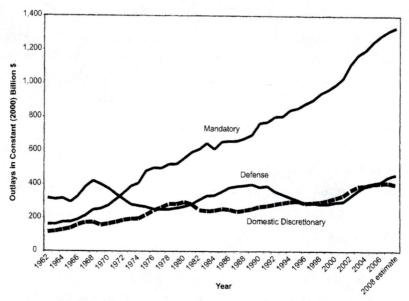

Source: Calculated from US Office of Management and Budget, Historical Statistics,
Table 8.1 (http://www.whitehouse.gov/omb/budget/fy2008/hist.html).

of Congress to pass a continuing resolution (on the grounds that
this procedure would over-fund agencies) led to shut-downs of
government programs.

Third, after 1975 the budget deficit expanded sharply. This
was more a consequence of revenue losses than any lack of spending control. But though the typical subfunction was brought under
control by the new budget procedures, and the rampant culture of
spending and new program development had been curtailed, outlays overall were still growing. This was mostly a function of the
growth in mandatory programs. Domestic discretionary expenses

were exactly the same in 1992 as they were in 1978, adjusting for inflation, but entitlements grew 54 percent.

More importantly, tax receipts failed to keep pace with past patterns as a consequence of the "stagflation" of the 1970s and the recessions and massive Reagan tax cuts of the early 1980s. The congressional budget process better controlled spending than it did the deficit. Also, the process better controlled discretionary spending, which could be adjusted in the annual appropriations process, than mandatory spending, which required changes in the statutes governing the mandatory benefit levels for programs.

In the end, the critics were wrong. Expenditures were brought under control, and though this did not occur immediately, it would not have been possible had a legislative budget process not been in place. Budget battles among factions of Congress and between the president and Congress continued, perhaps a permanent feature of the hard and honest numbers forced on both branches by their expanded analytical capacities. Nevertheless, the implementation of the Congressional Budget and Impoundment Control Act marked a watershed in budgetary politics and caused a shift from an era of increases in programs and expenditures to one of more limited governmental ambitions. The process has not been pretty, but budget battles go to the heart of the nation's public priorities and perhaps should not be smooth and consensual.

CONTROLLING THE DEFICIT

Fiscal prudence implies both budget discipline and the policies to ensure that revenue flows approximate expenditure needs. The budget process, as professional as it had become, addressed only the budget side of the equation. There was no mechanism available to enforce discipline on the revenue side of the equation. With the election of President Reagan, American political leaders lost the will to enforce revenue-side fiscal discipline, and it took more than a decade and much political conflict to achieve fiscal prudence.

After the Reagan tax cuts of 1981, the deficit burgeoned, and congressional politics gravitated toward deficit control. On December 11, 1985, President Reagan signed the Gramm-Rudman-Hollings Act (G-R-H), setting deficit reduction targets and automatic across-the-board cuts—termed sequestrations—if these targets were not met. When the Supreme Court declared the automatic reduction provisions unconstitutional, Congress re-passed a modified version of the act in 1987 and gave the president and the Office of Management and Budget authority to make the cuts.

Gramm-Rudman-Hollings exempted many budget categories from sequestration, including mandatory spending categories. In 1990 it became clear that the act's targets were going to be exceeded by a large amount, requiring sequestrations of 32 percent in defense and 35 percent in domestic discretionary programs. President GHW Bush and congressional leaders agreed to a budget "summit." The result of these negotiations was the Omnibus Budget Reconciliation Act of 1990, which reduced spending and raised taxes. This badly-needed tax increase, however, violated Bush's pledge at his party's 1988 convention that he would enact no new taxes and earned him the enmity of the right wing of his party. Congress also passed the Budget Enforcement Act (BEA), which substituted the Gramm-Rudman-Hollings deficit targets with pay-as-you-go (or pay-go) provisions that required new revenue sources for any program increases and program reductions for any tax cut.

The budget agreement initiated a period of serious fiscal prudence. The pay-go provisions were extended in the Omnibus Budget Reconciliation Act of 1993 and the Balanced Budget Act of 1997. Just as importantly, political conflict revolved around establishing and maintaining fiscal prudence. Beginning in 1985, much of the political dialogue centered on restraining spending and controlling the deficit. When a mechanism for enforcing fiscal prudence was put in place, conflict continued to swirl around government spending. The last gasp of the dialogue of fiscal prudence occurred during the 2000 presidential elections, when both candidates promised to enforce a "lock box" for Social Security revenues—a promise that in effect would ensure a budget in surplus for the foreseeable future. Nevertheless, in 2002, when the BEA came up for reauthorization, President Bush refused to agree to continue the provisions, demanding that they apply to spending but not to revenues. This marked the end of the era of fiscal prudence.

It was widely agreed that the Gramm-Rudman-Hollings method of enforcing deficit reduction contained a basic flaw in failing to fully recognize the role of recessions on both the revenue and expenditure sides of the equation. In recessions, revenues go down and expenditures directed at counteracting the decline in economic demand that characterizes recessions go up. This causes government budgets to fall very quickly out of balance, and in a big way. G-R-H required addressing the totals in the next budget cycle, which was virtually impossible. Nevertheless, G-R-H led to a far more successful experiment in prudent fiscal policy—the

Budget Enforcement Act expenditure control provisions. By operating primarily on changes in programs and tax policies (rather than trying to balance the totals), the BEA and its pay-go rules were less sweeping and hence more palatable. More importantly, the procedures operated on programs government officials could control, not the total deficit. The latter is influenced by spending policies, tax policies, and the state of the economy that generally is beyond the direct control of presidents and Congress.

Even more important than the specifics of G-R-H and BEA is what they signaled about the political process. Political leaders were struggling with a consensual goal: both parties were seriously committed to a path that would restore the federal fiscal balance between tax revenues and budgetary expenditures. This often unstated consensus endured from the institution of sound congressional budget procedures in the mid-1970s though 2001. If we reexamine the budgetary eras of the previous chapter, we see that the basic underpinning of the era of fiscal prudence is this consensus. But this was more than some vague consensus. By continuing to struggle with putting in place a system of budgetary rules that guided policy-making activities, political leaders ensured a continuing active and practical focus on the goal of fiscal responsibility.

Figure 5.4 documents the path of this struggle. There we show both federal outlays and receipts for the 1948–2005 period. The institution of congressional budget procedures in 1976 (the first fiscal year they were fully operative) and the beginning and ending of the BEA pay-go rules are noted by vertical lines on the graph. The congressional budget procedures altered neither the path of overall outlays nor the flow of revenues in the next few years. We claimed in Chapter 4 that the culture of spending was transformed

FIGURE 5.4
U.S. Revenues and Expenditures, 1948–2006

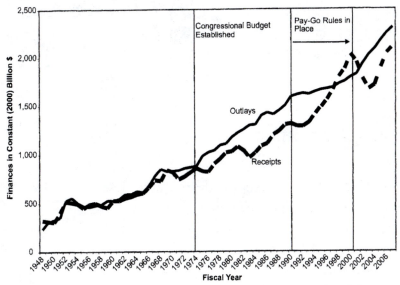

Source: Calculated from US Office of Management and Budget, Historical Statistics, Table 1.2 (http://www.whitehouse.gov/omb/budget/fy2008/hist.html).

during this period. Even when Congress has slowed the average growth of programs, it took a while for the effects to show up in aggregate figures such as those in Figure 5.4. Moreover, enough "automatic government spending" was in place to continue to drive spending upward.

During the Reagan presidency, the path of expenditures continued at about the same trajectory as during the Carter years, but there was a dramatic decline in revenues. The first occurred in the late 1970s and early 1980s, associated with economic stagflation and the subsequent recessions in 1980–1982. The second occurred as a direct consequence of Reagan's massive 1981 tax cuts; the fiscal balance was only restored with the tax increases of the late Reagan, GHW Bush, and Clinton years, and the 1995–2000 economic boom.

From the end of World War II through the Johnson administration, America experienced a quarter century of respectable fiscal balance. The deficit/GDP ratio never exceeded 1 percent per year in any of the presidencies during this time. Strong economic growth, adequate taxes, and informal means of enforcement kept the budget in balance. In the 1970s, as growth stagnated, the informal means of keeping the balance broke down. They first buckled on the budget side, as liberals were able to circumvent the appropriations committees, and then on the revenue side, when President Reagan adopted the radical economic theories of supply side and starve-the-beast.

Responsible fiscal policies were restored only through the long political struggle that took place between 1974 and 1990, resulting in the pay-go rules of the 1990s that pushed the political parties toward fiscal balance. Directly following the institution of these rules in 1991, the path of expenditures leveled off and did not resume rapid growth until 2001, when the pay-go rules were ignored and finally cast aside.

What happened seems simple enough: When the rules were in place, the nation moved toward fiscal balance, when they were removed, the nation moved away from fiscal balance. These results support our argument that institutional arrangements, either in the form of the informal system in place between the Second World War and the 1970s, or the formal pay-go rules of the 1990s, are necessary to achieve fiscal prudence.

TAX REDUCTIONS DO NOT
CONTROL GOVERNMENT GROWTH

Figure 5.5 is a simple summary reminder of what we have learned: tax reductions do not control the growth of government. The figure shows each of the major income tax rate changes since the Second World War along with the size of government relative to the economy. After the 1964 tax cut which was passed during the Kennedy administration but implemented after he was assassinated, government grew relative to the economy. After Reagan's tax cuts in the 1980s, there was no trend in the size of government—budgetary struggles between Congress and the president damped down

FIGURE 5.5
Tax Rates and Federal Outlays as a Percentage of GDP

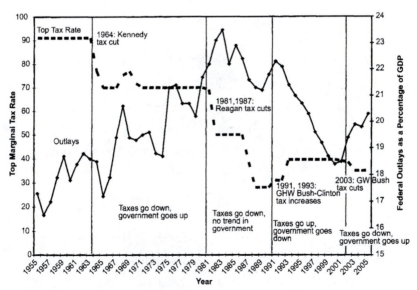

spending during this period. Clearly, however, the large tax reductions did not limit government growth, because the size of government relative to the economy was about the same when Reagan left office as when he assumed the presidency.

Presidents GHW Bush and Clinton raised taxes in 1991 and 1993, and an era of declines in the size of government followed, buoyed by strong economic growth. When GW Bush and Congress lowered taxes after 2001, the size of government resumed robust growth.

Starve-the-beast and supply-side theory do not work. Cutting taxes results in bigger government and structural deficits. Tax increases result in lower deficits and smaller government.

GOVERNING INSTITUTIONS AND RESPONSIBLE GOVERNMENT

The most important scholar of public budget behavior in the 20th century was the late Aaron Wildavsky of the University of California at Berkeley. His contributions centered on how budgets were actually made in practice, and how they had developed historically. Wildavsky came to the conclusion that the budget behavior of political leaders falls either in the "responsible" or the "irresponsible" categories—they either feel constrained by the realities of their nations' national fiscal balance sheets or they do not. He knew that institutions constrain behavior and was an early academic advocate of a balanced budget amendment.

Our analyses in the last two chapters indicate that Wildavsky was essentially correct in his analysis. Using budget data, we have shown first that eras of budgetary behavior can easily be detected in the United States after the Second World War, and that these eras alternate between high-spending eras and more constrained periods. Associated with careful spending is careful stewardship of the revenue stream. When an imbalance occurs, a combination of tax increases and expenditure controls are put into place. On the other hand, free spending eras are disassociated from the revenue stream, and tax reductions can occur during these times.

Academic economic analyses tend to downplay institutions, but even the most strident theoretical economist would admit a need for a defined structure intended to protect property rights, administer justice, and provide for the common defense. Somewhat similarly, some political scientists see elections as the only key to responsible government, but even the most ardent electoral theorist would admit the need for some form of institutional structure that channels the electoral results into decisions on policy matters. But elections do not enforce sound public finances. We have found no consistent relationship between the party in power and responsible financing. With the possible exception of 1992, no election in post-war America has been fought on the issue of responsible public finance. Even then it was the third-party candidate Ross Perot who raised the issue; President Bush and challenger Bill Clinton studiously tried to avoid discussing it. It is clear that bad public finances can lead to electoral change, but only after the situation becomes extraordinarily bad. Perhaps Argentina in the late 1990s is the model here.

We have shown that in fact hard-won agreement among political protagonists on a set of ground rules for public finance can lead to responsible budget behavior. If the protagonists can agree beforehand to a reasonable set of sanctions if the rules are violated, rules that all sides view as fair, then the likelihood for success is much greater. The pay-go rules imposed automatic sequesters of funds if targets were violated, and basically required sacrifices from both the domestic and defense sides of the budget. All sides grumbled, yet nevertheless carried out their responsibilities in a sensible manner.

What happens when (a) the rules and procedures established at one time no longer fit the circumstances; or (b) one side feels emboldened enough because of electoral successes to refuse to play by the established rules? This is exactly what transpired in 2001, when to most observers government was taking in too much in tax revenues. In the 2000 election, both candidates promised to abide by the so-called Social Security lock box, which essentially was a pledge not to finance the general fund with Social Security surpluses—a pledge that George Bush promptly violated with his tax cuts of 2001. He then went on to refuse to approve an extension of the pay-go rules—or rather he refused to agree to rules that would imply tax increases under any circumstances. He was proposing unfair rules, and he well knew that Democrats would refuse to agree.

Could the sound financing system of the 1990s have been saved? Yes. A sensible system for modification could have been established, and today we might be discussing a true American success story. Instead, Bush went "to his political base," with a policy that had been a bad idea from the start (starve-the-beast) and with the untested academic supply-side theory that would fail as discussed later. When Congress enthusiastically signed on, the sound system of fiscal prudence, on the verge of institutionalization in 2001, was destroyed.

CHAPTER 6

Big Government Republicanism
Costs Money

Limited government is enshrined in the Republican Party's platform—the 2004 version says, "We believe that good government is based on a system of limited taxes and spending." Yet that principle no longer guides the GOP. With power has come a huge increase in spending, the size of government, and borrowing to pay the cost. Theories justifying tax cuts without the fiscal discipline necessary to maintain a reasonable government balance sheet have resulted in structural, long-term budget deficits. The ideological, faith-based nature of tax cutting has pushed aside the hard choices of governing, and big government has emerged out of a lack of discipline rather than systematic programmatic considerations.

Nebraska Senator Chuck Hagel commented that the Republican Party "has presided over the largest growth of government in the history of this country and maybe even the history of man."[1] Though this is an exaggeration, against the backdrop of the limited government claims of Republicans it is shocking to see the vast spending increases engineered by Republicans.

In this chapter, we examine the explosive spending of George W. Bush when there were Republican majorities in both houses of Congress. We show that this spending binge that lasted until the Republicans lost control of Congress in November 2006 is not confined to defense and homeland security. It reaches virtually across the board, including the biggest entitlement program since 1965. The president and the Republican Congress passed the new Part D of Medicare that provides prescription drug coverage for eligible elderly who choose to participate in the program. The cost of this policy is estimated to be truly staggering—more than $120 billion per year by 2114.[2] Paired with huge tax cuts, the result of this undisciplined spending has been large deficits and a rapidly rising national debt. One of the most disturbing aspects of the spending explosion has been the destruction of the restrained fiscal regime that had been in place since the mid-1970s.

DISCRETIONARY SPENDING

Peter G. Peterson, who was secretary of Commerce in the Nixon administration and a lifelong Republican, writes in his book, *Running on Empty*, "This [Bush] administration and the Republican Congress have presided over the biggest, most reckless deterioration of American finances in history."[3] There isn't any doubt that

[1]Quoted in Joseph Lelyveld, "The Heartland Dissent," *New York Times Magazine*, February 12, 2006.
[2]Letter from Congressional Budget Office Director Douglas Holtz-Eakin to William "Bill" M. Thomas, Chairman of the House Committee on Ways and Means, February 5, 2005.
[3]Peter G. Peterson, *Running on Empty*. New York: Farrer, Straus, and Giroux, 2005, p. xliii.

President Bush and the Republican Congress have collaborated to grow government. Fiscal constraints collapsed, and the small government–fiscal prudence wing of the Republican Party lies in ruin. Many people were dimly aware of the emergence of a big-government Republican governing coalition, but few understood the magnitude of the initiatives, and many thought it had been caused by the vigorous response to the terrorist attacks of 2001. Though some of the expenditures had been a direct result of this, much of the story lies elsewhere.

From Bush's first inaugural until the Democrats recaptured Congress, the outlays (actual spending) of the U.S. government grew at an annual average of 4.35 percent above inflation, according to calculations made from the Office of Management and Budget's reported data. This compares to a per-year average of 1.22 percent during the Clinton administration, 2.96 during the administration of the senior Bush, and 2.66 during the two Reagan terms. This growth was not due simply to a burgeoning defense budget, as nondefense expenditures increased at a 3.13 percent annual clip, far higher than Clinton's modest 1.82 percent.

This fiscal record makes Bush the second biggest spending president in the postwar years. Recall that government expenditures can be categorized as *mandatory*, which are required by statute, or *discretionary*, which are budgeted year-by-year. Mandatory expenditures include Social Security, Medicare, and other entitlements; discretionary includes national defense, transportation, and a host of other government functions. Congress and the president must decide on the discretionary budget yearly, but existing laws govern mandatory expenditures through the "automatic government" features discussed in earlier chapters. Because existing laws determine mandatory expenditures, the president and Congress need to change the statutes governing the expenditures in order for there to be a different spending regimen. This is invariably more cumbersome than changing discretionary spending. In the Senate, votes on changing statutes are subject to filibuster, but the yearly budget bills cannot be filibustered. So we expect discretionary spending to be most sensitive to presidential influence.

Bush has used his power to encourage Congress to spend substantially more in the discretionary budget than during the Clinton or GHW Bush years. Indeed, he has increased the budget faster than all but one other postwar president. Table 6.1, drawn

TABLE 6.1
Largest Annual Increases in Real Discretionary Outlays in the Past 40 Years

JOHNSON, FY 1967	14.8%
JOHNSON, FY 1966	12.4%
GW BUSH, FY 2002	10.3%
GW BUSH, FY 2003	9.7%
GW BUSH, FY 2004	8.3%
JOHNSON, FY 1968	6.6%
REAGAN, FY 1985	5.5%
CARTER, FY 1978	4.3%
CLINTON, FY 2000	4.2%
CARTER, FY 1980	4.1%
40 YEAR AVERAGE	1.7%

Source: Veronique de Rugy, "The Republican Spending Explosion", (http://www.cato.org/pubs/briefs/bp-087es.html) Cato Briefing Paper no. 87, March 3, 2004. Washington, DC: Cato Institute.

from work by the Cato Institute's Veronique de Rugy, shows the largest annual increases in inflation-adjusted discretionary outlays for our most recent presidents.[4] Bush's record puts him second only to Lyndon Johnson as producing the largest increases in discretionary spending.

Discretionary spending includes defense spending, so what if we exclude defense? As Figure 6.1 shows, this changes nothing. In his first term, Bush increased domestic discretionary spending by more than 25 percent, second only to Lyndon Johnson. Moreover,

FIGURE 6.1
Cumulative Domestic Discretionary Spending Increases in First Term

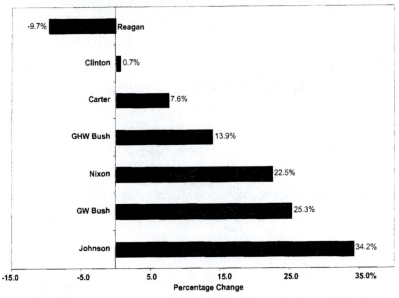

Source: Calculated from Veronique de Rugy, "The Republican Spending Explosion", (http://www.cato.org/pubs/briefs/bp-087es.html) Cato Briefing Paper no. 87, March 3, 2004. Washington, DC: Cato Institute.

---

[4]Veronique de Rugy, "The Republican Spending Explosion." Washington DC: Cato Institute Briefing Paper #84, 2004.

Bush and the Republican Congress broke an important mold by reversing the slow growth in discretionary spending that characterized every president from Carter to Clinton. Reagan actually reduced domestic discretionary spending during his first term, and Clinton held it to less than 1 percent.

Another way to look at the development of a spending culture since 2001 is to revisit our analysis of fiscal eras from Chapter 4. Here we do a very simple calculation of the proportion of federal government subfunctions that have received increased funding (in constant dollar terms, to be sure inflation is not a factor in the comparisons). By this measure, the Bush fiscal revolution has produced an across-the-board receptiveness to spending that exceeds any other era in the period since the Second World War. More than three quarters of subfunctions received year-to-year increases on average during the era. This exceeds even the first extended growth regime, from the mid-Eisenhower years to 1976, when 70 percent of budget subfunctions received increases annually. During the Reagan through Clinton era of fiscal restraint, only 58 percent did so.

In eras of budget restraint, political leaders are able to deflect demands from many constituencies and focus more intently on particular areas that they believe need attention. During eras of more robust growth, most programs will be able to achieve increased budgets. It is clear that Bush and the Republican controlled Congress were smack in the middle of the latter, regardless of the Republican tax cuts that so severely limited government revenue.

In the eras of spending growth, vast new government programs are invariably created, and Big Government Republicanism has been no exception. "No Child Left Behind" promised states increased education funding, and the act itself is the most extensive federal intrusion in the field of K–12 education ever. The prescription drug benefit and the costly new subsidies for Health Maintenance Organizations and insurance companies to provide health insurance for the elderly have created new requirements for spending that are projected to grow enormously in future years. Add to this increased national police powers developed in the USA Patriot Act, the important but expensive Homeland Security initiatives, the vast increase in farm subsidies, the aggressive new energy policy full of subsidies for Big Oil, and the unprecedented centralization of legal matters from state to federal courts, and one gets a rush toward big national centralized government matched only by Franklin Roosevelt's New Deal and Lyndon Johnson's Great Society.

As president during the Golden Years of economic growth, Johnson operated in starkly different economic circumstances from those of Bush. First, rising tax revenues from strong growth allowed for increases in discretionary expenditures to pay for the War on Poverty and the Vietnam War while still maintaining a rough balance between revenue and expenditures. Whether the added spending was good or bad policy need not be addressed; our concern here is with the deficit and the debt ratios that remained favorable. Second, Johnson's increases in domestic discretionary spending were measured against a lower starting base, which magnifies percentage increases; Bush's percentage increases that are nearly as high as those of Johnson began from a much higher level of relevant expenditures. Third, Bush reversed the debt/GDP ratio that had finally started to decline during the late Clinton years.

MANDATORY SPENDING PROGRAMS

More ominously, during the Bush administration major new entitlement programs have been established, requiring vast sums in the future even if present expenditures are modest. The Medicare drug reform law—the largest health policy initiative since Lyndon Johnson—will necessitate spending of $100 billion per year by 2015, or a total of $750 billion from 2006 to 2015, according to Bush administration estimates.[5]

It is not as if the pre-Bush entitlement programs were inexpensive. The big categories are Social Security and Medicare. Social Security expenditures are running at some 4.3 percent of GDP today, but the program is in reasonably sound actuarial shape. The payroll taxes collected to fund the Social Security trust fund are adequate to fund the system many years into the future. The trust fund itself, which since Congress acted on the recommendations of the Greenspan Commission in 1983 has collected more in taxes than it needed to pay in benefits, will run a surplus until around 2018. Then the taxes collected will not cover the benefits that will need to be paid, but reasonably simple, relatively low-cost changes can keep the trust fund in balance for at least 75 years.[6] Nevertheless, the quicker these changes are instituted, the easier the transition will be. People today who now live longer

[5]Robert Pear, "New White House Estimate Lifts Drug Benefit Cost to $720 billion," *New York Times*, February 9, 2005. Congressional estimates are even higher. See Note 2 above. Estimates of future spending in programs are difficult. Drug benefit expenditures are coming in at a little less than the initial estimates.
[6]Office of the Chief Actuary, Social Security Administration, *The Financial Health of Social Security and Medicare: Summary of the 2005 Annual Reports*. Washington DC: Social Security Administration.

and have fewer children can be called upon to contribute payroll taxes. The likely compromise would involve increases in taxes (probably on the better-off, who do not pay payroll taxes on salaries above around $100,000), some slight increases in the age at which citizens become eligible for Social Security, and some curtailing of the rate of growth in benefits.

The same is definitely not true for Medicare, where the long-term fiscal situation is much grimmer than Social Security. Currently Medicare expenses are 2.9 percent of GDP, and expenses are rising much faster than for Social Security. The aging population affects both programs, but medical expenses are projected to rise much faster than retirement benefits. The addition of the prescription drug benefit to coverage for hospital and doctor costs has caused a huge increase in these expenses.

Figure 6.2 shows the differences in the growth of Medicare and Social Security, projected into the future. The combined growth of Medicare Hospital Insurance (HI), Supplementary Medical Insurance (SMI), and Part D (the new prescription drug benefit) is on a rapidly increasing trajectory. This is certainly the case compared to the restrained growth of Social Security that combines Old Age and Survivors Insurance (OASI) and Disability Insurance (DI).

The percentage of GDP taken by Medicare is projected to exceed Social Security in 2024. The original Social Security program began in the mid-1930s, and Disability Insurance was added in 1950. Medicare began in 1965 and has been growing at a much more rapid pace than Social Security throughout its history.

It is strange indeed that the Bush administration cried "wolf" over problems of long-term financing in Social Security in the Spring of 2005, when the President made Social Security privatization

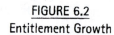

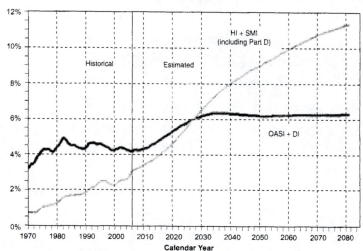

Source: The 2007 Annual Report of the OASDI Trustee Report, Actuarial Publications SocialSecurityOnLine (www.socialsecurity.gov).

his premiere domestic agenda. Fiscal problems in Social Security could have been easily corrected by simple, relatively low cost changes if Bush, who then controlled Congress, had acted responsibly. Instead he tried to partially privatize Social Security in a way that would have increased the national debt in a major way, and additionally created a huge new entitlement that will cause serious financial issues in the immediate future and massive ones in the long run. The administration pushed Medicare Part D through Congress despite the deep concerns of House Republicans about costs by claiming that the first ten-years' costs would not exceed $400 billion. Bush deceived his own party when he hid from Republicans that his administration's top Medicare analyst at the time estimated the costs to be around $550 billion. It is highly unlikely that the bill would have passed the House if the higher estimates had been released (more about this later).

THE OVERALL PATTERN

This frenetic activity has had a profound effect on the growth of government. It is easy to detect a strong shift in government spending starting at the time Bush took office. Figure 6.3 shows the important shifts in the path of federal spending that came about after his election. Compare that trajectory with the pattern established in the period directly preceding his presidency,

FIGURE 6.3
Inflation-Adjusted Federal Outlays, 1955–2005

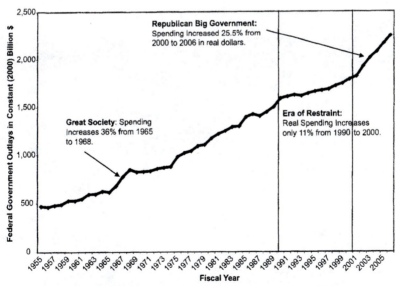

Source: Calculated form US Office of Management and Budget, Budget of the United States Government, FY 2008, Historical Statistics, Table 1.3 (http://www.whitehouse.gov/omb/budget/fy2008/hist.html).

when the United States really did have a culture of spending restraint in place.

These differences become even more graphic if we calculate the projected path from the era of fiscal restraint to the Bush era. Using simple projections, we calculate that if the fiscal path pursued by GHW Bush and Clinton had been continued during the GW Bush presidency, expenditures would have been approximately 15 percent smaller than they actually are today.

The Grand Old Party has had itself a real party! It has been able to spend as if there were no tomorrow, yet still offer tax cuts that, as we saw in Chapter 3, are justified only by the lamest of economic notions. The consequences are completely predictable. The massive

Borrowing to Sustain the (Grand Old) Party

Source: *Seattle Post-Intelligencer*, February 16, 2006.

new government programs initiated during the Bush presidency are being, and will be for the foreseeable future, funded from borrowing. Bush's tax cuts, which were supposed to stimulate revenue growth to offset their costs, have instead driven federal revenues down from almost 21 percent of GDP in 2000 (Clinton's last year) to 18.4 percent in 2006. Simultaneously, outlays have grown from 18.5 percent of GDP to 20.1 percent, leading to large deficits that, as just noted, replaced Clinton's declining debt/GDP ratio with a rising one.

Tax cuts failed to stimulate enough growth to recoup the lost revenue, and economists predict they will not do so in the foreseeable future. Table 6.2 shows the growth in outlays and revenues for the years 2001–2006, calculated as a percentage of GDP, along with two other ways of calculating outlays. The bottom line: revenues as a percentage of GDP have declined, and expenditures have increased. The result is increased borrowing.

We have shown in previous chapters that spending was brought under control in the mid-1970s when Congress established a method of budgeting that required explicit consideration of the whole spending package. This review process offered the necessary financial transparency, and the pay-go rules that were in place in one form or another from the mid-1980s to 2001 locked the regime of fiscal responsibility in place.

Figure 6.4 shows the gross federal debt as a percentage of GDP from 1940 through 2006. The federal government engaged in massive borrowing to fund the war effort during the 1940s, but immediately after the end of conflict began to pay down the debt. The debt declined relative to the size of the economy from 1946 to 1981, when it reversed direction. From 1981 to the present it rose

TABLE 6.2
Federal Outlays and Revenues during the Bush Years

FISCAL YEARS:	2001	2002	2003	2004	2005	2006	PERCENT GROWTH 2001–2006	ANNUAL AVERAGE
NOMINAL OUTLAYS (BILLIONS)	1863	2011	2160	2293	2472	2655	42.5%	7.0%
REAL OUTLAYS (BILLION $2000)	1821	1929	2018	2082	2167	2247	23.4%	3.9%
							PERCENTAGE POINT GROWTH OR DECLINE	
REVENUES, % OF GDP	19.8	17.9	16.5	16.3	17.5	18.4	−1.4	−0.23
OUTLAYS, % OF GDP	18.5	19.4	20.0	19.9	20.1	20.3	1.8	0.30

Source: Calculated from US Office of Management and Budget, Budget of the United States Government, Fiscal Year 2008, Historical Tables, Table 1.3.

as a percentage of overall national economic activity, save only for much of the Clinton presidency.

What happened? We know that spending patterns could not have accounted for the trace of the debt, because when spending was increasing most rapidly the debt was declining. So one of two things must have occurred. First, a recession in a particular year that has eroded that year's GDP from its level in the prior year can increase the debt/GDP ratio even if the actual amount of that debt had not changed. That is, the same amount of debt in the current

FIGURE 6.4
Gross Federal Debt as a Percentage of GDP, 1940–2006

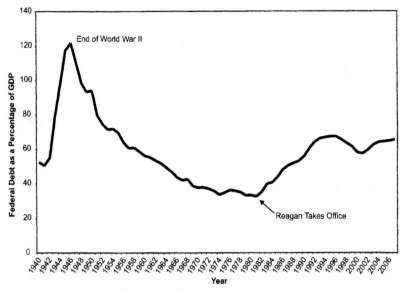

Source: Calculated from US Office of Management and Budget, Budget of the United States Government, FY 2008, Historical Statistics, Table 7.1 (http://www.whitehouse.gov/omb/budget/fy2008/hist.html).

year as in the prior year will grow relative to this year's GDP that is smaller than the previous one. To keep the percentage stable, spending would have to be cut. Or, second, without such spending reductions, tax cuts would cause the debt to increase.

We can have a look at this by returning to the trace of the top marginal tax rate charged citizens across time. Recall that this measure is a pretty good proxy for the entire complex federal tax structure. When the top rate is cut, most all taxes are cut. Figure 6.5 diagrams these tax rates and the gross federal debt.

Basically there have been four incidences of major tax changes since the Second World War. The first was enacted in 1963 with

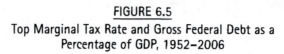

FIGURE 6.5

Top Marginal Tax Rate and Gross Federal Debt as a Percentage of GDP, 1952–2006

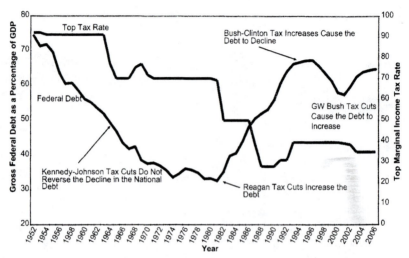

Sources: Calculated from US Office of Management and Budget, Budget of the United States Government, FY 2008, Historical Statistics, Table 7.1 (http://www.whitehouse.gov/omb/budget/fy2008/hist.html). Tax rates as described in Chapter 2.

the Kennedy tax cuts, intended to stimulate economic growth in an already growing economy. That tax cut did not deflect the continuing decline in the national debt that had begun in 1946. The Reagan tax cuts did, however. The reversal occurred just as soon as the tax cuts were enacted—that is, the debt as a percentage of GDP began to grow. At first this growth in debt occurred because of a sharp economic recession, but subsequent economic growth did not reverse it.

This growth in the indebtedness of the national government continued until the tax increases imposed by Presidents GHW Bush and Clinton finally stopped it in 1995. The national debt leveled off, declined as borrowing slowed, and finally ceased after strong economic growth. The GW Bush tax cuts immediately caused an increase in borrowing and a subsequent increase in the size of the debt, both absolutely and as a percentage of the economy.

Of the major tax cutting events, only one—Kennedy's 1963 cut (implemented in 1964)—did not result in increases in the national debt. Only after this tax reduction did the economy grow enough to offset the increased borrowing necessary to fund government programs. Reagan's tax cuts resulted in increased borrowing from future generations, as did GW Bush's tax cuts.

Figure 6.6 is a scatterplot showing the top marginal tax rate levied by the national government and the annual change in the gross federal debt (as a percentage of GDP). As the tax rate goes up, the debt goes dowm, and as the tax rate goes down, the debt goes up. Charging high tax rates reduces the debt, just as common sense would tell you. Charging low rates increases the debt, again, as your common sense would suggest. Put another way, government has to borrow, thereby adding to the debt, to fund reductions in the tax rate.

What happened to the debt/GDP ratio tells much about fiscal policy in the postwar years. The ratio in the 1950s, 1960s, and 1970s declined 37 percent, 31 percent, and 14 percent, respectively. In the three decades prior to 1981, there were vigorous debates about the size of government, its assumption of new programs, and even the size of the federal deficit and debt. The first two decades benefited from strong economic growth, whereas the 1970s were a time of economic problems. Although the presidents in the main did not pursue explicit policies of fiscal prudence, the debt ratio declined in each decade while the deficit ratio went somewhat above parity in that decade.

But President Ronald Reagan's 1981 tax cut opened the door for a flood of massive deficits that swept over his budget constraints, radically increased the deficit/GDP ratio, and halted the decline in

FIGURE 6.6

Top Marginal Tax Rate on Individuals and the Annual Change in Federal Debt as a Percentage of GDP

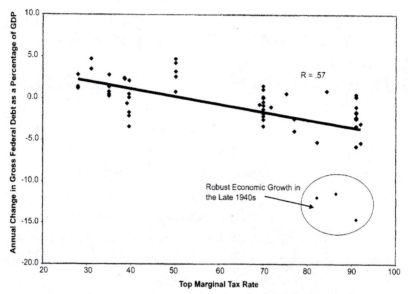

Sources: Calculated from US Office of Management and Budget, Budget of the United States Government, FY 2008, Historical Statistics, Table 7.1 (http://www.whitehouse.gov/omb/budget/fy2008/hist.html). Tax rates as described in Chapter 2.

the debt ratio that had begun shortly after the end of World War II. Over the rest of his presidency, the administration raised taxes in total to equal roughly one-half of the original tax cut, but Reagan's bad economic ideas had unwisely initiated a new tenet in Republican Party doctrine. Tax cuts rather than fiscal balance became the party's mantra. The prudent fiscal policies of the two presidents during the 1990s and by far the best level of economic growth since the 1960s that came in the last half of the decade during the Clinton presidency yielded four years of budget surpluses and restarted the falling deficit/ratio.

But the mantra had not been suppressed. George W. Bush went far beyond Reagan, based on bad economic ideas that he continued to adhere to, despite overwhelming evidence refuting them. He decreased taxes several times by an overall amount much greater than Reagan's 1981 tax cut. Simultaneously he refused to support any tax increases and destroyed the budget controls he inherited.

Some conservatives, including *New York Times* columnist David Brooks, have tried to justify GW Bush's aggressive big-government conservatism as "Hamiltonian," after the greatest conservative who never became president, Alexander Hamilton. The claim made no sense. Hamilton had supported a strong central government and large-scale spending for infrastructure development to support the development of the infant nation's commerce. But Hamilton was also the man who launched the United States on the right fiscal path by constructing the fledgling nation's financial structure as George Washington's secretary of Treasury. He regarded the integrity of government bonds as sacrosanct, and he surely would never have supported massive public borrowing to support tax cuts, domestic welfare spending, and benighted foreign adventures.

CONCLUSIONS

The unified Republican control of Congress and the presidency led to big spending increases and bigger government. On almost every indicator imaginable, the ascendancy of GW Bush to the presidency represents the end of a period of slow growth in government and an initiation of spectacular growth in both discretionary and mandatory programs. These programs have spanned the gamut of what government does—from education and health to defense and transportation. Spending has been higher in defense and "homeland security," but that is scant comfort to those advocating limited government.

There is one category of government size that has not grown during the era of Big Government Republicanism: revenues as a proportion of the economy. As Republican government has grown, taxes have been cut, and revenue has declined. The result has been massive borrowing and a basic deterioration in the fiscal balance sheet.

CHAPTER 7

Politics, Economics, and Tax Theories

In the previous several chapters, we examined the economic theories that have been used to justify tax cuts in light of the actual fiscal performance of the federal government, and we found them wanting. Now we take a more detailed historical examination of how these theories emerged and how they became lodged as basic tenets in the ideological framework of the modern Republican Party, despite their failure to produce the intended effects. In doing so, we'll take an historical bird's eye view of American postwar economic, political, and public policy development.

In Greek myth, the goddess Athena was born when she sprung in full armor from the forehead of Zeus, but theories relevant to the policy process don't generally spring full-formed out of the minds of economists and political theorists. There is always a context, and, in turn, the theories influence subsequent policy history. In this chapter, we put the conservative tax theories in historical context by examining postwar economic and political developments as they have affected, and in turn have been affected by, the conservative tax theories.

AMERICA'S POSTWAR ECONOMY

It is useful to distinguish three distinct periods of economic history of the postwar era: (1) the Golden Years, 1947–1973;[1] (2) the Years of Downturn and Despair, 1974–1980; and (3) the Roller-Coaster Years, 1981–2007.

The Golden Years

In his impressive study, Brown University historian James Patterson pointed to the great economic dominance of the United States in the period 1945–1974: "With 7 percent of the world's population in the late 1940s, America possessed 42 percent of the world's income and accounted for half of the world's manufacturing output. American workers produced 57 percent of the planet's steel, 43 percent of electricity, 62 percent of oil, 80 percent of automobiles."[2] Per capita income greatly exceeded the United States' closest rivals.

How such dominance came about is no mystery. America's major economic rivals had been devastated by the war in Europe and the Pacific. In addition, the United States built an amazing reservoir of skilled workers and of physical assets from plants to transportation systems. "By 1943–1944 the United States alone was producing one ship a day and one aircraft every five minutes!"[3]

---

[1]The starting year reflects the fact that the several months after Japan surrendered involved demobilization.
[2]James T. Patterson, *Grand Expectations*. New York: Oxford University Press, 1996, p. 61.
[3]Paul Kennedy, *The Rise and Fall of the Great Powers*. New York: Random House, 1987, p. 355.

It built close to half of all armaments produced in 1943 by the combatants in the war—that is, by both friend and foe.[4] By the time the United States had demobilized, it was indeed the world's great economic power. And its economic strength paid off for American citizens: the quarter century from 1947 to1973 still stands as the longest period of strong economic growth and high productivity in American history.

This unique period became even more wondrous for those who had experienced deprivation during the Great Depression and the wartime shortages. Suddenly, ordinary people found themselves with money they had saved during the war and more goods available than there had been since the late 1920s. An exceptionally high productivity rate of more than 2.5 percent led to truly astounding gains in real household income during the Golden Years. Massachusetts Institute of Technology economist Frank Levy wrote: "[1947] was the beginning of a period of substantial growth during which family income (adjusted for inflation) never went more than three years without setting a new record. By the early 1970s, median family income had more than doubled."[5]

The growth was shared reasonably equally across economic classes. Of course the United States had rich and poor, but the poor and the rich enjoyed similar percentage gains in their incomes—indeed, the poor actually were gaining on the rich. In the period 1947–1969, the percentage of income share gained was the greatest for the poorest fifth of the population and less for each quintile thereafter, and the highest quintile experienced an actual decline.

---

[4]Ibid.
[5]Frank Levy, *The New Dollars and Dreams*. New York: Russell Sage Foundation, 1998, p. 205.

However, though income inequality lessened, this was hardly a massive redistribution. The richest quintile gained a much greater actual amount of income and prospered even if its share of income for that period declined slightly. This was historically unique, true neither before World War II nor after 1969. Indeed, only the richest quintile experienced a gain in income shares after 1969 while the offsetting declines grew larger and larger moving from top to bottom.[6]

Both the size of the increase in real median family income and in the rising equality in the shares of national income during the Golden Years created a broad middle class. It is in these years that the American Dream became a reality. Families came to expect that the parents would do better and better and the children would enjoy even greater prosperity as their standards of living moved higher and higher. America citizens looked to the future with great confidence, believing that American ingenuity could overcome all limits. Patterson's critique of the Golden Years characterized them as a "grand quest for opportunity . . . [that] resulted in significant and lasting improvement in the economic and legal standing of millions of people. No comparable period of United States history witnessed so much economic and civic process."[7]

Years of Downturn and Despair

The Golden Years ended abruptly when the Organization of Petroleum Exporting Countries (OPEC), composed of nations mainly in the Middle East that controlled much of the world's

---

[6]All of the statistics used in this paragraph were derived from Levy, *The New Dollars and Dreams*. P. 199 (Table A. 1).
[7]Patterson, *Grand Expectations*, pp. vii–viii.

oil reserves, sharply raised oil prices in 1973. Despair and fear set in with the shocked realization that the wondrous economic performance might not continue. This was particularly so for those born in 1946 or later—the baby-boom generation—who had never faced the hardships many of their parents suffered for well over a decade during the Great Depression and World War II.

Many of the baby boomers had seen their parents become part of a prosperous middle class that had an ever-rising standard of living that allowed them to send their children to colleges and universities. And these young people did not graduate with large debts for that education hanging over their heads. Those with degrees in hand likely had begun their work careers with the expectations formed in the Golden Years of a good life that got better and better as their incomes grew. Even those who left high school after graduation had seen their parents do well in high-paying assembly line jobs in the automobile industry and elsewhere. They had no idea that the Golden Years had been the heyday of such good jobs and that the decline in high-paying manual labor opportunities would be precipitous.

Starting in 1965, the United States experienced rising tensions. Riots in the predominantly black ghettoes of a number of major cities and widespread protests against the Vietnam War became increasingly violent. But it was only after the 1973 OPEC oil price increase that everything seemed to unravel. President Richard Nixon was driven from office by the Watergate scandal. Vietnam became an ever-bigger disaster with tens of thousands of American troops being killed for what increasingly seemed to be a meaningless cause. In 1979, OPEC again greatly increased the price of oil, and gasoline shortages brought long lines and much anger as people waited restlessly at filling stations.

Jimmy Carter's star-crossed presidency made the gloom more palpable yet. The OPEC price increase in 1979 exploded into double-digit inflation at a time his presidency already was in deep trouble. To make matters worse, Carter made a national speech naming the public as a culprit in the excessive use of gasoline. The last shoe dropped with the failure of President Carter's badly-bungled attempt in 1979 to rescue employees of the U.S. embassy being held hostage by Iran. The economy and the government seemingly had let the people down. The nation's leaders looked particularly inept in light of their collective failures to restore either America's economy or its military power to dominance.

The Roller-Coaster Years

Americans were on an economic roller coaster in the quarter century following the inauguration of Ronald Reagan. The up-and-down ride did not simply follow the business cycle but came in part from the public's wide mood swings that reflected concerns about their own future and that of the nation. During the Golden Years, the several recessions did not crush the public's confidence in the efficacy of the federal government or dampen the expectation of a continuing strong economic performance. Then came the anguish that began in 1973 and crystallized into despair toward the end of Jimmy Carter's one-term presidency.

Once in office, Ronald Reagan moved quickly to restore public confidence. He believed without reservation that federal policies were the main roadblock holding back the unlimited potential of free-market capitalism. Reaganism's two most basic tenets held that tax cuts at the top offered the magic fix and that federal government regulations stifled businesses, the two premises reinforcing each other. The president sought to unleash the American entrepreneurial spirit through massive reductions in income tax rates and in the government's regulatory power. His tax reduction strategy disproportionately favored the tax filers at the top of the income distribution because they were considered to be the group most likely to use tax cuts for productive investments.

Even though the United States had been hard hit by the 1981–1982 recession that still ranks as the deepest of the postwar era, President Reagan persevered, promising a strong recovery even as the recession worsened. And recover it did. Economic growth in 1984 rose more than 7 percent—a level not seen since the 1950s. President Reagan claimed it was morning again in America, the notion of "again" recalling the Golden Years. Economic realities were far more complex, however, and the Golden Years had by no means been restored. Though the last six years of the Reagan presidency showed a distinct improvement over the earlier period of economic weakness, they were nevertheless marred by a low productivity rate, declining real average weekly earnings for the 80 percent of the labor force in production and nonsupervisory work, increasing income inequality, and the highest budget deficits in U.S. history to that time.

Increasing economic growth driven by record deficits fit the expected pattern from an extraordinarily large Keynesian countercyclical tax cut. Although the results did not match those of the early postwar period, they were better than the 1970s, and Reagan's infectious optimism prevailed. Americans had found the leader who could restore their confidence and their belief in the nation's exceptionalism. Reagan's confidence was a critical bromide to the deep gloom of the 1970s, but his optimism begot overconfidence in a still-fragile economy.

Lou Cannon, an admirer whose Reagan biography ranks among the best and fairest accounts of the Reagan presidency, wrote, "Because of his ability to reflect and give voice to the aspirations of his fellow citizens, Reagan succeeded in reviving national confidence at a time when there was great need for inspiration. This was his great contribution as president. But because he believed in happy endings obtained with too little sacrifice, this revived confidence became an end in itself that Reagan rarely sought to focus on higher goals."[8]

A year after President Reagan left office, slow growth returned. The deficits that reached new highs blighted the one-term presidency of George H. W. Bush and continued into Bill Clinton's first years. Then, much to everyone's surprise, the economy accelerated in 1995 and kept right on going until the end of the 20th century. Those years yielded levels of sustained, noninflationary economic growth, high productivity, and increasing real average weekly earnings for production and nonsupervisory workers not witnessed since the Golden Years.

The performance of the 1995–2000 economy exceeded that of the last six years of the Reagan presidency, yet the policies were diametrically opposite. When President Clinton raised taxes in 1993, he did so by increasing the rates for the top three

---

[8]Lou Cannon, *President Reagan*. New York: Simon & Schuster, 1991, p. 837.

income tax brackets. He hit the trifecta: strong economic growth, increased productivity, and an end to the long string of budget deficits. Economic growth yielded a bonanza in new federal tax revenues so great that it bestowed the legacy of a large budget surplus on George W. Bush at the outset of his presidency.

Nor did investment by the richest taxpayers dry up after Clinton's 1993 tax rate increases. Vast sums flowed into the rapidly growing high-technology sector, driven by cutting-edge improvements exemplified by the Internet. The productivity rate made a quantum leap, approaching the level of the Golden Years. Ever-increasing confidence—and finally overconfidence—came as the stock market led by the high-tech sector soared far beyond previous highs. The market's favorite Internet stocks—mainly new companies that had never shown a profit—rose to astonishing prices. Euphoric investors envisioned the economy and the stock market continuing onward and upward.

Even though the law of gravity held and a downturn came, Clinton's tax strategy directly challenged the supply siders' unswerving conviction that all tax increases, particularly for those paying the highest tax rates, deterred investment and economic growth. Indeed, Clinton put the onus on those who support the supply-side approach to explain why these spectacular economic successes do not refute their claims that tax cuts are good for economic growth and tax increases block it.

The reason that tax increases do not invariably harm economic growth is not difficult to understand. After the Clinton 1993 tax increase, the most robust economic growth since the Golden Years followed in 1995–2000. Historian James Patterson wrote "[The] enactment of the budget package of 1993 was widely credited with contributing to the turnabout. It sent a message to skittish American investors that the federal government was finally serious about reforming its fiscal affairs."[9] That is, the investors responded positively to President Clinton's fiscal prudence after the yearly budget deficits that had started early in the Reagan administration continued through the GHW Bush presidency. Fiscal prudence is good policy, and it turned out to be good politics as well. Clinton was solidly reelected in 1996, in large part because of economic prosperity. He demonstrated that tax increases, rather than genuflecting to the ideological claim that all increases are bad, should be in any president's policy kit.

Clinton argued the case for a New Economy, telling the members of Congress in his January 27, 2000 State of the Union Message that "never before 'has our nation enjoyed, at once, so much prosperity and social progress with so little internal crisis and so few external threats.'"[10] Although Clinton could legitimately point to the first period of extraordinary economic performance since 1973, there was still a good degree of political puffery here. His remarks ignored a number of serious problems, including the rapidly rising trade deficit and dangerously high level of consumer debt. Claims that a New Economy had been born were premature. The British journalist and historian Godfrey Hodgson, who had spent a number of years in the United States and much admired it, came much closer to reality in pointing out that the period 1974–2000, despite the boom years

---

[9]James T. Patterson, *Restless Giant*. Oxford, England: Oxford University Press, 2005, p. 333.
[10]Godfrey Hodgson, *More Equal than Others*. Princeton: Princeton University Press, 2004, pp. 2–3.

that ended it, was "for many, probably for most Americans, years of disappointment and denial."[11]

A few statistics underscore Hodgson's statement. Median family income (in 2003 dollars) rose from $21,201 in 1947 to $43,219 in 1973, a gain of 104 percent.[12] From then to 2000, an increase of $10,972 brought real income in 2000 to $54,191, a gain of 25 percent. Had real income in 1973–2000 risen at the same rate as in 1947–1973, it would have increased by more than $56,000 so that real median income would have soared to roughly $110,000. Also, real wages for men below the 50th percentile actually declined in 1973–2000. These men were forced to work longer hours or their wives had to join the labor force or increase their hours worked to maintain family living standards. And the income share of the top 10 percent—especially the top 1 percent—rose markedly. This was true in part because of the huge increase in capital gains from the sale of common stock, the great bulk of which is held by the top 10 percent.

The roller coaster started down again when the economy went into a mild recession in March 2001. The new Bush administration was already pursuing a tax cut that passed in June 2001. Overall it was of a size similar to the Reagan 1981 reduction, and like its predecessor disproportionately benefited the richest Americans. Although the administration touted the stimulative effects of the cuts, at the time they were originally justified on supply-side grounds.

---

[11]Hodgson, *More Equal than Others*, p. xvii.
[12]All of the data in this paragraph were either drawn from Lawrence Mishel, Jared Bernstein, and Sylvia Allegretto, *The State of Working America 2004/2005*. Ithaca, NY: Cornell University Press, 2005, pp. 42 (Table 1.1) and 124 (Table 2.7), or calculated by the authors.

President Bush's tax package contributed to years of budgetary deficits that replaced the surpluses of the late Clinton years. Unlike Reagan, whose record tax cut in 1981 was followed by moderate tax increases in the face of rising deficits, George W. Bush continued to seek lower taxes. The September 11, 2001 terrorist attacks and the 2002 mid-term election, which increased the Republicans' House and Senate majorities, greatly strengthened President Bush's political power. In 2003, Bush pushed through another tax reduction for individuals, one that again favored the wealthiest families.

President Bush's deep tax reductions occurred along with significant increases on the expenditure side. Some of the new spending came from efforts to fight terrorism and the costs for running wars in Afghanistan and Iraq. However, even after removing the added defense and homeland security outlays, expenditures during the Bush years remain well above the comparable level in the Clinton administration. Since the start of the Bush presidency, federal spending has risen from $1.86 trillion to $2.71 trillion in nominal dollars.[13] After adjusting for price changes and population growth, the real outlays per person were a very high growth level of more than 16 percent from 2001 through 2005; spending went from 18.5 to 20.1 percent of GDP.[14] Despite the resulting imbalance between the federal government's revenue and outlays, the president and the Republican leaders in Congress were unwilling to reduce expenditures significantly and continued to support making tax cuts permanent. Finally conservatives realized they had a new

---

[13]Office of Management and Budget, *Fiscal Year 2007 Review, US Budget.* Washington DC: Office of Management and Budget.
[14]Data were finished by the Center on Budget and Policy Priorities.

form of Big Government; *New York Times* reporter Jonathan Weisman wrote in October 2005: "Conservative activists had begun pressing Republicans hard on what they saw as Big Government Conservatism."[15]

Given the massive tax cuts that greatly increased the yearly deficits and should have produced a short-term Keynesian stimulus, President Bush's economic performance has been surprisingly weak. The net increase did not exceed the jobs lost for almost four years; no president in the past 40 years has done so poorly in creating new jobs.[16] In his 2006 State of the Union address, Bush asserted that "In the last two and a half years, America has created 4.6 million jobs." Unfortunately the country lost more than 2.5 million jobs in the first two and a half years of his presidency.[17] The president's claim was technically correct and yielded a job gain per month of 184,000, a good but not outstanding increase. But looking at the first five years President Bush was in office, the average of 92,000 jobs per month is extremely weak.

In Chapter 8, when the Bush administration economic recovery is compared to the average recovery during the postwar era on key economic measures, we will see a mainly below average recovery compared to the previous postwar recoveries. Moreover, the economic gains from Bush's tax and budget policies came at a large price. Rising budget deficits from his tax cuts and the unfunded liabilities created by his costly Medicare prescription

---

[15]Jonathan Weisman, "House GOP to Push for $50 Billion in Federal Budget Cuts," *New York Times*, October 2005, p. A1.

[16]During his first 64 months in office Eisenhower's record was worse, leaving Bush next-to-last in the postwar period.

[17]Peter Wallsten and Maura Reynolds, "Some of Bush's Facts Don't Tell the Whole Story," *Seattle Times*, February 1, 2006, A13.

drug legislation have become long-run threats imperiling the fiscal solvency of the federal government and the standard of living of much of the American population.

The Bush tax cuts helped stimulate overall economic growth, but the gains bypassed the lower half of the income distribution. In its annual survey of income and poverty, the Census Bureau reported that by the end of 2006 median family income (adjusted for inflation) was still below its 1997 level even though family income had risen 1.1 percent during 2005 and 1.3 percent in 2006. But this followed four straight years in which median family income failed to rise. Moreover, the entire 2005 increase came for those over 65; for those under 65, median family income fell again, for the fifth straight year. It finally rose in 2006. The poverty rate remained higher than in 2001, and the number of Americans without health insurance rose to 47 million, up from 41.2 million in 2001. The earnings of full-time workers decreased for the third straight year; the increase in family income was due to more family members going to work.[18]

THE CHANGING POLITICAL ENVIRONMENT

Politics and economics go hand-in-hand. Postwar politics can be divided into two distinct periods: BR and AR (before and after Reagan). Until the late 1970s, American faith in government, and the politics of the New Deal coalition, survived, although cracks were appearing. Republicans won the presidency only when large

---

[18]U.S. Census Bureau, *Current Population Reports P60-231: Income, Poverty, and Health Insurance Coverage in the United States, 2006.* Washington DC: U.S. Government Printing Office, 2007; David Leonhardt, "U.S. Poverty Rate Was up Last Year," *New York Times*, August 31, 2005, p. A1; E. J. Dionne, "Perfect Storm for the Poor," *Washington Post*, September 1, 2006, p. A21.

Democratic majorities defected, creating what political scientists termed "deviating elections"—that is, elections that had deviations from the underlying Democratic party identifications of the majority of American voters. The terrible 1970s brought the critical systemic shift from the New Deal philosophy and a breakdown of many voters' firm identification with the Democratic party. Voters never accepted Reaganism as well as they had accepted Rooseveltism, but Reaganism has nevertheless defined the political landscape since 1980. Democrats have been on the defensive ever since.

Reaganism has two forms, its pure form reflecting the optimism and understated style of President Reagan, and a version based on the same underlying principles but pursued more vigorously and harshly. Understanding modern American politics requires appreciating the decline of the Democratic Roosevelt coalition, the rise of Reaganism, and the replacement of Reagan's optimistic tone with its harsher version pursued by Republican Speaker of the House Newt Gingrich and other partisans after the 1994 mid-term election.

The Postwar Rise and Fall of Liberalism

When President Calvin Coolidge spoke to the Society of Newspaper Editors in January 1925, he was able to set out the guiding philosophy of the United States in just six words: "The business of America is business." Except in wartime, the federal government was small until the 1930s and offered little or nothing to individuals and businesses needing help. Once the Great Depression brought massive problems, the Roosevelt government initiated numerous New Deal programs that provided jobs for the unemployed and aided struggling businesses. The ebullient Roosevelt restored public confidence and gave hope to a people who had experienced both the worst depression and the nation's widest and most extensive involvement in a foreign war. Victory in World War II added greatly to the national government's image of effectiveness.

Once peace came, Washington led the miraculous economic recovery of the next quarter century. At home the GI Bill of Rights provided educational benefits to nearly eight million veterans between 1944 and 1956, including more than two million who went to colleges at a cost of over 14 billion, a vast amount in that period.[19] Harry Truman's Marshall Plan became a pivotal factor in the rapid transformation of Western Europe and Japan that helped lead to sustained worldwide economic growth. The two remain among the most successful federal programs in American history.

Along with faith in government came faith in the economy and scientific progress. Historian Thomas Patterson notes that the exceptional performance of the economy, including the introduction of new goods and services and the futuristic design of products, "promoted grand expectations, especially among the educated middle classes, about the potential for further scientific and technological advances. This optimistic spirit—the feeling that there were no limits to progress—defined a guiding spirit of the age."[20]

The striking successes created such grand expectations that they finally could not be met. Although those economic Golden Years warranted optimism and confidence, they inevitably degenerated

---

[19]Patterson, *Grand Expectations*, p. 68.
[20]Patterson, *Grand Expectations*, p. 317.

into a consuming overconfidence that made the fall more shatter-
ing than the actual decline appeared to warrant. In intellectual circles, proponents of the libertarian theory of minimal government
attacked the size and intrusiveness of Washington. Even those
who had strongly favored the earlier government effort worried
that it had gone too far.

Reaganism and Its Harsher Version

In 1981 the new president brought to dispirited Americans a
message that combined ideology and myth. Its central ideological proposition—the federal government as the problem and
unregulated capitalism as the solution—stemmed in part from
Reagan's mistaken belief that the United States had achieved
greatness through the hard work of individuals without the help
of government. His biographer Lou Cannon wrote: "Of all the
myths in which Reagan believed, none was more fundamental to
his vision and his message than the notion that Americans had
taken control of their destiny without assistance from the federal
government."[21]

And the American people came to accept his shining vision
composed of ideological dogma and myths of nationhood. Because
of his unique persona, which combined unquenchable optimism
and unquestioning belief in American exceptionalism, Reagan likely
is the only postwar president who could have made the fictional
vision believable. He and Roosevelt were in a class by themselves,
the "Great Communicator" sweeping away the gloom of the 1970s

---

[21]Cannon, *President Reagan*, p. 793.

just as FDR had in the 1930s. Reagan's antigovernmentalism had sufficient power to continue as the dominant political philosophy over the 12 years during the presidencies of George H. W. Bush and Bill Clinton, even though neither were true believers. These presidents felt it politically necessary to adhere to its precepts, and Clinton went so far as to proclaim the end of big government.

Reaganism's harsh edge had been masked during the Reagan presidency. The doctrine, however, could easily be used to encourage individual greed, business recklessness and dishonesty in the pursuit of profits, and the severe judgment that society's "losers" did not deserve government support. What can be termed Harsh Reaganism burst out after the Republicans won 54 new seats in the House of Representatives and 8 seats in the Senate in the mid-term election of 1994, taking control of the House for the first time since 1955.

Georgia Republican Newt Gingrich brought the new version to the fore by putting the tenets of Reaganism in a confrontational style. Strident attacks on the Democrats in the House of Representatives, who had fallen into a governing style that tolerated considerable abuse and excess, made it easy for him to mastermind the 1994 victory. More than a House insider, Gingrich was also a party-builder, carefully constructing the Republican candidate base and aiding promising candidates as they built their political careers. The 1994 freshmen he recruited became his base for being elected Speaker of the House.

Gingrich, an intelligent strategist, would compromise when that tactic brought gains. The new Republican House members, in contrast, generally were hardcore ideologues who sought total adherence to doctrine. Their angry ideological behavior, which propelled the Clinton impeachment, heightened polarization to a point where reasonable deliberations and bipartisan agreements became almost impossible. The party's ideologues pushed Gingrich to make the 1998 mid-term elections a referendum on impeachment, and the party lost seats. Gingrich then was pressured into resigning as Speaker of the House. The ideologues, then led by Texas Representative Tom Delay and facing electoral repudiation and Clinton's increasing popularity ratings, nevertheless voted articles of impeachment. In the Senate, Republican majority leader Trent Lott of Mississippi, seeing that the votes were not there to convict, moved swiftly to get the matter off the agenda with a quick vote.

Even though Reagan had been out of office 12 years when the Clinton presidency ended, Reaganism still dominated the nation's political thought. George W. Bush came to office a true believer in Reaganism, especially the need for income tax reductions for the wealthiest citizens. Yale presidential scholar Steven Skowronek depicts Bush as "a man who came to believe that definitions effectively asserted can create their own reality," crafting "a political stance that renounced flexibility in the name of commitment."[22] Bush remained committed to the Reagan orthodoxy. His presidency became exemplified by his unwillingness to accept hard evidence refuting his premises and his relentless attacks on the conflicting evidence, using deception and denial as the main weapons. Nowhere is this rigidity more clear than in the continuing advocacy of tax cuts at the top as the

---

[22]Steven Skowronek, "Leadership by Definition: First Term Reflections on George W. Bush's Political Stance," *Perspectives on Politics*, 3, December 2005, pp. 817-831.

magic fix for America's economic ills and the use of starve-the-beast as the rationale for the mounting budget deficits.

THE RATIONALE FOR TAX CUTS

We've seen that supply-side economics actually has two variations—the miracle and the academic versions. Ronald Reagan's 1981 miracle tax cut had been the brainchild of economists well outside the mainstream, and it was viewed with disdain by many within it. The highly regarded Harvard University economist Martin Feldstein became the intellectual force behind the academic version and trained the two economists who led the later supply-side effort in George W. Bush's presidency. But despite its intellectual and mathematical sophistication, this version prescribed the same policy of cutting taxes at the top in the 2001 and 2003 tax packages as had the miracle version for the 1981 legislation. The mantra of the Bush administration became cut, never increase, taxes. Unlike the Reagan administration, which raised taxes several times, Bush refused to do so and repeatedly pushed for new tax cuts and extensions of earlier temporary ones.

Reagan's Supply-Side Economics

Keynesian theory developed in the 1930s proposed reducing federal taxes as a countercyclical strategy to stimulate the economy during a recession. It operated on the demand side, putting new funds from the tax cuts in people's hands so as to induce more spending. Tax cuts were not the only countercyclical measure. Unemployment insurance payments could be extended or public works initiated to hire unemployed individuals. The benefits in both cases were likely to be spent quickly by those out of work. Keynes also envisioned balancing the budget over the business cycle with deficits offset by tax increases after economic recovery. These various tax changes were simply tools available to decision makers to use in fiscal policy at different times during the business cycle.

Only later did politicians and some economists begin bally-hooing the magical properties of tax cuts. The miracle supply-side thesis fit perfectly with Reagan's ideologically driven demand to reduce tax rates—particularly the highest ones—and his political desire to have his policies be painless in not requiring reductions for the beneficiaries of federal programs.

The miracle supply-side thesis moved from theory to practice via the classic "back of the napkin" meeting at the Two Continents Restaurant, barely a block from the White House. Arthur Laffer emerged as the guru of the new doctrine, and Jude Wanniski, an editorial-page writer for the *Wall Street Journal* who had arranged the meeting, became the propagandist for the idea. Wanniski sold the concept to Robert Bartley, his boss as the head of the editorial page at the *Wall Street Journal*, who used his position to make supply-side economics a central concept in the conservative revolution.

By the end of the Reagan presidency, the budget deficit had hit record highs and personal saving had fallen. Harvard economist Benjamin Friedman in *Day of Reckoning*, the best book on "Reaganomics," underscored the key shift. He wrote that in the 1980s, the Reagan administration's "fiscal policy has steered more of our spending into consumption and less into investment in productive plant and equipment and housing than ever before in the post World War II era," with each having dropped by one-third, while the United States was becoming more dependent on foreign investment.[23]

Friedman highlighted the shift from creditor to debtor nation that occurred under Reagan. In 1915, America had became a net creditor. The total value of foreign assets owned by the United States exceeded the total worth of U.S. assets owned by the rest of the world. After nearly seven decades in that status, America slid to net debtor status in 1984 and by 1987 had become the world's biggest one.

Borrowing from abroad in much of the 19th century, particularly after the Civil War, had been a key factor in the nation's economic growth. As a net borrower, the United States had financed productive investment in such areas as transportation facilities and business plant and equipment. Successful investments helped the United States outgrow this need before the 20th century began. In the 1980s, borrowing from abroad had a different function. It financed consumption, both government and consumer debt. Americans became hooked on the credit-card syndrome, and that hard-to-cure malady continues to plague the nation and its people.

Reagan's huge 1981 tax cut started a debate as to whether it was a colossal economic error or a hidden plot—a Trojan horse—to reduce the role of the federal government. Reagan and the true believers may have actually thought the deficit would vanish. Such unrelenting confidence in convictions is the mark of true ideologues.

---

[23]Benjamin Friedman, *Day of Reckoning*. New York: Random House, 1988, pp. 174–175 and 185–186. The discussion in the rest of this paragraph and all of the next one is based on pages 226–227.

Lou Cannon wrote of the supply siders: "Many of them expressed their convictions with an evangelical fervor more appropriate for a religious crusade than an economic discussion."[24]

Wanniski told Haynes Johnson that Reagan too was a true believer: "It set off a symphony in his ears. He knew instantly it was true and would never have a doubt thereafter."[25] Reagan tended to embrace an idea that meshed with his underlying beliefs with total conviction and not question it thereafter. What could be more basic than a painless policy featuring deep tax cuts for the rich? It fit with his tough talk but general unwillingness to follow through with tough action. He liked to tell his inaccurate tale of the "Welfare Queen" who drove a Cadillac paid for by government overpayments and have red-meat Republicans cheer wildly when he spoke to them, but that generally was enough for the president. Major welfare changes with bite came only after Harsh Reaganism replaced the milder version.

Many other policy makers were well aware that the supply siders' claim of massive new tax revenues that would materialize from the growth generated by the supply-side effects of the tax cuts and replace the amount lost from lowering tax rates at the top, did not comport with reality. George H. W. Bush, competing against Reagan in the 1980 Republican presidential primaries, labeled the supply-side thesis "voodoo economics." If Reagan and the supply-side purists did in fact expect the miracle outcome, it is hardly surprising that the doubters near the president did not seek to dissuade him, or if they did, that they failed.

---

[24]Cannon, *President Reagan*, p. 236.
[25]Haynes Johnson, *Sleepwalking through History*. New York: Norton, 1991, p. 105.

The hidden agenda may well have gone beyond hubris and cockeyed economic reasoning to a more base intent. Economist Benjamin Friedman charged that it was "a carefully calculated plan for forcing the government to reduce its role in American life. . . . The economic costs of this subterfuge were not a surprise but the inevitable and fully foreseen by-products of a more important campaign in which the issue at stake was not economic well-being but the character of American life in broader terms and in which our economic prospects (not to mention our government's fiscal position) were merely a hostage."[26] Whatever the motive, the tax cuts, combined with excessive deregulation and considerable mismanagement, reduced the capacity of the federal executive branch to carry out its legislative mandates in the broad area of domestic policy.[27]

Bush's Supply-Side Economics[28]

Although tax cuts for the rich were a constant in both the Reagan and George W. Bush presidencies, a more sophisticated version of supply-side economics promulgated by reputable economists shaped the latter's 2001 and 2003 tax policies. Keynes had focused on the short run to alleviate a temporary downturn in the business cycle. Fix the puncture and get on with the trip. The supply siders led by Harvard economics professor Martin Feldstein emphasized tax cuts that were intended to induce more saving and in turn greater capital accumulation, which over time

[26]Friedman, *Day of Reckoning*, p. 23.
[27]Walter Williams, *Mismanaging America*. Lawrence, KS: University Press of Kansas, 1990, pp. 98–104.
[28]This subsection draws heavily on Daniel Altman, *The Neoconomy*. New York: Public Affairs, 2004.

would increase the nation's long-term standard of living. Focusing on the long-term economic effects of low taxes, they de-emphasized short-term concerns.

These mainstream supply siders employed sophisticated mathematical models to develop their new theory of economic growth that singled out capital investment, such as plant and equipment, as the missing ingredient. Increasing the rate of investment required either borrowing abroad or pushing up saving by Americans, who were at the low end among savers in the advanced industrialized nations. When the supply siders cranked up their sophisticated mathematical models to determine the appropriate federal policy for increasing capital investment, out popped the very same policy recommendation as that from Arthur Laffer's curve drawn on a napkin at the Two Continents. Both the napkin and the computer models proclaimed: Cut taxes so as to bring the most benefits to the wealthy, and America shall thrive as never before.

How did this correspondence occur? Daniel Altman, in a 2004 book called *The Neoconomy,* provides the best roadmap. Altman, who received his graduate training in economics at Harvard University under Feldstein, has written a well-reasoned, even-handed critique of supply-side economics.[29] ("Neoconomists" is the word Altman coined for the academic supply siders.)

As with much modern macroeconomics, supply-side theory is embodied in a set of mathematical equations. There is no question

---

[29]One expert observer noted that "Altman bases his arguments on merits, not motives. He accepts the neoconomists' goal of increasing the growth rate of the economy by stimulating saving and applies basic economic analysis to their arguments." Tom Gallagher, "The Unkindest Cut," *Washington Post National Weekly Edition,* September 13–19, 2004, p. 32.

of the value of mathematical models to the discipline of economics, but as is the case with any research tool, it has its limitations. The most important one for our purposes is that no matter how elegant the models and how competent the researchers, their basic orientation and choices can bias the model's results. One is well advised to approach mathematical models as one would a shiny vehicle on a used-car lot. Look under the hood and kick the tires—which means to economists and other social scientists to examine the data. Models are abstractions and must make predictions about real economic data. Even the best model may contain slanted assumptions that seem inconsequential until carefully assessed—not only by argument or more mathematics, but in light of real economic experiences.

The academic supply siders held that "the new task for government was to procure the best possible long-run equilibrium—the one with the highest living standards—for the economy."[30] Economic growth, they asserted, can be increased by changes in the supplies of technology, labor, and capital. Altman notes the assumptions used by supply siders to develop their models: "In the United States, the size and growth of the population, and therefore the labor force, were generally taken as given. So . . . was the rate of technological innovation. That left capital."[31] The supply siders went one more step by devising new models showing that innovation could be induced by increasing the stock of capital.

Capital investment took center stage for the supply siders, but they still needed two related assumptions. Postulating that tax

---

[30] Altman, *The Neoconomy*, 24.
[31] Ibid.

reductions would raise the country's saving rate and that the beneficiaries of the tax cuts would use their increased after-tax income to make the needed capital investment tied together the stock of capital and aggregate national saving. Available data showed clearly that those in the highest income tax brackets historically saved more than those at lower levels. Hence, reducing tax rates at the top should induce the most saving per dollar of tax cut. The supply siders also argued that targeting the tax cuts directly on taxable income from assets that paid dividends and interest or produced capital gains would be an even more powerful inducement to increase saving, because rates of return on these assets should rise.

In sum, the key propositions underlying the supply siders' high-powered mathematical models are as follows. First, an increase both in aggregate personal saving and in the amount of this additional saving going into capital investment is essential for attaining the main objective of moving the economy to a higher long-run equilibrium and a permanent rise in living standards. Second, tax reductions aimed at the highest income filers yield more saving than such reductions for working- and middle-class earners. Third, those at the top of the income distribution will use the newly available resources to increase the rate of capital investment. Fourth, the federal policies that are most likely to reach the main objectives will be targeted tax reductions on the taxable income from capital investments with the optimum strategy reducing income taxes on such investments to zero. Finally, the desired higher growth rate will not continue to increase indefinitely, so the government's task remains that of stimulating greater saving to increase capital investment. New jumps in capital investment over time will move the economy to higher and higher equilibria and permanent rises in standards of living. These leaps might take years, and when precisely they would occur could not be predicted. Hence, the supply siders mainly ignored the short run on the question of economic growth—their theories simply did not speak to immediate economic growth or its effects on the tax revenues of government.

The policy differences between Keynes' demand-side approach and that of the supply siders are now clear. In a recession, Keynesian demand-focused policies were short-run palliatives aimed at people likely to spend their benefits quickly and save little or nothing. Supply siders spurned quick fixes and sought benefits for those likely to save much or all of them and then use these additional funds to increase the long-run supply of capital investment. The Keynesians viewed the economic problem as mainly a cyclical downturn to be treated by putting the money in the pockets of those who would spend it quickly on consumption. These added expenditures were expected to kick-start the sluggish economy immediately toward higher growth.

Supply siders argued that there would be greater benefits to the nation if the funds instead would be targeted on those with the highest taxable incomes who would invest their new funds so as to increase the stock of capital. Even though the tax cuts initially produced disproportionate gains to those at the top of the income distribution, the supply siders argued that those with lesser incomes would benefit more than if a quick fix had been directed toward them. That is because the growing capital investment over time would raise their standard of living and keep it higher than it had been previously.

In assessing the sophisticated supply-side model, we underscore that the 1981 extreme version had been rejected by the economics profession as pie-in-the-sky theorizing, whereas the work of Feldstein and his colleagues had much going for it. Economists liked that the well-designed theoretical framework went beyond Keynes' total focus on demand to highlight policies addressing such factors as technology and capital. This brand of supply-side economics merits a careful assessment of its theoretical dimensions including the main assumptions, the orientation of the modelers, and how the concept has been put in practice in the Bush administration.

That the supply-side theory meets the academic standard of being logical (for example, it has no internal inconsistencies) and reasonable does not rule out legitimate challenges to assumptions or other aspects of the model. In particular, the pivotal assumption that only capital, not labor or technological or organizational innovation, can be increased by federal policies is questionable. Of course rising capital investment can indirectly induce more technological innovation, but how this might happen is not explored by the models. In fact, some of the most successful government policies have been directed at labor and technological innovation. The quality of the labor force can be raised through the federal government funding education and training. The GI Bill of Rights provided additional education for returning World War II veterans which increased the work skills of millions of them and carried the United States to higher and higher standards of living as real median family income doubled during the Golden Years.

Today, various federally funded programs help lower-income students attend college and support training either in classrooms or on-the-job settings. In the latter case, an individual firm may be reluctant to do in-house training on its own because of the risk that those trained may leave that company before the gains from higher skills are recovered. Government, however, can subsidize upgrading trainees' skills at a firm, and society will capture the total benefits even if the trained workers go to other companies.

The most interesting case is that of technological innovation, where there is a long history of government funding basic research, usually through universities. For example, innovations taking advantage of basic research results have contributed to commercial breakthroughs such as the Internet and other technological innovations that increased the quality and quantity of information and the speed of delivering that data. Godfrey Hodgson wrote: "The linking of computers into a national, then international, network was the work of the Pentagon's Defense Advanced Research Projects Agency (DARPA). . . . By the 1960s it was estimated that 70 percent of all research into computers and related sciences in the United States was being funded by DARPA."[32] The University of Washington's Edward Lazowska, an authority on the history of computers, has argued more generally that federally funded university research support has been the pivotal factor in the collaboration between the federal government, the private sector, and the nation's universities that has made the United States the leader in cutting-edge information technology.[33]

---

[32]Hodgson, *More Equal than Others*, pp. 79–80.
[33]Ibid., p. 66.

Given the track record of government-funded basic research in stimulating a higher rate of technological innovations, the indirect policy of tax cuts for the rich on dividends and capital gains as the sole mechanism for promoting innovation is not attractive. As Altman observed: "[If the supply siders] *truly valued innovation,* they were taking a rather uncertain, roundabout approach to it. . . . According to economic theory, it's likely that the private market spends too little on research and development. The reason is that the benefits companies reap from R&D are smaller than the benefits to society."[34] In such situations, economic theory indicates that the benefit will be undersupplied by the free market. The argument follows the same logic as in the case for federally funded training.

When George W. Bush came to office, he picked as his chief economists two academic supply siders, Lawrence Lindsey as the top White House economic advisor and Glenn Hubbard as the chairman of the Council of Economic Advisers. Both had been among Professor Feldstein's best students at Harvard and subsequently were among the strongest advocates for the supply-side thesis.

Critics argued that the Bush tax proposal provided little help for low-income taxpayers, but the administration denied a bias toward the rich. The critics were right. A Center for Budget and Policy Priorities (CBPP) report, based on data from the Urban Institute–Brookings Institution Tax Policy Center, found that the 2006 tax provided $740 on average to the middle quintile (40–60 percent) of the income distribution, $44,000 on average to the upper 1 percent, and $118,000 on average to those

[34]Altman, *The Neoconomy,* p. 61, italics added.

with incomes of at least a million dollars that year.[35] Moreover, the real income tax rates for the very rich dropped. A December 2006 Congressional Budget Office analysis indicated that between 2001 and 2004 the effective tax rate (income taxes divided by income) for the top 1 percent of income earners fell, but the rate for the middle quintiles did not change.[36] The middle class paid about the same proportion of its income in taxes in 2004 as it had in 2001, but the rich saw their tax burdens lowered. Although these statistics were not available at the time the 2001 tax bill was being considered, reasonable estimates by reputable research organizations showed that the rich would be disproportionately rewarded. Indeed, simply looking at the rates for the income tax brackets made obvious that the rich had to be the big winners.

Marketing the Tax Cuts

Neither the 2001 tax cuts on individual brackets, nor the later 2003 tax cuts centering on cuts in rates for investment income for individuals, were sold on their academic supply-side merits. The Bush administration misrepresented both the stimulative and the distributional effects of the cuts, aggressively attacking those who raised the issue. Lawrence Lindsey, the highest ranking supply sider in the Bush government, said in a July 19, 2001 talk at the Federal Reserve Bank of Philadelphia: "Proper macroeconomic management requires that the government 'lean against the

---

[35]"Tax Cuts: Myths and Realities," Center on Budget and Policy Priorities, Revised March 20, 2007, p. 8 (figure 4).
[36]Congressional Budget Office, "Effective Tax Rates, 1979–2004." Washington, DC: Congressional Budget Office.

wind,' or act as a shock absorber. This is what the recently enacted bill does."[37] Lindsey's first sentence could have been taken from an introductory economics textbook explaining the Keynesian demand-stimulus thesis aimed at increasing spending quickly.

But then Lindsey claimed falsely that the bill simply followed the Keynesian approach when the legislation in fact proposed a fundamental fiscal policy shift from the short-run stimulus orientation to the long-term saving/capital investment approach. When the supply siders were in an academic setting, they emphasized that their new thesis differed starkly from the Keynesian theoretical framework, which they considered to be outmoded. When the supply siders came to government their arguments morphed. Instead of making the best case for their thesis in the marketplace of ideas, the administration's top supply sider chose to package the approach in Keynesian wrapping paper to produce what the administration views as one of its greatest political successes—the selling of the huge 2001 and 2003 tax cuts.

Top Bush administration officials, including the president, were true believers in the efficacy of tax cuts for the rich and, as classic ideologues, blocked out sound evidence refuting their arguments and used hard-ball tactics to discredit critics. Bush's tax cuts and budget increases produced outcomes that disproportionately benefited those at the top of the income distribution while diminishing the long-term fiscal health of the nation and the economic status of ordinary Americans. Simply put, the cuts mortgaged the fiscal health of the country to benefit the rich.

---

[37]Quoted in Altman, *The Neoconomy*, p. 86.

CHAPTER 8

The Impacts of Recent Fiscal Policies on America

In this chapter, we consider in more detail President George W. Bush's fiscal policy record, because he is the most unrepentant practitioner of the economic theories we've been examining in this book. We show that tax and budget policies and the Medicare prescription drug legislation have been major causal factors in both the federal government's fiscal deterioration and the increased financial threat to the living standard of most of the American people.

Establishing that an administration's fiscal policies directly caused these deleterious outcomes is difficult, but three points in combination make the argument for causality powerful. First, the Bush administration undertook several major policies—the 2001 and 2003 tax cuts, the abandonment of tight budget spending controls, and the Medicare prescription drug program—that were almost certain to have a critical impact on fiscal outcomes. Though the Medicare program is not a direct fiscal policy, its impacts on federal fiscal solvency are likely to be massive over time. All of the policies came from a deeply held commitment to flawed economic ideas, buttressed by a flawed institutional decision-making process (discussed in subsequent chapters) and an unbending ideology. Moreover, the administration refused to change its policies when they were in the development stage or once in place, even after sound evidence became available to refute them.

The wars in Iraq and Afghanistan and huge increases in homeland security also contributed to the explosion in spending after 2001. Even if the administration had not moved so aggressively in these areas (and certainly some bold moves were supported by most Americans at the time), the fiscal picture would have been problematic. Moreover, tax cuts in a time of national emergency are not normal; indeed, Bush's refusal to raise taxes during a war is unprecedented in America. Surely fiscal prudence in the face of a national emergency would have dictated a "steady as she goes" on fiscal policy rather than the risky approach actually taken.

Second, the evidence shows that the performance of the Bush administration on several key economic measures fell short in comparison to the average levels of those variables in earlier administrations. On GDP, employment, wages and salaries, median family income, and the federal deficits and debt, the Bush administration fares relatively poorly.

Third, critics of the tax proposals had predicted the specific harmful results before the legislation had been enacted, just as proponents had predicted desirable outcomes. One critic observed: "It was clear to me that the Bush [2001 tax] plan would squander the hard-won budget surplus. What I didn't foresee was just how quickly things would fall apart, with record surpluses transformed in the blink of an eye into record deficits."[1] The generally poor results we document here were not cases of unanticipated policy failure. Critics of the tax policies both accurately spelled out the institutional deficiencies in the decision-making process and flaws in the design of the tax proposals, and they predicted the deleterious outcomes before the enabling legislation had passed. After its enactment, critics indicated implementation problems and the likely deleterious results.

In this chapter, we first lay out the criteria we use to assess the Bush administration's economic performance. Then we detail those aspects of his administration that are likely to have resulted in poor economic performance, including both the processes of decision-making used in his administration and the particular policies adopted. Finally, we assess economic performance in the Bush years and link that performance to decision-making in the administration.

OUTCOME CRITERIA

To assess the Bush administration's economic record in more detail, we have derived outcome criteria based on the Golden Years of 1947–1973, the quarter century of exceptional economic performance early in the postwar years after demobilization had been completed. When President Ronald Reagan spoke of it being "morning again" in America after the astonishingly high economic growth rate in 1984, his "again" referred to these years. We have drawn on the economic results of the quarter century from 1947 to 1973 to develop a useful measuring rod for assessing President George W. Bush's economic performance compared to that of his predecessors.

---

[1]Paul Krugman, *The Great Unraveling.* New York: Norton, 2003, p. 134.

We have selected a small number of criteria that should provide a fair assessment. The performance criteria that we use are 1) general economic performance; 2) the distribution of the gains in economic productivity across income classes; 3) federal government indebtedness; and 4) changes in the economic status of the middle class. For general economic performance, we use changes in the GDP, economic productivity, and inflation rates. For the distribution of the economic product, we use two measures. First, we compare the growth in productivity to changes in median family income to assess how much of the growth in productivity is translated into increases in income for the typical American family. Second, we compare the growth in real income for the top income class with the rest of Americans. For federal government indebtedness, we use the ratio of federal debt to GDP, a measure we have relied on previously. Finally, for the status of the middle class, we examine the capacity of the broad middle class to maintain or increase its standard of living over its life span. The middle class's capacity to at least maintain its living standard during its entire life depends on the level of income while working and in retirement. The latter can come from Social Security and private pension benefits and income from accumulated saving. Maintaining middle-class status during both periods depends on how much will be spent with the cost of health protection looming large.

Productivity. Economic productivity, the economic output produced by the average worker, is the critical factor in the economic equation. Strong productivity growth provides the base for healthy increases over time in the economy and in wage and family income with steady or decreasing inflation. From 1947 through 1973, American productivity rose by 104 percent, and median family income rose by the same 104 percent. Since then, however, productivity gains have grown much faster than median family income—by 3 to 1—and are no longer being translated into increases in family well-being.[2] After the Golden Years, the productivity rate dropped to around 1–1.25 percent and generally stayed there until the beginning of the economic boom in 1995. Then the productivity rate rose from 1995 to the 2.5–3 percent level of the early postwar years and has been robust since.

Distribution. A remarkable aspect of the Golden Years is that gains in income shares across the entire American population were distributed so equally. Income gains had actually been the greatest for the lowest fifth and declined for each succeeding quintile thereafter. Only the top 20 percent experienced a small decline, with the top 5 percent doing worst. How different from the modern period! Since 1973, the rate of income growth for those at the very top has diverged further and further from the rest of Americans. As a consequence, they are capturing a higher and higher share of total income. And the wealthiest 1 percent of the income distribution is running away from the merely "near wealthy."

National Debt. The federal debt to GDP ratio is such a useful indicator of fiscal performance because it encapsulates several aspects of government fiscal performance. If the ratio is rising, it may be because increased spending by the federal government is not covered by rising tax revenues. A large increase in the size of the federal government also can come about from inadequate budget controls. Strong gains in economic growth can generate sufficient new tax revenues to cover the cost of expanding the government, but this will occur only if the underlying structure of

---

[2]Harold Meyerson, "Devaluing Labor," *Washington Post National Weekly Edition,* September 4–10, 2006, p. 26.

tax rates is high enough to generate the additional revenue needed. A rising debt/GDP ratio can be likened to a person's waistline that has expanded from a combination of too much food and too little exercise with every added pound showing.

The Middle Class. Historically, the federal safety net applied mainly to persons in the labor force with limited job skills, who were much more likely than the middle class to be out of work or move from one dead-end job to another without much in the way of health or retirement benefits. The federal safety net for the relatively unskilled has become increasingly tattered in recent years. Now the middle class is facing many of the problems traditionally suffered by less fortunate workers.

In the past, once one got into the broad middle class, one stayed there. Not so anymore. Jacob Hacker shows that the probability of falling out of the middle class (and perhaps joining it again later) is much greater now than in the Golden Years. As he puts it, "The gap between Bill Gates and Joe Citizen is a lot larger than it used to be, but it's actually grown less quickly than the gap between Joe Citizen in a good year and Joe Citizen in a bad year."[3] Economic life is much riskier for Joe today than in the Golden Years.

The Golden Years was distinguished by steadily rising wages and family income. Because of this, the strong middle class had a personal safety reserve when trouble came. But since that time, the middle class safety net has grown increasingly porous as wage increases lagged while employers cut back on health and retirement protection.

---

[3]Jacob Hacker, *The Great Risk Shift.* New York: Oxford University Press, 2005.

INSTITUTIONAL DEFICIENCIES

The Bush administration developed its fiscal policies in a decision-making process that was strikingly different from those of most of his postwar predecessors. Ideology played too large a part, leading policy makers to dismiss sound data and analyses and to avoid serious deliberations about policy design and implementation. Once policy proposals emerged, they were too often defended by deception and misinformation. The Republican-controlled Congress pushed many proposals through the lawmaking process without hard scrutiny, and this same Congress—to avoid criticism—limited the role of Democrats.

The 2001 Tax Cut

In formulating the 2001 tax cuts, Bush administration economic policy makers relied on a reasonable but untested academic supply-side thesis that critics questioned because the tax reductions disproportionately favored upper income citizens. By far the biggest problem, however, was that the administration unrealistically treated the rough projections of the expected budget surpluses as if they were money in the bank. This was the case even though it was well-known that the ten-year projections indicating sufficient economic growth to produce large surpluses were artificial because of unrealistic congressional requirements for developing the projections.

When the new congressional budget process was put in place in the 1970s, the required projections were understood to be no more than rough ballpark guidelines, not realistic estimates to be used for detailed policy-making. Accurate predictions over such a long time period, both then and now, are simply beyond the ability of even the most skilled analysts. Economists, like everyone else, lack a crystal ball indicating the future.

The danger of a shortfall in economic growth that would yield huge budget deficits could have been averted by using "triggers." This device requires that the tax cuts must be tied to the availability of funds. If the expected budget surpluses do not materialize, the trigger would stop the federal government from borrowing to finance the tax reductions. No surplus, no tax reduction, no increase in the federal debt from paying for the proposed tax cut by borrowing translated into fiscal prudence.

Federal Reserve Board Chairman Alan Greenspan and Secretary of Treasury Paul O'Neill liked the 2001 policy proposal. At the same time, the two men were gravely concerned about the return of the large yearly budget deficits, which had finally disappeared in Clinton's last years, and were committed to avoiding such an outcome. Alan Greenspan in his 2007 book The Age of Turbulence wrote that before the 2001 tax legislation had been enacted, he had "declared" that, "We are not going back into the red."[4]

Could the Bush administration's dangerous policy of not using a trigger, despite the unreliability of the projections, been prevented? Greenspan argued that he had tried repeatedly to do but failed and blamed Bush for his recklessness. We read the evidence as indicating that Chairman Greenspan did not press President Bush hard enough at the time. His current critics continue to argue that Greenspan in his testimony before Congress in 2001 signaled his support of the Bush tax cut, and that was the common view then. Moreover, the 2001 tax package passed at a time when

---

[4] Alan Greenspan, The Age of Turbulence, New York: Penguin Press, 2007, p. 216. Ibid., 224, italics added.

President Bush did not have the prestige and power that came after September 11. Chairman Greenspan at the time did have great prestige and power as the oracle on economic policy after the strong economy in the Clinton years. We do not know what would have happened had Greenspan taken a strong public stand that the Bush's 2001 tax proposal would be acceptable to him only if triggers or some other device protected against the return of massive deficits. But he did not make a highly visible effort even though the FRB chair by law is independent of presidents and Congress so he can speak out in opposition in such circumstances.

Although we maintain that Greenspan shares the blame with President Bush for the quick return of large deficits, definitive evidence is not in. However the current controversy need not be settled conclusively for our purposes. Whatever Greenspan did, our point holds that President Bush's 2001 tax cut—based on shaky numbers and without a trigger—had fatal flaws from the start and seemed nearly certain to end up a calamitous fiscal policy error. A number of critics pointed out the problems before the bill passed in June 2001. The critics were right. As Greenspan wrote in The Age of Turbulence: "The vaunted surplus . . . was effectively wiped out overnight. Starting that July, red ink was back to stay."

The 2003 Tax Cut

By 2003 the yearly budget deficits were pushing the national debt up rapidly, and evidence indicated that the tax cuts at the top had not induced the increases in saving and investment as the administration had predicted. President Bush's 2001 version of the academic supply-side thesis was beginning to look like a failure in practice.

The short and mild recession of early 2001 had been replaced by tepid economic growth. Given this slow growth situation, a moderate, temporary fiscal stimulus aimed at those who would quickly spend most or all of the benefits received might have been reasonable. The stimulus would be directed at maximizing the amount of additional consumer spending per dollar of cost to the government, thereby minimizing any increase in the budget deficit. Several good policy choices were available, including some that did not involve cutting taxes. The administration chose instead a reduction in dividend taxes and capital gains, which had little chance of stimulating economic growth rapidly. Moreover, those with the highest incomes received the lion's share of the total tax cut, thereby expanding an already wide distribution of income.

Better options were readily available. For example, simply extending unemployment insurance (UI) benefits would generate 73 cents of economic stimulus per dollar of revenue lost, whereas dividend tax reductions would generate just 9 cents per dollar. That's eight times the stimulative impact in favor of the UI extension.[5] In other words, it required $8 in tax cuts to generate as much consumer spending as $1 of UI benefits. If the economy needed a short-term shot in the arm, the 2003 package of tax cuts was not the ticket.

An increasing number of people own stocks. Wouldn't the 2003 tax cuts benefit them? Not really, because the law pertained only to *taxable* dividends. Although more and more people have saving devices such as IRAs that pay dividends to their retirement accounts, these dividends are exempt from taxes

[5]Isaac Shapiro and Joel Friedman, "Tax Returns," Center on Budget and Policy Priorities, April 2004, p.33. See Author's Note at end of the chapter.

when received. The average citizen saving for retirement by investing in the stock market received no benefits from the 2003 tax cuts, but the wealthy surely did. Capital gains and taxable dividends go almost exclusively to those at the very top of the income distribution.

In an analysis of the distribution of dividend and capital gains tax cuts in 2005 (that is, two years after the 2003 legislation had been enacted), economist Joel Friedman of the Center on Budget and Policy Priorities concluded that: "Households with incomes of more than $1 million receive over half—53 percent—of the benefits of these tax cuts, even though they constitute only 0.2 percent of the households in the nation."[6] Because 53 percent goes to the tiny group of families with earnings of $1 million or more, it follows that the remaining 99.98 percent of the population that year received only 47 percent of the total pie. If the Bush administration aimed to mainly benefit only the very richest Americans, the tax cut hit the bull's-eye.

Medicare Prescription Drug Costs

The most costly new program of the Bush administration is Medicare Part D, which covers prescription drugs. Over the next 75 years, the unfunded liabilities for the prescription drug program, Medicare Parts A and B (the coverage for doctors and hospitals), and Social Security together run into the tens of trillions of dollars. A trillion equals 1000 billion, and that is a mind-boggling amount. The added unfunded liability incurred by the federal government

---

[6]Joel Friedman, "Senate Finance and House Ways and Means Reconciliation Tax-Cut Packages Flawed," Center on Budget and Policy Priorities, November 18, 2005, p. 1–5. The quote in this paragraph is from page 3. The percentage of families with a million dollars or more of income may have increased to 0.3 percent by 2007.

for Medicare Part D is estimated at $8.1 trillion for 75 years. Part D's unfunded liability is roughly twice as large as that of the retirement part of the Social Security system. Medicare Parts A and B have unfunded liabilities estimated to be between two and three times larger than Part D.[7]

This massive commitment to future payments presents a huge problem: The national government will not have enough dollars in its trust fund assets or coming in from future Social Security contributions and Medicare premiums to meet that responsibility—not by a long shot for the now expanded Medicare coverage. The federal government must use general tax revenues to make up the shortfall when health care expenditures exceed the available receipts.

Even before the new Medicare coverage, the government's unfunded liabilities loomed large. Fiscal prudence would require that government prepare for large new programmatic initiatives, but the Bush administration acted in a contrary fashion. The president eliminated the surplus he received as a legacy from the Clinton administration, and he failed to prepare for the broad new initiative he proposed. Moreover, the particular choices of policy instruments have caused needless spending. For example, various requirements and restrictions have made Part D more expensive and inefficient than it could have been with a better policy design. Subsidies had to be paid to insurance companies to induce them to participate, and the federal government was barred from using its bargaining power to lower the price of prescription drugs purchased from the pharmaceuticals.

---

[7]David M. Walker, "Saving Our Futures Requires Tough Choices Today" U.S. Government Accountability Office Fiscal Wake-up Tour. Presentation to the Union League Club, Chicago IL, August 24, 2006.

Chapter 10 will spell out how the administration maneuvered Part D through Congress by hiding a key cost estimate made by the Medicare actuary and promising that it would keep outlays below a certain amount that was much lower than the hidden estimate. In pushing the prescription drug program through Congress without full information, the administration deceived Congress and the public as it dug the fiscal hole deeper yet.

OUTCOMES

The administration's flawed decision-making process has yielded a number of poor fiscal policy choices. Once enacted, there were predictable policy failures that became major causal factors in both the fiscal deterioration of the federal government and the increasing financial threat to the living standard of many Americans. Legislation has added $2.3 trillion to the budget deficit since 2001 with tax cuts accounting for 51 percent of the deficit increase (international and homeland security outlays added 33 percent). The Office of Budget and Management's Mid-Session Review estimates show that absent the Bush tax cuts, the federal budget in 2007, instead of having a deficit of $205 billion, would actually be in surplus. There would still be a budget surplus despite the security outlays that accounted for one-third of the rise in the total deficit.[8]

President Bush and the Republican Congress produced income redistribution for the rich with regressive income tax cuts. As we

[8] The data in this and next two paragraphs are from "Tax Cuts: Myths and Reality," Center on Budget and Policy Priorities, Revised March 20, 2007, pp. 1–2, 7–8; and James Horney, "Smaller Deficit Estimate No Surprise: New OMB Estimates Do Not Support Claims about Tax Cuts," Center on Budget and Policy Priorities, Revised July 13, 2006, p. 7.

noted in Chapter 7, in 2006 households with a million dollars or more in income received on the average $118,000 from the administration's tax cuts, while the middle 20 percent of the households received $740 on average. That is roughly 160 times as many dollars going to the top as to the middle. Moreover, those at the top of the income distribution were also experiencing a materially larger percentage increases in pretax incomes in the period 2001-2006 than other households. The Bush tax cuts further increased the maldistribution of income in the United States that was already the worst among the advanced nations. The rich were getting richer and government policies were increasing the gap.

These wide disparities in America's income distribution have been justified by the claim of much greater upward mobility in the United States than other advanced nations. It's another American myth. Intergenerational mobility is lower in the U.S. than all the Scandinavian countries and several others in Western Europe and Canada.[9] Clive Crook, a British citizen and *Atlantic* senior editor, wrote in June 2007: "Myths that defy the common experience can persist for only so long. Perhaps in the future the country will try harder to foster the opportunity it thinks it already provides. Or perhaps the culture will come to accept this un-American reality: a society of rigid economic orders, maintained by inheritance, blessed by its elites, and impotently endured by its underclass."[10]

Fiscal Stress

President Bush's flawed fiscal policies that increased the yearly budget deficits and the national debt and created massive new

---

[9]"The Land of Opportunity?," *New York Times*, July 13, 2007.
[10]Clive Crook, "Rags to Rags, Riches to Riches," *Atlantic*, June 2007, p. 24.

unfunded liabilities with the Medicare prescription legislation were ill-timed. The huge baby-boomer generation born between 1946 and 1964 stands on the brink of eligibility for Social Security checks and Medicare coverage.

The administration's fiscal policies that have disproportionately benefited the top of the income distribution at the expense of the rest of the population make it harder for the latter to maintain their living standards. Personal saving has fallen below zero for the first time since the Great Depression. If the saving rate remains low, inadequate resources at retirement can leave retirees with such low incomes that political pressure will be put on the federal government to raise retirement benefits. Responding to these demands arising from financial strain would increase fiscal stress. Yet politicians may be so fearful of losing their seats that they vote for costly new benefits paid for by borrowing. If so, the considerable damage from Bush's failed fiscal policies during his presidency may pale compared to the negative future impact caused by these policies.

The 2001 and 2003 Tax Cuts

Based on its ideologically-driven supply-side notions, the Bush administration believed that the 2001 and 2003 tax cuts would bring extraordinary increases in GDP, non-residential investment, and tax receipts and the ensuing strong economic growth would drive up other macroeconomic variables such as employment. The first two years of the Bush presidency included a mild recession and the expected outcomes did not materialize. After the 2003 tax reductions on dividends and capital gains, GDP and non-residential investment rose, and somewhat later tax receipts started to increase.

President Bush and the Republican Party declared that the tax cuts had succeeded. The Senate Republican Policy Committee on the fourth anniversary of the 2003 Tax Relief Law that reduced the tax rates on dividends and capital gains claimed that these reductions had "contributed to today's strong pro-growth economy . . . and led to a surge in tax receipts."[11] Such claims can only be validly tested by taking the role of the business cycle into account. In considering the validity of this claim, we first compare the economic outcomes from the trough of the recession from November 2001 to early 2007 (the latest time period for which data were available) with comparable periods after earlier postwar recessions on the basis of the annual growth rates for GDP, non-residential investment, employment, and wages and salaries, and then separately for tax revenues.

The Bush Tax Cuts since 2001. The average results for the first four factors during recovering from comparable recessionary periods since the end of the Second World War were markedly better than the economic performance for the recovery in the Bush years.[12] The GDP growth rate for the Bush recovery is only two-thirds as high as the postwar average. Yet it is the highest relative growth rate among the four economic factors. Non-residential investment grew at a little over one-half that of the average level of investment in the earlier postwar economic recoveries, and the growth rate for wages and salaries is one-half of the comparable experience in the earlier postwar recoveries. Finally, the extremely low employment growth rate for the recovery in the Bush years is

---

[11]Senate Republican Policy Committee, "Marking the 4th Anniversary of the 2003 Tax Relief Law: A Boon to Taxpayers, Tax Receipts, and the Economy," May 15, 2007.
[12]The growth rate data are from Aviva Aron-Dine, Chad Stone, and Richard Kogan, "How Robust is the Current Expansion?," Center on Budget and Policy Priorities, Revised June 28, 2007, p. 6 (Table 1). The CBPP study is based on statistics developed by the Bureau of Economic Analysis and the Bureau of Labor Statistics.

only three-eights as high as the average growth rate from the end of the Second World War to 2000. Bush administration performance for these variables during the entire recovery period is sub-par at best and exceptionally low in areas of employment and wages.

The 2003 Tax Cut on Dividends and Capital Gains. In 2003 the recovery picked up as compared to the initial two years, including a marked rise in non-residential investment. The Bush administration achieved considerable success in selling the tax reductions on capital gains and dividends as the magic supply-side fix that caused the stronger growth rate in non-residential investment. However, the results clearly did not mean that the benefits from the 2003 tax legislation caused the faster growth in non-residential investment or the other key economic variables.

Such improvements are the expected results in the later years of a recovery with or without tax reductions and come about from the dynamics of economic recoveries over the business cycle. The impact of the 2003 tax cuts would have been surprising only if the four economic variables had decreased after the first two years of the recovery. Any claim of causality from the 2003 tax reductions must rest on direct evidence from a comparison with earlier recoveries, not just with the first years of the same business cycle.

The proper comparison is with the average growth rates in the postwar era up to 2000 that we used to assess the Bush administration's economic performance since 2001. In such a comparison, the growth rates starting from 2003 are not impressive in terms of the four economic variables. Although the growth rates for GDP, wages and salaries, and employment exceeded those in the earlier comparison that included the first two years of the Bush presidency, all still ended up lower than the comparable averages for the postwar years. Non-residential investment did improve sufficiently to come up to the average postwar growth rate. This improvement, however, is only an average outcome, not an exceptional one.[13]

Even more damaging to the Bush administration claim of the power of reducing taxes on investment income is a comparison to the 1990s when there were substantial income tax increases in 1990 by GHW Bush and in 1993 by Bill Clinton. The 1990s recovery from its trough, just as the later one, began with limited growth during its first part, but grew at a faster pace after that than did the Bush recovery featuring the supply siders' tax cuts targeted on highest income earners. Aviva Aron-Dine observed:

> *Overall investment growth in the 1990s business cycle, with its large tax increases in 1990 and 1993, was substantially stronger than the current business cycle with its tax cuts in 2001 and 2003. If major economic developments were generally attributable to tax policy, then the 1990s experience could lead one to conclude that tax increases provide more potent economic stimulus than tax cuts. The more appropriate lesson to draw, however, is probably that weak recoveries tend to return to historic norms, whether taxes are cut, increased, or left unchanged.*[14]

In sum, the claim that the 2003 tax cut on investment income caused much higher non-residential investment holds no water. It is also clear that the basic ideological belief that tax cuts are always good and tax increases are always bad is a myth unsupported by any sound empirical evidence.

---

[13]The data used in the comparisons in this and the following paragraph are from Aviva Aron-Dine, "The Effects of the Capital Gains and Dividend Tax Cuts on the Economy and Revenues: Four Years Later, a Look at the Evidence," Center on Budget and Policy Priorities, Revised July 10, 2007, pp. 2 (Figure 1), 3, and 7 (Figure 4).

[14]Ibid., p. 3.

Tax Revenues

Bush tax cut makers claimed that the reductions have generated increased tax revenues. Yet, once again tax was a factor in the role of the business cycle. Tax revenues always decrease in recessions and increase after them. The performance by the administration looks poor in comparison to postwar results through 2000. From the start of the recession in 2001 to the time of the 2007 estimate, tax revenues grew by 3.1 percent; the rise in revenues averaged 12 percent in the comparable postwar recoveries. The most damaging comparison of all is the striking revenue gain of 16 percent in the comparable recovery period in the 1990s after two tax increases.

These poor results have not deterred Bush administration officials from their incessant claims. In the Office of Management and Budget's July 2007 Mid-Session Review, tax revenues were estimated to be $34 billion higher and spending $6 billion lower so the yearly deficit (after rounding) is estimated to be $39 billion less as compared to the President's February budget prepared by OMB.[15] The administration argued that the estimated increase in tax receipts and decline in the deficit from $244 to $205 billion came about because of the president's tax and budget policies. Available evidence makes clear that the 2007 claim is wrong. What we have is the administration's ploy of making unwarranted claims by ignoring its own earlier results and the historical record of tax revenue estimates over the business cycle by OMB and the Congressional Budget Office.

Actually, the $34 billion reestimate of revenues is 1.3 percent of the 2007 projected revenues and well below the historic average.

---

[15]The data in this and the next two paragraphs are from Horney, "Smaller Deficit Estimate No Surprise: New OMB Estimates Do Not Support Claims about Tax Cuts," 1–7.

Based on 25 years of experience with its revenue estimates, CBO has either overestimated or underestimated a year's revenue by an average of 2.8 percent of the actual number. Moreover, the tendency is to underestimate revenues as a recovery lengthens. The Congressional Budget Office's historical data leaves no doubt that the administration's claim its fiscal policies were succeeding because the July revenue estimates by OMB and CBO were higher than those in February is not only wrong but highly deceptive.

The best numbers available on President Bush's supply-side-economics-driven tax cuts show overwhelmingly: (1) income tax increases raise tax revenues, (2) income tax cuts decrease tax revenues unless offset by an equal amount of budget cuts and/or increases in other taxes, and (3) income tax cuts do not necessarily raise the economic growth rate more than no change in taxes or a tax increase. No sound evidence to date supports the claims of the efficacy of the Bush administration tax cuts. The bottom line is that the supply-side thesis as practiced in the Reagan and Bush administrations has proved to be a bad policy idea that should be labeled: BEWARE: DANGEROUS TO THE NATION'S HEALTH.

Deficits and Debts

At the end of World War II, the United States emerged as the economic colossus. It was the only nation among the major prewar economic players not devastated by the war. America became the world's creditor by selling products and lending funds that helped revive the world economy.

The ratio of the gross federal debt to gross domestic product, which assesses the size of the debt relative to the capacity of the economy to sustain it, illuminates the march of the United States from fiscal good health to growing fiscal stress. As we illustrated in figure 4.6, at the end of World War II, the debt/GDP ratio stood at 122 percent.[16] It went down rapidly during the sustained economic growth in the Golden Years, falling to 33 percent by 1973. After President Reagan's 1981 tax cut, the United States experienced large yearly budget deficits and rising debt relative to gross domestic product, a trend that has continued up to the present, with the exception of the years 1995–2000. The ratio during Reagan's two terms increased from 33 to 52 percent and kept going up to 67 percent by 1995. Then it fell.

Strong budget controls, the 1991 and 1993 tax increases which restored fiscal prudence to the national government and high economic growth after 1995 finally turned yearly budget deficits into surpluses. The debt/GDP ratio started rising again in George W. Bush's presidency with the end of budget controls, huge tax cuts, and large spending increases. As the conservative economist Bruce Bartlett has noted, "The Bush administration's economic policy has been built largely on a massive increase in the public debt—both on-budget and off-budget."[17] Having failed to stimulate the economy enough to fund his policy priorities, Bush borrowed to fund his spending increases and tax cuts.

During the first six years of the presidency of George W. Bush the budget went from a surplus/GDP ratio of 2.4 percent in 2000, Clinton's final year, to a 1.9 percent deficit ratio in 2006. The 4.3 percent swing from a surplus at the start of the Bush presidency is the second worst six-year fiscal deterioration in the

---

[16] Gross debt figures will be generally used in discussing the debt/GDP ratio. Net debt figures are used generally because the gross amount includes debt owed within the government itself, but the latter provides a better perspective on total claims that need to be paid.

[17] Bruce Bartlett, *Impostor*. New York: Doubleday, 2006, p. 102.

postwar era.[18] Since fiscal year 2001, yearly deficits have brought an upsurge in both the gross national debt, which is the total debt held by all entities, and the net national debt, which is outstanding debt not held by U.S. government agencies. The nation has experienced a remarkable increase of 50 percent in both the net and the gross amounts, with the latter rising from a little more than $5.5 trillion in 2001 to nearly $8.5 trillion in 2006.

There is a second disturbing debt problem that the U.S. faces today—the trade deficit. From being the world's banker in the early postwar years, the United States morphed into the world's largest debtor. Its monthly trade deficit generally stayed below $10 billion before the mid-1990s. In 2006, this deficit averaged more than $60 billion per month and reached $763.6 billion—the fifth consecutive year that the trade deficit hit a record high.[19] The 2006 deficit was 5.7 percent of GDP. Paul Krugman, a *New York Times* columnist who is also one of the world's foremost experts on the international economy, termed the size of the 2005 trade deficit "amazing," and observed: "This huge trade deficit means that America is living beyond its means, spending far more than it earns. In 2005, the United States exported only 53 cents' worth of goods for every dollar it spends on imports."[20]

We don't argue that President Bush's policies have been a major cause in the rapid rise in the trade balance, although his protectionist policy with steel and his raising of agricultural subsidies were harmful.[21] But he failed to undertake efforts to control

---

[18]Robert Greenstein, "Despite the Rhetoric, Budget Would Make Fiscal Problems Worse," Center on Budget and Policy Priorities, Revised February 7, 2007, p. 5. Greenstein observed: "The worst six-year deterioration occurred between 1998 and 2004 and also reflected the impact of the tax cut as well as other factors."
[19]Steven R. Weisman, "For 5th Year, Trade Gap Hits Record," *New York Times*, February 14, 2007, p. C1. Jonathan Jacoby, "Attention to Deficit Disorder: U.S. Trade Deficit Demands Long Term Focus," Center for American Progress, February 13, 2007, p. 1.
[20]Krugman, "CSI: Trade Deficit," *New York Times*, April 24, 2006, p. A23.
[21]For a discussion of Bush's trade policies, see Bartlett, *Impostor*, pp. 85–101.

the widening trade balance that is one of the elements in the nation's fiscal deterioration. The huge federal deficits, caused by his tax cuts, augmented the trade deficit, resulting in what economists call the 'dual deficit'. The huge trade deficit did not produce a major economic disturbance because Japan and China chose to block painful increases in the U.S. interest rates by purchasing Treasury offerings. These purchases allowed American consumers to continue buying the two counties' goods and services and set record trade deficits year after year. Even though the United States and its citizens fell deeper and deeper into debt, the Bush administration took no corrective actions. And the trade deficit sets record after record. Both the nation and its citizens continue to go deeper and deeper into debt, but the Bush administration does nothing.

The fiscal outlook continues to grow increasingly grim over time. David Walker, the comptroller general of the United States, is leading his Fiscal Wake Tour to a number of American cities to discuss the grave dangers of the rising national debt. He and the other experts joining him on the tour offered this warning: "If the U.S. government conducts business as usual over the next few decades, a national debt that is already $8.5 trillion could reach $46 trillion or more, adjusted for inflation. . . . A hole that big could paralyze the U.S. economy."[22]

Walker himself said: "We need to recognize that the United States is going to last more than ten years and move beyond *the flat Earth theory for budget analysis* and to recognize that our real problems are not the next five or ten years. They are not short-term deficits. *They are long-range growing, structural*

---

[22]Matt Crenson, "Economists Warn of Nation's Fiscal Meltdown, Call for Hard Choices," *Seattle Times*, October 29, 2006.

deficits and related debt burdens that could swamp our ship of state."[23] The threat from the national debt is far down the road compared to lesser dangers and may not be viewed as critical until it is too big to stop. The Flat-Earth theory of budgeting is so widespread because it allows the leaders of government to ignore what is too distant to bring a public outcry. Also, the public adheres to its own Flat-Earth theory not only for the national debt but for its own individual debts. In the case of the growing financial burden of Americans, the day of reckoning may be much closer than for the threat to the nation's fiscal solvency, as the next section indicates.

Financial Strains

Foreign observers of the United States often are more perceptive about America than we are. That has certainly been the case for one of the best of these observers, the Englishman Godfrey Hodgson, who wrote: "The experience of the years from Richard Nixon's resignation of the presidency until the millennium, in contrast to the advertisement that was so often screened, of universal prosperity at home and cost-free triumph abroad, were in reality for many, probably for most Americans, years of disappointment and denial."[24]

Here we explore why the period from Nixon's resignation to the end of the Clinton presidency was generally so dismal, at least for the average American, and then focus on what George Bush did for Joe and Joanne Citizen. Those below the middle-class income levels have experienced increasing problems as well, but the discussion that follows focuses on the broad American middle class.

[23]Quoted in Mark Trahant, "Bush Tax Cuts Don't Pay for Themselves," *Seattle Post-Intelligencer,* August 5, 2007, p. C2, italics added.
[24]Godfrey Hodgson, *More Equal than Others.* Princeton: Princeton University Press, 2004, p. xvii.

■ Median Family Income: 1947–2000[25]

From 1947 to 2000, real median family income (in 2003 constant dollars) rose from around $21,000 to $54,000—an increase of $33,000. The Golden Years accounted for two-thirds of the gain, or $22,000; the later period added the remaining one-third or $11,000. If real median family income in 1973–2000 had increased at the same rate as the Golden Years, it would have risen to roughly $110,000 as compared to the $54,000 real median family income actually attained.

The later years can be divided into two periods: 1973–1994 and 1995–2000. Although the first of the periods is about four times as long as the later one, each contributed $5,500 to the total $11,000 gain in real median family income. So the years 1973–1994 were the worst of the entire period.

In 1995–2000, the growth rate for real median family income averaged 2.2 percent per year, coming close to the 2.8 percent growth rate for the Golden Years. Although the Clinton administration and others claimed that Americans were far better off than ever before, that was not the case. The boom ran for only six years and was followed by zero real median family income growth during the period 2001–2005. This brief boom followed the years from 1973 to 1995, which had an anemic growth rate of less than 1 percent. The brief boom may have elicited great optimism, but it did not begin to wipe out the financial damage suffered by the middle class in the twenty plus years before it.

Even if we exclude the years 1973–1980 in the analysis, supply-side theory does not perform well. Median family income grew more

[25]The data on real median family income and some of the calculations come from Lawrence Mishel, Jared Bernstein, and Sylvia Allegretto, *The State of Working America 2004/2005*. Ithaca, NY: Cornell University Press, 2005, (Table 1.1), p. 42.

in the 1973–1980 period than during the Reagan years. Although the Reagan presidency began with the worst in the postwar recession years and family income suffered, the economy then recovered nicely. Yet there was no supply-side effect that brought significant gains in tax revenues or productivity. The massive Reagan deficits continued until 1995 without any significant jump in the productivity rate. Reagan himself raised taxes after 1981 and employed tight budget controls as did his two successors. However, it was only after the Clinton tax hike that strong increases in economic growth and productivity rates, as well as in real median family income, occurred.

■ Declining Real Median Family Income and Rising Inequality: 2001–2006

The 2006 Census data on real median family income (the most recent available) show an increase in that year that was enough to return all households in this category to their 2001 level.[26] The gains that returned the entire group to the 2001 level in 2006 went mainly to median income families over 65 years of age. After declining for five straight years, median income for working-aged families finally rose by $725 in 2006. However, it remained $1336 beneath the 2001 level for working-aged families and $2375 under their 2000 level at the end of the Clinton administration.

In the economic recovery which President Bush praised so highly, median income working families experienced a real decline in their incomes despite the strong productivity. The Center on Budget and Policy Priorities summed up the latest available income data on the Bush administration reported by the federal government

---

[26]The data in this and the next paragraph are in Number and Percentage of Americans Who Are Uninsured Climbs Again: Poverty Edges Down but Remains Higher, and Median Income for Working-Age Households Remains Lower, than When Recession Hit Bottom in 2001," Center on Budget and Policy Priorities, Revised August 31, 2007, pp. 1–6. The quote at the end of the next paragraph is on page 3.

for the period 2001–2006: "The current economic recovery has been exceptionally uneven and . . . an unusually small share of the income gains have reached low- and middle-income families. Data recently issued by the Commerce Department illuminate the trend. They show that a smaller share of the income gains from the current recovery are going to workers' wages and salaries and a larger share are going to corporate profits than in any other recovery since World War II." For the first time in the years since World War II, ordinary families generally did not benefit from their labor, which helped produce strong productivity gains. The link between productivity growth and income growth has been broken. After low productivity growth since the early 1970s, strong gains started again in 1995 and continued in the Bush presidency.

Productivity in 1995–2000 rose at roughly 2.5 percent annually, and real median family income followed by increasing at about a 2.2 percent annual rate.[27] Productivity has grow at a higher rate in George W. Bush's presidency, but, as just noted, real median family income decreased for working-age families. They were not the only ones losing out in the Bush years.

Almost everyone lost ground relative to the richest Americans. In 2004, after excluding capital gains, the average real income of the top 1 percent of the income distribution rose 12.5 percent while the rest of the population gained only 1.5 percent.[28] As Paul Krugman noted: "Growth didn't just bypass the poor and lower middle class, it bypassed the upper middle class too. Even people

[27]*Seattle Times*, "The U.S. Work Force Has 2 Faces," September 4, 2006, p. A3. The percentages used are drawn from *The State of Working America 2006/2007*, forthcoming.
[28]Brian K. Bucks, Arthur B. Kennickell, and Kevin B. Moore, *Recent Changes in U.S. Family Finances: Evidence from the 2001 and 2004 Survey of Consumer Finances*. Washington DC: Federal Reserve Board, August 2006.

at the 95th percentile of the income distribution—that is, people richer than 19 out of 20 Americans—gained only modestly. The big increases went only to people who were already in the economic stratosphere."[29] For example, while wages and family income stagnated, the salaries of corporate executives soared. In 1993 the average corporate executive officer (CEO) received compensation of around 120 times the average pay for hourly workers. By 2006 that ratio had grown to almost 370.[30]

How much more those at the top earn than ordinary workers is shown in a report from Northeastern University's Center for Labor Market Studies. The number of production and nonsupervisory workers (excluding farmworkers), the bulk of the national workforce, is 93 million. In 2001–2006, this massive group had a $15.4 billion gain in their combined aggregate real annual earnings. This amount was less than half the 2006 Christmas bonuses (estimated at $36 to $44 billion) paid by the top five Wall Street financial firms.[31] The productivity gains generated during the Bush presidency were consumed by the corporate superrich; almost none trickled down to the worker.

Census Bureau data showing the full income distribution by quintiles is based on a sample that is only large enough to support breaking out the income of the top 5 percent. Another data source, the Internal Revenue Service household data from individual income tax returns, is large enough to permit a statistically valid determination of family income at the top 1 percent of the income distribution

[29]Krugman, "Left Behind Economics," *New York Times*, July 14, 2006, p. A19.
[30]Joann S. Lublin and Scott Thurm, "Behind Soaring Executive Pay, Decades of Failed Restraint," *Wall Street Journal*, October 12, 2006, p. A1.
[31]Bob Herbert, "Working Harder for the Man," *New York Times*, January 8, 2007, p. A23.

and beyond.[32] Economists Emmanuel Saez at the University of California, Berkeley, and Thomas Piketty at the Paris School of Economics, have been leaders in analyzing these data. Their findings leave no doubt that the top of the income distribution has benefited disproportionately in the past quarter century, with their share of total income by 2005 rivaling 1928, the peak of the 1920s.[33]

The latest data from Saez and Piketty are mind-boggling when you compare the richest families to ordinary ones: (1) as a group, the top 300,000 Americans received nearly as much income as the 150 million at the bottom; (2) these top 300,000 Americans—on a per-person basis—had 440 times as much income as the average individual in the bottom 50 percent of the income distribution, almost doubling this gap since 1980; (3) the 1 percent at the top received a little more than one-fifth (21.8 percent) of all reported income in 2005, more than twice their share in 1980; and (4) the 21.8 percent share of total income received by the top 1 percent was the highest share in the postwar era and came close to the 1928 peak of 23.9 percent.[34]

Thus, in a quarter of a century, the top 1 percent had more than doubled its share of the economic pie, with that 2005 share approaching the peak share of the highest 1 percent in the "Roaring Twenties. " The widening gap between the top 1 percent and everyone else started before the Bush presidency. But no president in the postwar era has pursued fiscal policies so favorable to the richest of the rich, as exemplified by Bush's 2003 tax cut on capital gains and taxable dividends. And the distributional results, combined with longer-run economic trends, have been severe.

---

[32]No individuals can be identified by those using the IRS data set.
[33]David Cay Johnston, "Income Gap Is Widening, Data Shows," *New York Times*, March 29, 2007, p. C1.
[34]Ibid.

In 1980 the United States had the greatest inequality among the rich, industrialized nations. A quarter of a century later, its lead had lengthened, as Bernard Wasow, a senior fellow at The Century Foundation, pointed out: "To the degree that families gauge their well-being relative to other families in the society, the American middle class has been falling behind. *This disconnect between the experience of the middle class and those at the top makes the United States stand out among the rich countries.*"[35]

Rising Debt and a Weakening Safety Net

A number of factors in the years since Nixon's resignation to 2005 have made it harder for most Americans to maintain their living standards throughout their working lives and during retirement. After strong, steady yearly income growth stopped, the broad American middle class faced serious tradeoffs. If people choose to incur more and more debt to live in their accustomed style during their working lives, saving for an adequate retirement becomes increasingly difficult. But setting aside sufficient savings for an adequate retirement puts the current living standards in jeopardy.

At one point an adequate overall retirement program seemed likely, but the outlook today is grim. The combination of limited income growth, a precipitously declining rate of savings, and an increasingly inadequate pension system has put much of the middle class in great jeopardy of failing to maintain their working years' standard of living at retirement.

In the Golden Years, confident middle-class families felt that they would maintain their standard of living at retirement through a combination of Social Security, company pensions, and personal

---

[35]Bernard Wasow, "Standing Alone in Inequality," The Century Foundation, September 22, 2006, italics added, www.tcf.org/list.asp?type=NC&pubid=1403.

saving. Prevailing expert opinion held that sound private pension programs would expand to a point where most middle-class families would receive generous retirement payments. Rising incomes would support a reasonable level of personal saving. For the middle class, the still relatively small Social Security program would at least top off the other two components to provide sufficient income to continue the pre-retirement lifestyle. As for the working class, rising earnings would carry more and more of them into the middle class.

Jump forward to the 21st century and the picture has changed radically. Personal saving is on the endangered species list. The experts were wrong—the growth of private pension systems stalled and pension plans became less generous. Only Social Security thrived. It had become a political favorite later in the Golden Years and greatly expanded to become the strongest of the three components. But Social Security growth alone will not take up the slack.

Saving. Many Americans lacking steady income gains are on a borrowing treadmill. *Washington Post* staff writers Jeffrey Birnbaum and Chris Cillizza observed in a September 2006 article: "According to a study by the Federal Reserve Board, the ratio of financial obligations—primarily mortgages and consumer debt—to disposable personal income rose to a modern record of 18.7 percent earlier this year. The amount of mortgage debt alone has more than doubled since 2000, to nearly $9 trillion."[36]

Historically, Americans have not been among the biggest savers compared to people in other rich industrial nations. But what is happening now is unprecedented. The rate of saving to disposable personal income that ranged from 8 to 11 percent from the Second

---

[36]Jeffrey H. Birnbaum and Chris Cillizza, "Just Can't Get Ahead," *Washington Post National Weekly Edition*, September 11–17, 2006, pp. 18–19.

World War through the 1980s now has dropped below zero. It has been so since the second quarter of 2005.[37] This is hardly a good sign in the struggle to retain families' standards of living at retirement.

Although it is not unusual for people to go into debt early in their earning careers, today the saving rate for those under 35 has dropped to minus 16 percent. Mark Zandi, chief economist at Moody's Economy.com, noted that "The post-boomer generation feels very cavalier about saving. They've been very aggressively dis-saving and have borrowed significantly."[38]

Mortgages have become an increasingly important factor for homeowners as they took second liens on houses that had appreciated in the booming real estate market that marked the early years of the 21st century. Alan Greenspan, former chair of the Federal Reserve Board, and James Kennedy have estimated the amount of cash that homeowners have borrowed in the residential mortgage market and indicated that the equity extracted from homes between 2001 through 2005 averaged roughly a trillion dollars a year, over three times the average in the period 1991-2000. Since 2005 the amount extracted has moved back toward the average of the earlier period.[39] With the end of the housing bubble in 2007, this method of stretching household finances may no longer be available.

When the net value of a family's assets rises appreciably, there may be "wealth effect" that induces the family to consume more of its yearly income and save less. But the apparent decline in saving may be misleading if a gain in the net value of the assets more than

[37]Eileen Alt Powell, "Retirement Savings Fall Way Short in Nation of Spenders," *Seattle Times*, July 15, 2007.

[38]Quoted in Steven Greenhouse, "Many Entry-Level Workers Feel Pinch of Rough Market," *New York Times*, September 4, 2006, p. A10.

[39]All data in this and the next two paragraphs are drawn from Alan Greenspan and James Kennedy, "Sources and Uses of Equity Extracted from Homes," Federal Reserve Board, Finance and Economics Discussion Series 2007-20. The papers in this series are preliminary and can be acknowledged but cited only with the express permission of the authors.

makes up for the decrease. For example, if the net asset value of a home had increased by $50,000 in a year (not uncommon in the Seattle housing market before 2007) and the family chose not to save $15,000 that year as it usually did, its net assets would still be higher.

Extracting equity from the house necessitates increasing the mortgage and hence the interest payments. Greenspan and Kennedy estimated that total mortgage debt since the 1980s grew faster than total housing values, thereby decreasing housing wealth as a share of the housing values. This is an extremely complicated area with lots of controversy and unanswered questions. The wealth effect from housing could indicate that the decline in the savings rate has occurred in response to asset appreciation and did not represent a retreat from retirement goals. Our view, however, is that both the rising consumption and the falling savings rate have lasted long enough to support the claim that the latter is not simply a reasoned response to the wealth effect. The Greenspan and Kennedy estimate that total mortgage debt rose more rapidly since the 1980s than total housing values supports our view, as does the slow growth in income for all but those at the top of the income distribution. The end of the housing 'bubble' in 2007 means that families are facing declines in the values of their homes, adding to financial strain.

Pensions. In the United States, employers have offered two different pension programs to their workers, the traditional or "defined-benefit plan" and the "defined-contribution plan." The former is funded by the employer alone and provides either a continuing monthly income or a lump sum payment at retirement. How much an employee receives under a traditional plan generally is determined by the person's salary, age, and years of service. Income payments each month at retirement will be a specific amount, such as $300 a month. Employers, who have the responsibility for paying retired employees the defined benefit per month, do the investing for the pension fund because of the retirement payment obligation. Thirty years ago these were the predominant type of pension, covering 39 percent of employees. But they have now declined to 19 percent.[40]

In recent years, traditional plans have become much more costly. The apparent explanation is that lower than expected investment returns forced employers to pay in additional funds so that pension assets will be sufficient to meet future obligations. In response, employers shifted to defined-contribution plans, the most common being the 401 (k). These plans have a specified contribution per month by employers, pass the responsibility for investing to employees, and finally pay employees a lump sum equal to the market value of their accumulated assets at retirement.

Defined-benefit plans leave employers with a continuing financial responsibility after employees retire. In defined-contribution plans, employers have no financial responsibility after employees receive the check for their accumulated assets. As a consequence, this is now the plan of choice for companies. Defined-contribution plans covered 17 percent of the workforce in 1978 and increased to 56 percent by 2003. As Bill Fleming, managing director in the private-company service group at PricewaterhouseCoopers, noted in August 2006: "The days of the good old mother company taking care of you with a pension as a retiree are gone."[41]

In the face of rising company costs for defined-benefit plans, the good old mother companies turned to the cheaper and more predictable defined-contribution plan. Once employees retired, companies were off the hook and retirees alone had to cope with

---

[40]Kathleen Day, "Retirement Plans, Squeezed," *Washington Post National Weekly Edition*, September 25–October 1, 2006, p. 19.
[41]Quoted in "Pension Changes: What Do You Need to Know," *Seattle Times*, August 16, 2006, p. A1.

the vicissitudes of the investment market. This generally leaves retirees in a riskier situation. Moreover, most employees are unable to achieve a saving and investment plan capable of generating a retirement comparable to that provided by a defined-benefit plan. As a consequence, the rapid growth of defined-contribution plans materially weakened the private pension system.

Social Security and Health Care. The zero savings rate and the weakened private pension system put much greater pressure on Social Security to help the struggling middle class meet its retirement needs. Despite fears that it will not deliver, the Social Security system can be fixed, and much more simply than other entitlement programs. But it is unlikely that benefits will increase sufficiently to meet the growing retirement needs of the middle class. Prospects have diminished because of rapidly growing health costs that affect families directly and impact Medicare as well.

According to a 2006 Kaiser Family Foundation survey, the cost of family health insurance coverage has risen 87 percent, far more than increases in workers' pay.[42] The deleterious impact of these added health costs reverberates through the fiscal and financial systems. It becomes harder for retirees and workers to keep up their standard of living, for workers to save for retirement, and for the federal government to increase Social Security retirement benefits. As health costs rose rapidly and incomes stagnated in the first years of the 21st century, the number of uninsured people grew. Census data show that a record 47 million people were uninsured in 2006, an increase of 7.2 million since 2001.[43]

---

[42]Milt Fruedenheim, "Health Costs Rise Twice as Much as Inflation," *New York Times*, September 27, 2006, p. C1. Note: Health costs have risen more than twice as much as inflation since 2000. The headline referred to the latest one-year increase.

[43]Center on Budget and Policy Priorities, "Number and Percentage of Americans Who Are Uninsured Climbs Again," p. 1.

AN ASSESSMENT

Let us now assess the economic outcomes in the period 2001–2006 by using the four criteria discussed earlier in the chapter. The Bush administration did fairly well on the first criterion of broad macroeconomic performance. Economic growth has been moderate relative to comparable earlier periods, the inflation rate has stayed low, and the rate of productivity growth has been outstanding. Growth in GDP has been about two-thirds the post-war average for comparable periods, but inflation has remained in check (mostly due to the efforts of the Federal Reserve Board and high productivity growth). The high productivity growth began in 1995, and hence cannot be due to Bush's policies but certainly some credit is due for maintaining it.

On the second, the distribution of economic gains has fueled greater income inequality. The correspondence between real median family income growth and strong productivity growth in the Bush presidency is the worst in the postwar era. During both the Golden Years and the period 1995–2000, high productivity gains produced strong real median family income growth. But the link did not hold under GW Bush. Instead, the growth in income went mainly to the richest of the rich. Although economic growth and the skill distribution are important in explaining the disproportionate gains at the top, Bush's highly skewed tax cuts too had a role.

In the case of the third criterion, the fiscal health of the government deteriorated markedly with the return of yearly budget deficits, an absence of budgetary control mechanisms, and the weak growth in tax revenues. Concomitantly, the federal government debt to GDP ratio that had been declining in the years 1995–2000 started to rise again.

Finally, the capacity of families in the broad middle class to maintain or increase their standard of living during the working years and at retirement declined markedly. In the face of limited income growth, middle-class families took on increasing debt loads and drastically reduced their saving. The middle class faced higher health costs, less health coverage, and significant deterioration in the private pension system. In addition, the federal government's increasing debt/GDP ratio and mounting unfunded liabilities are likely to lessen the federal government's fiscal capacity to aid the broad American middle class in its financial plight. Working Americans now face greater difficulty in maintaining their living standards than at any time since the end of World War II.

Although the Bush administration legitimately can boast of a strong overall economy, the bulk of the American population has every right to complain of limited income gains at best and increased stress on the well-being of their families. Their underscores that the Bush administration passed on the first criterion and failed on the other three.

New York Times columnist Bob Herbert wrote in his January 8, 2007 column: "The way the great wealth of the United States is distributed . . . [is] eating away at the structure of society and undermining its future. The middle class is hurting, propped up by the wobbly crutches of personal debt. The safety net, not just for the poor, but for the middle class as well is disappearing."[44] Roughly six decades ago, the broad American middle class emerged, prospered, grew rapidly, and embraced the American Dream that their income would continue to grow and their children (the baby

---

[44]Herbert, "Working Harder for the Man."

boomers) would do better yet. With productivity and real median family income increasing in lock step during the Golden Years, that dream had a realistic base. As the baby boomers stand on the brink of retirement today, the available data raise the question of whether the American Dream will vanish and the broad middle class itself will decline toward its pre–World War II level.

In sum, the available hard evidence presented in this chapter supports our argument that the Bush administration drew on bad economic ideas, mainly based on ideology, not facts, to craft policies that consequently failed. The bad policies included refusing to use triggers with the 2001 tax cut, instituting the 2003 tax cut in the face of rising deficits and an increasing debt/GDP ratio, the removal of budget controls, enacting the Medicare prescription legislation that greatly increased the already huge unfunded liabilities of the federal government, and refusing to use evidence that showed the policies were failing. In the latter case, the administration defended its failed fiscal policies through secrecy and misinformation. Failed policies have diminished the fiscal solvency of the federal government, left the middle class facing the greatest danger to its standard of living since the end of the Second World War, and could, if not corrected, in the future paralyze the American economy with the interest payments required to service a massive national debt.[45]

---

[45]Author's Note: The Center on Budget and Policy Priorities heads the list of sources of information in this chapter. We should note that CBPP is a left-of-center nonprofit think tank. At the same time, it has an impeccable reputation for sound and careful analyses. In general, the Center does not develop primary data but relies instead on major government sources such as the Department of Commerce, the Internal Revenue Service, and the Congressional Budget Office and major nonprofits such as the Urban Institute/Brookings Institution Tax Policy Center. Not only does CBPP produce trustworthy data and analyses, they work on issues that are particularly relevant for the paper and provide insightful interpretations. The authors know the center's founder and executive director, and he and members of the CBPP staff commented on an earlier version of this chapter. We observed firsthand how carefully the organization treats its data. However, the authors alone are responsible for how information and analysis has been used in the chapter, not CBPP or any other sources.

CHAPTER 9

The Rise and Decline of Reality-Based Policy Making in the Federal Government: 1945–2006

In government, as in life, poor analysis supports bad ideas; sound analysis restricts their harm. This chapter examines the shift from the high analytic capacity assembled by federal policy makers from the end of the Second World War to the Reagan administration, and its general deterioration in the executive branch since then. The deterioration of the analytic capacity of the executive branch and the tendency of recent presidents to pay less attention to the analysis that is available has contributed to the survival of bad ideas in the policy-making process. Bad ideas survive where they find a hospitable environment, and the fact-based systems of policy analysis constructed by federal agencies since World War II proved inhospitable to them. As this capacity declined, and a more ideologically-based decision-making process replaced it, the bad ideas we've been examining in this book found a more receptive environment.

The end of World War II forced America to confront simultaneously the problems of moving to a peacetime economy, reviving war-ravaged Europe's economic capacity, and thwarting the challenge of a resurgent and aggressive Soviet Union. After the successful wartime experience in policy planning, the federal government incorporated the available information techniques and decision-making procedures to develop hard data and sound analysis as the basis for postwar policy choices.

Postwar presidents before the Reagan years understood the value of valid data and analyses in a well-designed decision-making process. Studies of presidential policy making in that period indicated that the best internal decision-making processes featured (1) strong involvement by a knowledge-oriented president, (2) a competent policy staff, (3) sound data for assessing the pros and cons of alternative policies, and (4) a viable decision-making structure to support deliberations and needed compromises based on the reality of hard data.[1] This policy making model does not guarantee successful policy outcomes, but, absent blind luck, it is a necessary condition for them.

After his inauguration, Reagan cut back in size and downgraded in status analytic staffs throughout the executive branch. The new administration distrusted policy analysis and associated it with growing government and interference with the freedom of the marketplace. Rigorous analysis did not fit with President Reagan's style of thinking, which relied on his intuition and unalterable

[1]Walter Williams, *Honest Numbers and Democracy*. Washington DC: Georgetown University Press, 1998.

beliefs and drew on vivid examples, sometimes based on his own movie roles or films he had seen. The GW Bush administration went even further in creating an internal decision-making process that limited contradictory information and searched actively for evidence that supported its policy choices.

NEUTRAL COMPETENCE

Nowhere did the commitment to developing the best available numbers and policy options for presidential decision-making become stronger than in the Bureau of the Budget (BoB; now the Office of Management and Budget [OMB]). President Franklin Roosevelt brought the BoB from the Treasury to become part of the new Executive Office of the President in the late 1930s. The relatively small prewar BoB staff grew rapidly during the war years and emerged as a central component in the presidential decision-making process. The Bureau's basic creed held that it should provide the president the best available information analyzed without political spin as the foundation of his administration's internal decision making.

This creed of providing the unvarnished truth to the president was set out eloquently by Paul O'Neill, who had been highly respected for his competence and integrity during his lengthy BoB/OMB career in which he rose to the number two slot (a political appointment) before leaving the government at the end of the Ford administration. In 1988 he admonished young OMB staff members that their "guiding light" should be "a standard which says . . . in every decision the president has to make, he has from you . . . *the best and clearest exposition of the facts and arguments on every side of the issue that it is possible for a human mind to muster.*"[2]

Both the terms "neutral" and "competence" were critical. The Bureau sought out the brightest young analysts and used senior staff to mentor them, honing their skills. Its career analysts, at least until the coming of OMB when political appointees took over the top echelons of the organization, were viewed as the elite career staff in Washington. The career civil servant division chiefs who reported directly to the BoB director and deputy director (who often was a careerist too) were the most competent, respected, and powerful career civil servants in the federal government.

"Neutral" went beyond high technical skills alone. Career BoB analysts were nonpartisan, but not apolitical. Bureau of the Budget analyses prepared as a base of support for a president's policy deliberations and choices were expected to be (1) competently-crafted and sufficiently broad-ranging to cover the programmatic, organizational, and political factors relevant to the decision and (2) without any political spin that tailored recommendations to fit the particular president's political predilections.

The distinction between relevant political factors and political spin was central to BoB's concept of neutral competence. Bureau political critiques might include a political history of earlier attempts to pass similar policy proposals or an estimate of the likely amount of political support and opposition for the policy alternatives within Congress and the major interest groups. But in both cases, the BoB information and critique would not vary for presidents because of their political predilections or different

---

[2]Paul H. O'Neill, a presentation to Office of Management and Budget staff, The Center for Excellence in Government, Washington DC, September 6, 1988, p. 4, italics added.

approaches to the policy problem. It would be information necessary for reasoned deliberations to reach a final choice among the
policy options. To be sure, a president might want political spin,
but that fell outside of BoB's responsibilities. First and foremost,
neutral competence in BoB meant telling truth to power, even
when that was the president. And why wouldn't presidents want
hard facts and straight analysis because all the discussions and
documents used in internal decision making were shielded from
Congress and the public by executive privilege? It is a question
central to our later discussion.

POLICY ANALYSIS IN THE FEDERAL
AGENCIES AND CONGRESS

Agencies responsible for various aspects of domestic policy making
began to add analytic offices in the early and mid-1960s, a time
when Americans had great confidence in the capacity of the federal
government to solve problems and in the power of science to aid
that effort through research and analysis. Some heads of the new
analytic offices became key advisors to cabinet secretaries and
agency directors. Their offices also had the responsibility for
developing the agencies' policy and budget proposals submitted to
BoB/OMB that managed the president's policy planning and
budgeting system. Extended interaction with the budget staff provided the analytic offices the key linkage with that powerful office.

The dominant actors in the first strong agency analytic offices
were mainly economists from universities and prestigious think
tanks such as the Brookings Institution. They adhered to rigorous
academic research standards that demanded objectivity so that the

results would not be biased by questionable research techniques or the researchers' biases. Hard data and analyses were as important to these new agency policy analysts as to BoB/OMB staffs. Neutral competence became the order of the day, not only in the Bureau of the Budget, but in the agency analytic units.

Congress moved to create greater analytic capacity in the 1970s by strengthening some existing independent agencies and adding the Congressional Budget Office (CBO). The latter employed policy analysts who had similar backgrounds to members of the strong agency analytic offices. They too put great emphasis on the quality of the data and analyses. These independent agencies differed from the typical committees and subcommittees with their two partisan (majority and minority) staffs. They served the entire Congress. If an independent agency favored either the Republicans or the Democrats, even in a case where one of the parties controlled Congress, the other would cry foul and jeopardize the agency's credibility. Not only did the independent agencies take pride in their staunch nonpartisanship, that commitment became a means of survival.

On several occasions, the Congressional Budget Office's adherence to neutral competence made it unpopular with the majority party. Douglas Holtz-Eakin, who had been a member of GW Bush's Council of Economic Advisers staff, was chosen by the Republicans in 2003 to head CBO. A December 27, 2005 *New York Times* editorial noted that Holtz-Eakin had recently informed Congress that more tax cuts would not stimulate economic growth and raise tax revenues, and wrote:

That's startlingly straight talk, given that the Republicans are determined to pass tens of billions in unpaid-for tax cuts come

January. But it is typical of Mr. Holtz-Eakin, who is retiring this week after three years as director. In those years, he has delivered nonpartisan, data-driven research on some of the most controversial issues. . . . By going where the facts and figures led, Mr. Holtz-Eakin also protected his agency, which may be the last bastion of neutral government in Washington.[3]

Actually, Congress' other two independent agencies—the Congressional Research Service and the General Accountability Office—have also remained solidly nonpartisan, a telling comparison with the decline of neutral competence in the executive branch.

THE ATTACK ON NEUTRAL COMPETENCE

Paul O'Neill's troubled two years as President Bush's first secretary of Treasury exemplifies the conflict between neutral competence and the demands of the president for loyalty in justifying his programs.[4] As the Treasury secretary, O'Neill became a statutory member of the National Security Council and hence one of the few people at the table when the administration made the decision to invade Iraq. But O'Neill's firm belief in speaking the truth to power, which had not dimmed over the years, proved to be his undoing in the ideological fervor that dominated the decision to attack Iraq.

O'Neill's service in the federal government as a standard bearer for rigorous data and analyses, which gained him respect in an earlier era, made him an outcast in the Bush administration.

---

[3]*New York Times*, December 27, 2005, italics added.
[4]Ron Suskind, *The Price of Loyalty*. New York: Simon & Schuster, 2004.

What had been his great strength during his BoB/OMB years had become a cardinal sin in the Bush presidency, where "hard-eyed analysis would be painted as disloyalty."[5] President Bush once derided O'Neill for gaining "quite a reputation as a truth-teller" and fired him after two years as secretary, in good part because telling the truth in public branded him as disloyal.[6]

In George W. Bush's presidency, the standard of submitting data to rigorous scrutiny that existed prior to the Reagan administration reached a low point. Centralization became the order of the day. Why did the executive branch turn away from using sound policy information and analyses when the congressional agencies continued to embrace neutral competence?

The conventional wisdom is that the incentives in Congress for the independent agencies that answer to 535 bosses push toward competent, nonpartisan staffs. In contrast, incentives in the executive branch are viewed as unfavorable to the practice of neutral competence. There is only a president or an agency head, not the many congressional pressure points from members of both parties. If an independent agency engages in partisanship to help one of the parties, it will bring the wrath of the other party and undermine the agency's credibility. If a president demands the answers he wants to hear, neutral competence can be rejected, and there may be no competing, voices within the executive branch to counteract this, at least none with much power.

George W. Bush could have had an ample flow of nonpartisan information and analyses, but he chose a top-down, ideologically driven style, rather than reality-based data and analyses.

---

[5]Suskind, *The Price of Loyalty*, p. 69.
[6]Suskind, *The Price of Loyalty*, p. 263.

Presidential demand for honest numbers and analyses declined precipitously. Why demand fell is a complex question, but one thing is clear for the Bush administration: The president's demand did not decline because the underlying need for sound policy data and analyses in effective presidential governance had lessened.

THE RISE OF EXECUTIVE BRANCH POLICY ANALYSIS

After World War II, the RAND Corporation, a nonpartisan research organization, developed a rigorous model for government decision making, termed *systems analysis*. The approach, grounded in economics and statistics, moved from the RAND drawing board in 1961 when President John Kennedy's Defense secretary, Robert McNamara, asked Charles Hitch, his chief budget officer, to create a policy analysis office. Hitch, a former head of RAND's economics department who had a hand in developing the basic principles in the RAND system, established a powerful analytic staff and became a key advisor to Secretary McNamara.

The Planning-Programming-Budgeting System

In 1965, President Lyndon Johnson decided that the Department of Defense (DOD) analytic unit could be the model for introducing a new Planning-Programming-Budgeting (PPB) system in executive branch agencies. He observed: "Under this new system each cabinet and agency head will set up a very special staff of experts who, using the most modern method of program analysis, will define the goals of their department for the coming year. . . . This system will permit us to find the most effective and least costly alternative to achieving American goals. . . . It will insure a much sounder judgment through more accurate information.[7]

Johnson assigned BoB the responsibility for implementing and managing the PPB system. It issued an October 1965 circular to guide department secretaries and agency heads in establishing the policy analysis offices. The BoB directive set out all the right words about achieving national objectives through greater effectiveness and efficiency, and using accurate data to reach better judgments. In retrospect, President Johnson and the October 1965 circular overstated by a considerable degree what could be done immediately across the federal government. Both competent policy analysts and relevant policy data were in short supply except in the areas of defense and economic policy. Such shortages hit particularly hard in social policy, where the new War on Poverty placed heavy demands.

Moreover, the PPB system grossly underestimated how difficult it would be to synthesize complex information and make it relevant for real policy decisions. A serious and continuing problem in the policy-making process is how to combine information and analysis in a manner to improve decision-making capabilities. That automatic decision-making systems like PPB tend to fail does not mean that analysis is irrelevant. It implies only that policy makers must find a way to make sure they both receive relevant information and are able to comprehend its implications, while at the same time not being overwhelmed by its detail.

---

[7]Quoted in Walter Williams, *Social Policy Research and Analysis*. New York: American Elsevier, 1971, pp. 5–6.

The BoB directive provided for agency analytic offices, which had the needed status, responsibilities, and staff to make these units significant actors in agency policy making. The analytic offices had the primary agency responsibility for overall policy planning and became their representatives to work with BoB, which managed the yearly budget process for the president.

Over time the analytic offices became institutionalized as central elements in the decision-making process. This could happen only because agency and department heads served by the chief policy analysts wanted sound data and analyses in the decision-making process and were willing to expend the resources demanded in obtaining them. Chief policy analysts simply cannot succeed without continuing support from their bosses for reality-based decision-making processes.

The attempts to analyze systematically policy choices in the Johnson years marked an important point in the development of sound, data-based decision making in government. Lawrence Lynn, who had been an analyst at DOD under Hitch and later led two domestic policy analysis offices, pointed out that the most distinguishing feature of the new planning-programming-budgeting system was "the self-conscious incorporation of policy analysis and policy analysts as a matter of principle into the central direction of large, complex government organizations. . . . Henceforth the result of bureaucratic policies would reflect the influence of these policy analysts—the influence both of their ideas and of their access to power."[8]

---

[8]Lawrence E. Lynn, Jr., "Policy Analysis in the Bureaucracy: How New? How Effective?" *Journal of Policy Analysis and Management*, Summer 1989, pp. 374–375.

RONALD REAGAN AND THE
ANTI-ANALYTIC PRESIDENCY

President Reagan's inauguration ended the 20-year analytic revolution in the domestic policy area. The new administration began immediately to make what would become the most sweeping changes in the executive branch since Franklin Roosevelt created the Executive Office of the President (EOP). Reagan's anti-analytic presidency reduced the importance of executive branch policy analysis units by making large reductions in such factors as bureaucratic status, staff size and competence, and the funds available for large-scale policy research. For example, the Department of Health, Education, and Welfare (now Health and Human Services) policy analysis office had around 300 staff members in the Carter administration and supported major social policy experiments over time. Under Reagan, the office suffered a loss of two-thirds of its staff and ceased funding new large-scale social projects of this type.

Several factors worked to reduce the importance of policy analysis in the Reagan administration. First, control shifted to the top at the outset of the Reagan presidency. Major decisions about agency programs were handed down from above without necessarily involving the agencies concerned, thereby cutting the secretaries and their policy analysis offices out of the process. Second, President Reagan's ideological convictions were immune to hard evidence that raised questions about the validity of his beliefs. Finally, many Republicans felt that the analytical capacity of the federal government had operated to generate new demands for government programs; cutting back on the analysis would lead, they thought, to reduced demands for these programs. They saw entirely too many self-serving bureaucracies with staffs dedicated to finding problems that would yield more government, and hence more work for career civil servants.

White House Control

In asserting top-down control over government, Reagan established what came to be labeled the "Triumvirate," composed of chief of staff James Baker, deputy chief of staff Michael Deaver, and Edwin Meese, Governor Reagan's chief of staff in California. Meese was the White House policy chief, a new position with cabinet rank. The three men stood between President Reagan and essentially everyone else in the administration, including the cabinet secretaries and the Executive Office of the President (EOP).

Shifting major domestic program decisions to the White House decimated the social agencies' policy analysis and research support capacity, but unfortunately analytic capacity in the EOP was not expanded. The EOP included the National Security Council and the domestic Office of Policy Development. Prior to 1981 the National Security Council (NSC) had an important role in developing national policy, and it drew on strong NSC policy staffs for information and analysis. Dick Kirschten, the White House correspondent for the *National Journal*, minced no words in his 1981 description of the 99 members of the NSC: "[The staff] is seen as generally unskilled in dealing with the bureaucracy and possessing a hard-line, ideological tilt unsuited to a staff that is supposed to coordinate policy, not shape it. Their academic and professional reputations are regarded as rather mediocre."[9] Their role in decision making was inconsequential, but the staff appeared to fare better than their domestic counterparts in the Office of Policy Development (OPD). Ronald Brownstein joined Kirschten in spelling out the fate of the OPD staff: "From the time Reagan moved into the Oval Office, no one has ever bothered to turn on the lights at the White House's Office of Policy Development."[10]

Conservative Think Tanks

The Reagan administration downplayed analytical capacity in part because it had locked in on an agenda that had been developed well before the president took office. This agenda had its roots in the work of conservative intellectuals in think tanks, universities, and elsewhere. The think tanks were crucial. A small number of wealthy, extremely conservative Republicans had begun pouring funds into them in the early 1970s. Three of these think tanks—the American Enterprise Institute (AEI), the Institute for Contemporary Studies (ICS), and the Heritage Foundation—had critical roles in helping to develop and articulate the Reagan agenda.

The Heritage Foundation had been founded in 1973 by two congressional staff members, Paul Weyrich and Ed Feulner, to market conservative ideas aggressively. Political scientist Joseph Peschek wrote: "Nearly all of the hard-line positions developed at the AEI and ICS during the Carter administration were translated

[9]Dick Kirschten, "His NSC Days May Be Numbered but Allen Is One for Bouncing Back," *National Journal*, November 28, 1981, p. 2115.
[10]Ronald Brownstein and Kirschten, "Cabinet Power," *National Journal*, June 28, 1986, p. 1589.

into concise policy proposals for the incoming Reagan team in the Heritage Foundation's *Mandate for Leadership*."[11] Heritage had scored a coup with the successful packaging of other think tanks' ideas and marketing them to the incoming Reagan administration.

The One Man Band

Guidance drawn from *Mandate for Leadership* and other work in hand before President Reagan entered office helped provide the administration a firm policy agenda at the outset. But it still needed a strategy for turning the conservative agenda into legislation. The annual budget provided the vehicle. David Stockman, a member of Congress in his mid-thirties, joined the administration as OMB director, coming to the position with an amazing knowledge of the federal budget for someone who had not spent years at that agency.

The president and the Triumvirate wanted to move quickly, and Stockman combined the ideological commitment and stamina necessary to work night and day. In doing so, he had no qualms about hiding or distorting information that could be used by opponents. Stockman's reckless arrogance led him to race ahead on his own, even relegating OMB's professional staff to checking out numbers for him, rather than treating them as intellectual peers available for critiquing his ideas.

Once Stockman launched into selling the budget agenda, he operated with little or no input from above or advice from

---

[11]Joseph G. Peschek, *Policy Planning Organizations.* Philadelphia: Temple University Press, 1987, p. 158; and Charles H. Heatherly (ed.), *Mandate for Leadership.* Washington DC: Heritage Foundation, 1981.

below. Neither President Reagan nor the Triumvirate was knowledgeable about the intricacies of the federal budget. Of the three, only Baker had the skills to get up to speed on that budget, and he did not do so. Stockman viewed Meese and Deaver with contempt. The Triumvirate stood between President Reagan and Stockman so that the latter never talked to the president except in meetings involving a relatively large group of staff members. Stockman moved with such speed that the major choices were made before cabinet members had redecorated their offices and much of the sub-cabinet had been approved by the Senate.

Stockman's purpose was not to undermine the Reagan agenda. Both men had similar radical ideological worldviews and objectives. Though Stockman with his great energy may have wanted to go faster and further than the president did, the two sought the same goals. But Stockman's ambition and over-confidence led him to race on, mainly unchecked by criticism or commands from above or policy analysis from below. In his 1986 book, *The Triumph of Politics,* which remains one of the most insightful accounts of the administration, Stockman con-fessed to his less-than-honorable behavior and his ultimately foolhardy efforts.[12] In his chapter about the quick start that Stockman aptly named "Blitzkrieg," he observed: "I installed so much confidence by appearing to know all the answers, but I was just beginning to understand the true complexities and mysteries of the federal budget. . . . Designing a comprehen-sive plan to bring about sweeping change in national economic

---

[12]David A. Stockman, *The Triumph of Politics.* New York: Harper & Row, 1986.

governance in forty days is a preposterous, wantonly reckless notion."[13]

Stockman later became a strong advocate of budgetary prudence, including tax increases, and tried to convince the Reagan image-makers of the dangers made clear by the budget and tax data. But he had found religion late in the process, after he had been the primary operator opening the floodgates from which the mounting deficits poured forth.

Reagan as Manager

After President Reagan's landslide victory in 1984, political scientist Terry Moe and others hailed his administration as the model of how a successful president should operate. They claimed that success came because President Reagan grasped the big picture and chose outstanding subordinates for day-to-day management so that he had the time to stay on top of the major issues. In his assessment of President Reagan, published in 1985, Moe wrote: "He built a set of administrative arrangements that by past standards prove coherent, well integrated, and eminently workable . . . and could well establish him as the most administratively influential president of the modern period."[14]

By 1985 proponents appeared to believe that the reality-driven policy making model employed during the analytic revolution that featured an involved, knowledgeable president; policy staff competence; and a decision-making process informed by sound

[13]Stockman, *The Triumph of Politics*, pp. 80 and 91.
[14]Terry M. Moe, "The Politicized Presidency," in John E. Chubb and Paul E. Peterson (eds.), *The New Direction in American Politics*. Washington DC: Brookings Institution, p. 271.

information and analysis was obsolete. The improved managerial approach with a new kind of leader in Ronald Reagan worked far better than earlier management models, they claimed. Then came the Iran-Contra affair. Arms were sold covertly to Iran and the profits were diverted to help the Nicaraguan rebels fighting the leftist Sandinista government in that country. Even though Congress had banned such aid either directly or indirectly, the Reagan administration kept trying to free American hostages held by Iran and supply the anticommunists in Nicaragua, and so undertook the illegal arms-for-hostages deal. When the scandal became public, there was great dismay at both the Reagan administration's staggering ineptitude and the gross illegality of its efforts.

Reagan, to his credit, appointed a blue-chip commission to investigate the Iran-Contra affair, chaired by former Senator John Tower.[15] The bipartisan Tower Commission had broad powers and undertook scrupulously fair hearings with the key people involved in the arms-for-hostages debacle. Its extensive report that ran more than 500 pages exposed a terrible breakdown in the administration. Reagan was hardly on top of the game. His allegedly outstanding advisors not only badly mismanaged the effort but engaged in numerous unlawful practices.

The Tower Commission found the president so confused that they wondered if he could complete his term. R. W. Apple, then the chief Washington correspondent of the *New York Times*, wrote in the introduction to the report: "The board painted a picture of Ronald Reagan very different from that the world had become accustomed to in the last six years. . . . This portrait is

[15]*The Tower Commission Report.* New York: Times Books, 1987.

of a man confused. . . . At times, in fact, the report makes the president sound like the inhabitant of a never-never land of imaginary policies."[16]

REAGAN'S IMMEDIATE SUCCESSORS

Reagan's successor, George H. W. Bush, was certainly not overtly anti-analytic, and he assembled competent people around him. But Bush did little to restore an analytic approach throughout government, and he suffered harsh criticism from his own party when he worked to restore prudent fiscal policies. Conservatives in his party attacked him repeatedly when he agreed to a package of tax increases and expenditure cuts to forestall the automatic sequesters of the Pay-Go budget procedure that had been established in the 1990 Budget Enforcement Act. The act was passed with bipartisan support to control the huge Reagan-era deficits, and Bush was simply doing his job as chief executive and political leader. Nevertheless, this act of reality-based policy making deeply harmed his reputation among Republican Party faithful, who recalled his election-year pledge: "Read my lips: No New Taxes!" It seemed clear that partisan Republicans were in no mood to face facts.

President Bill Clinton himself had a penetrating analytic mind and engaged in extensive policy discussions with his top staff, but several factors worked against a full effort to revive policy analysis in the executive branch. Clinton followed the trend toward greater centralization at the top, so the agencies had less of a role

---

[16]R. W. Apple, Jr., "Introduction," *The Tower Commission Report*, pp. xii–xiii.

in the presidential decision-making process. Moreover, his often disorganized style mitigated against a systematic decision-making process involving orderly policy analysis. At the same time, he did restore serious policy analysis to the presidency and is the only chief executive since 1981 who fits the mold of the pre-Reagan presidents. This effort stands out as a real achievement and one that paid off in good policy decisions.

In the area of fiscal policy, Clinton raised top income tax rates and worked with Congress to control the federal budget. These policies were based on good information and reasoned analyses. They cemented in place the prudent fiscal policies that the federal government had pursued since the later Reagan years and were buttressed by the 1990 budget law imposing pay-go procedures and a bipartisan consensus in Congress that deficits should be controlled. Though Clinton's fiscal policies were not the main cause of the 1995–2000 economic boom, his sound fiscal policies facilitated the best period of sustained economic growth without rising yearly budget deficits since the 1960s.

"A COMPLETE LACK OF POLICY APPARATUS"

Policy analytic capacity, restored temporarily under GHW Bush and Clinton, suffered under President GW Bush. John DiIulio, a Princeton University scholar who served as the first head of Bush's Office for Faith-Based Initiatives, told the reporter Ron Suskind in late 2002 after leaving that position, "'There is no precedent in any modern White House for what is going on in this one: a complete lack of policy apparatus. . . . I heard many, many staff discussions but not three meaningful substantive policy discussions. There were no actual policy white papers on domestic issues.'"[17] The top-down centralized policy-making structure and belief-based policy thinking in the president's inner circle led to neglect of bottom-up policy development. Rather than thinking about goals and evaluating in a clear-headed manner the various policies that could be employed to achieve those goals, the administration tended to become irrevocably committed to a course of action, ignoring or refusing to consider alternate strategies.

Bush compounded the problem by refusing to make the needed changes to modify his policies even when reasonable alternatives were available to correct the excesses or errors. The president was loath to make reasonable corrections that could be seen as admitting his basic policies that were based on unchallengeable beliefs, not strategies to achieve goals, were not working.

Ronald Reagan and GW Bush: A Comparison

Similarities between the presidencies of Ronald Reagan and George W. Bush are striking. Both were large-state governors, but neither had much relevant policy knowledge or seemed concerned about the lack of facts. Because both presidents had leadership skills but knew little and cared less about organizational issues and tended to avoid them, they became heavily dependent on their main advisors. Each man had serious decision making and governance problems, yet we believe most will agree that Reagan performed much better

---

[17]Quoted in Paul Krugman, "State of Delusion," *New York Times*, February 3, 2006, p. A27.

than Bush, a judgment that is likely to develop into a consensus over time.

The Reagan administration did grave damage to the institution of the presidency by weakening its information-processing capacities and its commitment to hard data and analyses conducted by competent staff. However capable he was as a political leader, Reagan generally failed as chief executive. Yet he appointed two outstanding advisors capable of guiding him away from trouble and toward sound policies—Secretary of State George Shultz and Chief-of-Staff James Baker—and he listened to them.

A major component of Baker's job was protecting the president against foolhardy ideas coming from outside the White House, and he generally succeeded during Reagan's first term. Then Reagan allowed the secretary of the Treasury in his first four years, Donald Regan, to swap jobs with Baker, who wanted a major cabinet position. Regan lacked Baker's political and organizational savvy, and he failed in guiding Reagan away from poor advice in the Iran-Contra affair, leading to a major scandal.

George Shultz had been warned at the start of his tenure that the State Department career staff would not cooperate with him and should be left out of the decision-making loop. But he had had an outstanding record in managing high-level civil service experts from his time as OMB director and as secretary in two cabinet agencies (Labor and Treasury) in earlier Republican administrations. Shultz "understood both that his job was to give political leadership to the department and that to do so, he had no choice but to use the career staff to the fullest, because a secretary and his or her political executives alone cannot make and execute policy effectively."[18]

In his memoir, *Turmoil and Triumph*, Shultz noted that Foreign Service officers "bring a fund of knowledge and institutional memory not available anywhere else," and that the government "is basically full of people who are here because they want to help and they're honest. . . . I have never worked with more able and more dedicated people."[19] By rejecting the administration's misguided views on civil servants, the secretary made the greatest contribution to sound policy making of anyone serving President Reagan.

Shultz understood one of the most basic management principles for the head of a cabinet department: however great the secretary's leadership skills, he or she still must have the help of career experts with knowledge and analytic skills in order to govern successfully. Only a large cadre of career specialists with "knowledge and institutional memory" can provide their political superiors the information and analyses needed for reasoned policy decision making, sensible choices, and realistic implementation.

Bush's First Term

When George W. Bush became president 12 years after Ronald Reagan stepped down, Reaganism's antigovernment and pro-market stances still dominated political thinking. The extreme political polarization in Washington generated by Harsh Reaganism pointed

---

[18]Walter Williams, "George Shultz on Managing the White House," *Journal of Policy Analysis and Management*, 13(2), p. 373.
[19]George P. Shultz, *Turmoil and Triumph*. New York: Schribners, 1993, pp. 33 and 917.

to a close relationship between the new Republican president and the Republican-controlled Congress.

Although President Bush's huge 2001 tax cut won approval in June, his power did not solidify until several commercial airline aircraft were hijacked by foreigners and used to murder U.S. citizens on September 11, 2001. This was the first attack within the nation's borders carried out by foreigners since the War of 1812, and threw into question the fundamental assumption of citizens that they were safe from such a threat on their own soil.

Factors That Shaped GW Bush's Decision Making

These attacks early in President Bush's first term so greatly enhanced his political power that he generally faced only limited opposition to his flawed policy proposals from Congress and the public for the rest of his first term. We need to ask what factors led Bush to make such poor policy choices.

Personal Loyalty. Even before ascending to the presidency, George W. Bush was known for demanding that his subordinates display total commitment to the man himself. He knew there would always be subtle and not-so-subtle comparisons with his father. The elder Bush had more policy knowledge and experience generally, and particularly in foreign policy. Because of the new president's personal insecurity or not, total loyalty translated into not bringing discordant information to the president.

Unwillingness to Change Course. President Bush is renowned for his "resolve" and tenacity, an admirable trait in the proper circumstances. But in the wrong circumstances, resolve is simple stubbornness. Too often he has refused to shift policy direction because it implied the wrong initial choice, confusing sensible changes in direction with lacking commitment to stay the course. This dogged unwillingness to change in the face of contrary evidence led Bush to stick to bad policies with clear negative consequences. This certainly characterizes his tax cuts. It is interesting to compare Bush to Ronald Reagan, who has been hailed as the foremost enemy of federal taxes, on this score.

In crowning him as the tax-cutter supreme, Reagan's supporters forget that his administration increased taxes more times than it cut them. Bruce Bartlett, a conservative think-tank economist and Reagan administration official, found 11 tax increases compared to 4 tax decreases legislated during the Reagan presidency. All were not income tax changes, and the dollar size of the Reagan decreases were only half as great as the increases.[20] But the Reagan administration, as well as the administrations of George H. W. Bush and Bill Clinton, raised taxes to combat the debilitating deficits they all experienced. By the early 21st century, however, George W. Bush and the other true believers had ruled out all federal tax increases, however high the deficits and despite the Reagan record.

Creating Reality versus "Spin." As presidential scholar Steven Skowronek notes, Bush the politician has always thought that a premise repeated often enough and with enough conviction becomes reality.[21] This conviction goes far beyond the typical political ploy of spin, which is interpreting the facts in a favorable light to one's preferred program.

---

[20]Bruce Bartlett, *Imposter*. New York: Doubleday, 2006, p. 214.
[21]Steven Skowronek, "Leadership by Definition: First Term Reflections on George W. Bush's Political Stance," *Perspective on Politics*, 3: December 2005, pp. 817–831.

Ron Suskind, in a *New York Times Magazine* piece in 2004, explored the phenomenon in detail; and it remains the best analysis on the subject. A Bush aide boasted that Suskind and others like him were part of the "reality-based community," where people "believe that solutions emerge from your judicious study of discernible reality . . . . "That's not the way the world really works anymore," he continued. "We're an empire now, and when we act, we create our own reality. And while you're studying that reality—judiciously, as you will—we'll act again, creating other new realities, which you can study too."[22]

Bush sought to impose his own version of reality on Congress and the public in the realm of domestic policy making. One administration critic put it this way: "As a political strategy, reality control has worked very well. But as a strategy for governing, it has led to predictable disaster. When leaders live in an invented reality, they do a bad job of dealing with real reality."[23]

Bush administration leaders constructed an alternative reality that fit with their ideological beliefs, worked relentlessly to sell their reality to the public as the "real reality," and then used that new reality in governing. The main weapon in this campaign became the untruth that continues to be repeated even in the face of contradictory evidence. The key exhibits are statements by Bush, Vice President Dick Cheney, Treasury secretary John Snow, and the then–OMB director Josh Bolten in the Spring of 2006 that tax cuts cause increases in federal revenue. Readers of this book know this not to be true, but so do these leaders—the professional budget analysts have told them so. Indeed, the Budget of the Federal Government

---

[22]Ron Suskind, "Without a Doubt," *New York Times Magazine*, October 17, 2004.
[23]Paul Krugman, "Ignorance Isn't Strength," *New York Times*, August 8, 2005, p. A27.

for Fiscal Year 2007, which Bolten and Bush both signed, estimates that the Bush tax cuts will cause revenue losses.

Uncomfortable with Government. New *York Times* columnist David Brooks wrote in his May 14, 2006 op-ed piece that President Bush "has never felt comfortable with government and its institutions."[24] Brooks suggests that the president is "caught in a hangover from the old conservatism" that can only attack the federal government to limit its power, and does not see how government can be used in a positive way. . . . In part, Bush has had trouble governing because he and some of his advisors have been aloof from and often openly hostile to the institutions of government in this country. The first job of any Republican administration is to figure out how to use government agencies, which are staffed by people who may be liberals, but who are also professionals." Brooks got it right: The Bush White House simply could not or would not govern, because the president was uncomfortable with the institutions that must be used in governing.

A Paucity of Reality-Based Advisors. Bush did not have a James Baker or George Shultz in his inner circle, and he jettisoned the one noted analytic practitioner he took on in his administration, secretary of Treasury Paul O'Neill. But he did turn to seasoned professionals in foreign policy—Donald Rumsfeld at Defense and Colin Powell at State. With Dick Cheney as vice president, this would seem to be a group of first-rate policy practioners.

---

[24]The quotes in this paragraph are from David Brooks, "From Freedom to Authority," Opinion Section, New *York Times*, May 14, 2006, p. 12.

One of the great mysteries of the Bush administration is why Vice President Dick Cheney and Secretary of Defense Donald Rumsfeld, both of whom had good reputations as providers of "adult supervision," did not play the role Shultz did. We do not know the answer, but it is unlikely that Shultz, or O'Neill, were insufficiently conservative in comparison to Cheney and Rumsfeld. Rather, the answer seems to be that Shultz and O'Neill understood the continuing need for hard evidence and reasoned analyses and advice from men and women who have spent years becoming professional experts in complex areas. They were comfortable with the give-and-take of policy arguments offered by career civil servants.

On the other hand, Rumsfeld was a man with a mission at Defense, determined to bring a new conception of force deployment even if the generals did not like it. Powell, under a different chief executive, might have been a superb secretary of state, and he made reasoned arguments to the president concerning the Iraq invasion. Yet in the end he allowed Bush's demand for loyalty to trump his professional judgment, and became the key person in the public justification of invasion.

BUSH AND HIS ADVISORS: A LAST WORD

In the end, presidents get the advice they want. And this president brooked no internal criticism. As a consequence, his advisors did not stop, and even actively contributed to an unwillingness to govern realistically. In the case of fiscal policy, this ruled out facing up to looming budgetary problems, problems so severe that they demand wrenching changes, including both making significant overall tax increases and controlling expenditure levels. The obliviousness of the Bush administration to the obvious fiscal problems the nation faces has been abetted by the general decline in the analytic capacity of the executive branch since Reagan. Yet ultimately, the lack of good advice came about because President Bush only wanted to hear numbers and recommendations that fit with his unreal world views.

CHAPTER 10

The Role of Institutions

The institutions of government usually fall below the radar of pundits and professors. Only occasionally does institutional performance become egregiously bad and attract attention. The Federal Emergency Management Agency (FEMA) took center stage when its inefficiency endangered the inhabitants of New Orleans and other locales hit by Katrina and became a symbol of the Bush administration's seeming lack of governing competence. Now congressional scholars have begun to analyze the general performance of Congress in terms of institutional failure.[1] Are these governing failures tied to the politics of bad ideas? If so, how?

Thus far, we've discussed how bad economic ideas became incorporated into Republican Party ideology, how those ideas have caused serious deterioration in the fiscal health of the federal government, and how Presidents Reagan and GW Bush particularly undermined the traditional mechanisms of policy analysis to pursue their ideology-driven policy ideas unchallenged by rigorous scrutiny. Here we show how these trends

---

[1] A good example is Thomas E. Mann and Norman J. Ornstein, *The Broken Branch*. Oxford: Oxford University Press, 2006.

have interacted to weaken the quality of our governing institutions.

After the Second World War, a political consensus emerged in which both parties generally agreed that whatever policies they pursued would be based on sound analysis from competent policy professionals. The consensus experienced sharp breaches, as in the case of President Johnson's misleading claims about the Vietnam War. Despite this, the broad understanding extended to the operation of our governing institutions. They functioned admirably in meeting the great challenges of the Cold War, furthering the civil rights of minorities (if belatedly), and addressing issues from the environment to stabilizing the economy. Even in the case of the resignation of the disgraced president, Richard Nixon, Congress worked well in carrying out its constitutional responsibilities.

Now our political institutions no longer function properly. The decay of our governing structure in the face of increased partisanship and the destruction of the postwar consensus on policy analysis have allowed the politics of bad ideas to self-perpetuate. How that has happened is the story we tell in this chapter.

PAST INSTITUTIONAL DECLINE IN THE TWO BRANCHES

Not since the structural changes made by Franklin Roosevelt that included the creation of the Executive Office of the President had a president made such basic institutional changes in the executive branch as did Ronald Reagan. Chapter 9 documented how his presidency contributed to the deterioration of that branch's capacity to generate sound policy analysis and diminished the managerial capability of the federal agencies.

Reagan appointed several ideological political executives who too often had limited managerial skills. Many distrusted the civil servants working under them, often keeping them out of policy discussions. Excessive centralization of power at the top, reliance on ideology rather than sound analyses, and the misuse of the careerists all contributed to weakening the capacity of the executive branch to carry out the laws of the land.

Bill Clinton was a much more analytic president than his immediate predecessors, and used sound information and analyses more extensively in the executive branch. At the same time, as Howard Kurtz, the *Washington Post* media expert, pointed out, the Clinton administration created a "well-oiled propaganda machine—arguably the most successful team of spin doctors in history."[2] It became the first full-blown White House propaganda machine and offered a model for Bush in 2001. "Clinton and his supporting staff molded spinning into an institutional weapon that in capable hands could be devastatingly effective. But it was a performance that had routinized lying in the White House and that had used lying in trying to cover up behavior that much diminished the internal and external credibility of the presidency."[3]

In the 20 years between the inaugurations of presidents Reagan and Bush, Congress too suffered institutional damage. Both campaign contributions and the Washington lobbyist corps, of limited size and importance in the early postwar years, have

---

[2]Howard Kurtz, *Spin Cycle*. New York: Free Press, 1998. The quotation is from the dust jacket.
[3]Walter Williams, *Reaganism and the Death of Representative Democracy*. Washington DC: Georgetown University Press, 2003, p. 114.

grown exponentially in recent years. The number of registered lobbyists doubled—from 16,342 to 34,785—between 2000 and 2004.[4] Though lobbyists come from citizen groups, religious organizations, and even other levels of government, many represent corporate interests. All helped increase the flow of money to incumbents and worked the halls seeking favors for their clients.

The 1994 mid-term election brought a higher level of polarization to Congress than at any time in the postwar years, but polarization had been on the increase since around 1970.[5] The landslide Republican gains in the House of Representatives elevated Newt Gingrich to Speaker and provided him a phalanx of first term conservative ideologues. As a consequence of polarization, the deliberative process, which the Constitution's Framers considered essential to democratic governance, ceased to function properly. Of course the parties have always used the legislative process to score points and frustrate the opposition, but the constitutional strictures that make it relatively easy for minorities to block legislative progress have generally caused the parties to cooperate, if begrudgingly. What began to occur in the 1990s is that parties began to value symbolic attacks on the opposition rather than positive legislative accomplishments.

CONGRESS IN THE YEARS OF REPUBLICAN CONTROL

Congress surely reached a low point in 1998 during the House of Representatives' impeachment of President Bill Clinton.

---

[4]Jeffrey Birnbaum, "The Road to Riches Is Called K Street," *Washington Post*, June 22, 2005, p. A01.
[5]Nolan T. McCarthy, Keith T. Poole, and Howard Rosenthal, *Polarized America*. Cambridge: The MIT Press, 2006.

Congressional scholars Thomas Mann and Norm Ornstein thought at the time that the impeachment brought Congress as a competent functioning institution to rock bottom, at least during their three plus decades of watching Congress. By 2006, they observed: "We didn't think they could sink any lower. We were wrong."[6]

What accounted for this decline? One reason is certainly the increased polarization that has characterized recent American politics. In addition, small Republican legislative majorities put a premium on internal party loyalty. Strong party discipline and deference to the policy wishes of the Republican president led to a Republican party much closer to the textbook characterization of parties in parliamentary democracies than the generally more independent ones in the United States. Perhaps as a consequence, reasoned deliberations among members and rigorous oversight of the executive branch have both declined during the past decade.

In recent years, legislative partisanship reached a level not seen since the 1890s. Increased partisanship, in which two unified and ideologically polarized parties face one another, did not start in 1994. Its beginnings may be traced back to the 1970s.[7] The partisan climate after 1994 became much hotter. This intense polarization brought considerable arrogance and a win-at-any-cost attitude after September 11, 2001. President Bush, with his avowed intent to raise the power of the chief executive, demanded loyalty from Republican legislative leaders, and he mostly got it. The Republican leadership in turn behaved ruthlessly toward the minority Democrats and their own dissidents.

---

[6]Mann and Ornstein, *The Broken Branch*, p. 140.
[7]McCarthy, Poole, and Rosenthal, *Polarized America*.

This extremely partisan climate likely became the precipitating factor undermining Congress' fundamental institutional responsibility—the separation of powers, by defending their institution against the incursions of presidents. Naturally legislators were more suspicious of a president of the opposition party, but they also thought of themselves as representatives of the institution as well as their party. For much of the Bush presidency, Republican leaders in both houses of Congress dropped any pretense of defending the institution against a determined president. Congress, the institution the Framers considered the first branch, assumed a clearly subservient role.

During the years of one-party control, the marching orders for the Republican congressional army boiled down to two simple commands: push through the president's agenda and make sure they did nothing to embarrass him. Republican leaders in the House of Representatives rushed bills through to block questions and comments by Democrats and suspect back bench Republicans, excluded Democratic representation from conference committees, and limited the ability of the minority to offer floor amendments. House Republicans had forgotten their commitment to open government, pledged in 1995 after spending many years in the minority. Although the Republican majority had at first honored the pledge, they complained later that when the Democrats were allowed to participate they offered amendments and bills that were sure to be defeated and later used in 20-second sound-bites during elections. The Senate pursued a more collegial style, but it came to crisis itself over court nominations.

Legislative Oversight of the Executive

Our system of separated powers with checks and balances seldom works properly without considerable institutional tension between Congress and the presidency. It works best when this tension is channeled into policy disputes, with vigorous oversight from Congress through its committee system. The strong party system characterized by the GW Bush era caused a breakdown of this function. When the Republicans took control of the government, their legislative leaders valued party discipline over institutional loyalty. The cost was inordinately high—the system of checks and balances ceased to perform properly under these conditions. This dysfunctional result led to calls for divided government as a bromide to what many view as irresponsible unified government, but if the American governing system requires divided party control to work properly, then it is clearly not functioning as it was designed.

In Federalist Paper #51, James Madison wrote:

> (T)he great security against a gradual concentration of the several powers in the same department, consists in giving to those who administer each department the necessary constitutional means and personal motives to resist encroachments of the others . . . Ambition must be made to counteract ambition. The interest of the man must be connected with the constitutional rights of the place.[8]

So the Constitution establishes a system that gives means and motives for occupants of the branches of government to defend their branch and try to dominate the other branches to achieve their personal

---

[8]Alexander Hamilton, James Madison, and John Jay, *The Federalist Papers*. New York:/Mentor, 1961, p. 322.

goals. The Founders hoped that this system of mutual interference would prevent bad policies from being enacted, yet allow the necessary ones to survive—a strong but limited government was the aim.

From September 11, 2001 to January 2007 when the Republicans lost the control of Congress, this system failed to work. Party loyalty trumped the constitutional responsibility of Republican congressional leaders to thwart a determined and resolute executive determined to bend the legislature to his will. The president was highly successful in accomplishing his major objectives, and simultaneously the will of Congress to investigate the behavior of the Republican administration withered. In 2005 the *Boston Globe* reported that during the mid-1990s the Republican Congress conducted 140 hours of testimony on whether President Bill Clinton had used the White House Christmas card list to find Democratic donors. But it took only 12 hours of testimony on the abuse of prisoners at Iraq's Abu Ghraib prison during 2004 and 2005.[9] The *Globe's* analysis of the House Government Reform Committee indicated that the Democratically controlled Congress of 1993–1995 aggressively investigated the Clinton administration, conducting 135 hearings, whereas the Committee during the Republican Congress of 2003–2005 held but 37.

The Center for American Politics and Public Policy has carried out a more complete analysis of congressional oversight hearings of the executive branch in the postwar period. As shown in Figure 10.1, the study confirms and extends the results of the *Globe's* analysis, and puts it in perspective.[10] Oversight of the executive branch experienced two sharp spikes, in 1972, when a Democratic Congress

---

[9] Susan Milligan, "Congress Reduces Its Oversight Role," *Boston Globe*, November 20, 2005.
[10] We used data from the Policy Agendas Project to calculate the chart, plotting nonlegislative hearings in the following subtopics of the major topic of government operations: government efficiency, government procedures, scandal and impeachment, IRS, and other.

FIGURE 10.1
Number of Oversight Hearings on Government Operations

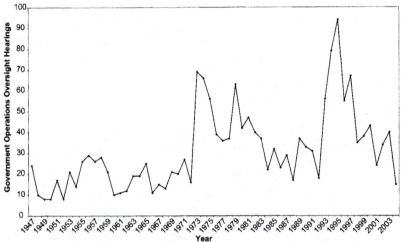

Source: Policy Agendas Project, Center for American Politics and Public Policy, University of Washington.

became concerned with the Nixon government's administrative effort to exert much greater control over the executive branch, and in 1993–1995, when both Democrats and Republican majorities energetically investigated the Clinton administration. A major decline in interest occurred in 1998 (perhaps the devastating loss in the Clinton impeachment trial demoralized conservatives). Nevertheless, the interest in investigating the administration fell to a 30-year low in 2001 and after.

After the Democrats took control of both the House and the Senate in January 2007, there have been more oversight investigations, but we do not know whether party change alone will restore the institutional integrity of Congress. Under the highly polarized conditions of today, it is hard to believe that the old system of collaborative government in Congress can be restored.

■ Deliberation and Information

Congress must develop its own sound information both to fuel a robust deliberative process and to determine that the law is being carried out faithfully by the executive branch. James Madison envisioned the process of deliberation as the essential mechanism for an effective legislative body. He wrote: "[Deliberations] refine and enlarge the public view by passing them through the medium of a chosen body of citizens, whose wisdom may best discern the true interest of their country and whose patriotism and love of justice would be least likely to sacrifice it to temporary or partial [that is, partisan] considerations."[11] Mann and Ornstein reaffirmed that centrality: "The essence of lawmaking in Congress is deliberation. . . . [It is] the signature comparative advantage of Congress as a legislative body. . . . [An] arduous process of going through multiple levels and channels of discussion, debate, negotiation, and compromise . . . make up a robust deliberative process."[12]

To be robust, the deliberative process requires orderly procedures and clear rules that support comity and a degree of bipartisanship so that an acceptable compromise can be sought. Deliberations do not, and should not, guarantee an agreement among the parties. But a robust process does demand a reasonable effort in working together to seek one. During the first years of the Bush presidency, the Republican congressional leaders rejected such an approach and sought a pro forma process that gave the appearance of substance.

Historically, congressional committees or subcommittees have used hearings to obtain information and commentary on

---

[11]Hamilton, Madison, and Jay, *The Federalist Papers*, p. 82.
[12]Mann and Ornstein, *The Broken Branch*, pp. 170, 215, and 216.

their own from persons in the executive branch and elsewhere such as experts from state and local governments, advocacy groups, and universities and think tanks. The independent agencies, particularly the General Accountancy Office with its extensive field work, and committee staffs also have had important roles in gathering information about government programs and doing analyses of it.

Members and their staffs engage in a number of other activities, such as visiting their districts to talk to constituents that may provide useful information too such as showing program deficiencies or additional needs. However, oversight through hearings and field investigations has long been Congress' primary means for gathering needed data directly from their own sources. Congress simply cannot satisfactorily carry out its constitutionally-mandated function as an independent branch without this extensive oversight effort.

During the years their party controlled Congress Republican congressional leaders abandoned meaningful oversight. The development by the legislative branch of independent sources of sound information would have conflicted with pushing through the president's agenda as expeditiously as possible. Since January 2007 the Democrats have re-instituted vigorous oversight, but whether the system of tensions between the two branches has been restored will not be tested fully until a unified government returns. The system of checks and balances fails if it works only during periods of divided government. Congress was charged with defending its separate and equal status against a president without regard to party control. Indeed, the system was designed before the emergence of the modern party system. It operated well in periods of divided and unified governments, but failed for five years during the GW Bush presidency and Republican unified government.

The Presidency

The Constitutional framers worried about an excessively strong chief executive—a King George III running roughshod over the Parliament—and deliberately constructed a government that was capable of preventing that. Yet the fear of an all-powerful president unconstrained by Congress or the judiciary seemingly had been swept aside during the first extended period of Republican governance since the 1920s. September 11, 2001 and the most polarized political environment in the postwar era helped pave the way for an increasingly powerful president. But such a presidency would not have emerged without two critical institutional changes by the Bush administration.

The first is the institutional shift that concentrated decision-making power in the hands of the president and a small inner circle. Historically important players were shut out, including most of the cabinet secretaries with the exception of Secretary of Defense Donald Rumsfeld. In this centralized pattern, Vice President Dick Cheney became the pivotal player, assembling a large and able staff to monitor decisions made throughout the federal bureaucracy and to intervene in the process where he thought it desirable.

Though pundits and political scientists have recognized the increasing politicization in Congress, they have tended to overlook a similar trend in the executive branch. Politicization strengthens the relative power of presidential appointees over career civil servants—political forces exert control over bureaucratic ones. President Richard Nixon established the Office of Management and Budget to replace BoB in order to gain greater control over his government. He justified the change on the sound grounds of exerting control over the vast bureaucracy that was rapidly growing in the wake of President Lyndon Johnson's aggressive domestic policy initiatives. But a consequence of the move to exert top-down control was increased politicization. Political appointees replaced the BoB careerists who had achieved great influence by using their neutral competence in advising presidents. Responsive competence, a public administration theory that emphasizes the duty of federal bureaucrats to hew to the program of the president regardless of its factual and analytical base, emerged as the standard for presidential advice in the Reagan administration. It reached its high point in George W. Bush's presidency a dozen years later.

The administrations of Ronald Reagan and George W. Bush both wanted policy information and analyses that conformed to the administration's ideology, but with the latter the demand became more insistent. Bush's highly centralized decision-making structure was fueled by the desire to impose total responsiveness to the wishes of the chief executive, and led to bad policy decisions and inept implementation. These results, in turn, necessitated the second key institutional change that made for a presidency with excessive power.

The Bush administration, eying the successes of Clinton in controlling the interpretation of complex information in the political discourse, built an even larger and more sophisticated propaganda operation and used it relentlessly to sell the administration's policies. This extensive propaganda effort moved beyond the characteristic Clinton "spin" aimed at protecting or improving his image to a more aggressive use of misinformation and deception.

A good example of this propaganda effort came with the surge in tax revenues in 2006. The Bush administration argued that the tax cuts had been successful in generating greatly increased levels of economic growth and new tax revenues. By the close of the 2006 fiscal year on September 30, the nonpartisan Congressional Budget Office (CBO) estimated that the federal deficit had fallen to $250 billion.

It is interesting to see how the more politicized Office of Management and Budget (OMB) handled the news in comparison to the CBO. The latter agency simply announced its estimates in a regularly issued Monthly Budget Review posting. The OMB website ballyhooed the estimated drop in the deficit in a headline that read: "Meeting the Priorities of the Nation While Achieving Spending Restraint." What followed included several "gee whiz" charts that were highly misleading, particularly on the president's alleged successes in reducing the deficit. Even the headline has been misleading. Spending increased 7.5 percent in Fiscal 2006, according to CBO, which is somewhat higher than the past several years as a percentage of GDP. The OMB acted as the poster agency for responsive competence—basically spinning the budget numbers to support the president rather than reporting the numbers and projections the nonpolitical way CBO did.

As discussed in detail in Chapter 8, the deception is reflected in the administration's claim of exceptionally strong growth in revenues from its tax cuts when available historical data make clear that tax revenue growth in the Bush administration had actually been quite weak as compared to earlier postwar data.

The top OMB political appointees, working no doubt with the White House, did the spinning to pass off the failed tax policies as successes. In contrast, the OMB career civil servants, who usually were well-trained analysts following the concepts of neutral competence when preparing the detailed Budget of the United States Government, provided honest numbers. Alas, this information had been buried in a publication that matched the size of big city telephone books. Only specialists, not citizens, were likely to find and recognize the significance of the accurate data.

RESPONSIVE COMPETENCE

In recent decades, we have witnessed an important shift in the basis of public administration in the United States. Many readers probably had the urge to skip this section as soon as their eyes lit on the words *public administration*. But this change is a major piece of the puzzle that explains why bad ideas persist. In this case, the bad ideas are put forth not by Keynes' "defunct economist," but by several influential political scientists. Their new theory of public administration is a primary contributor to the increasing dysfunctional nature of the executive branch. If the executive branch is broken, as we think it is, the emergence of responsive competence as the basis of governance is a major reason.

The New Theory of Responsive Competence

In embracing the Reagan administration's approach to policy making, political scientist Terry Moe wrote, "[The president] is a politician fundamentally concerned with the dynamics of political leadership and thus with political support and opposition, political strategy, and political payoffs . . . what he seeks is 'responsive competence,' not neutral competence."[13] If presidents go wrong,

---

[13]Terry M. Moe, "The Politicized Presidency," in John E. Chubb and Paul E. Peterson (eds.), *The New Direction in American Politics*. Washington DC: Brookings, 1985, p. 239.

the argument goes, they will be punished in subsequent elections. But elections are blunt instruments in which voters are asked to judge candidates across a wide range of issues, and in any case the notion that all hinges on electoral accountability delays feedback for up to four years.

Sometimes we get to observe a direct clash between responsive competence and the older notion of neutral competence. In a telling anecdote in his 2005 study of the Reagan presidency, Richard Reeves highlights what he termed "the incessant struggles" between Secretary of State George Shultz, one of the outstanding cabinet members of the postwar years, and Secretary of Defense Cap Weinberger. Weinberger had begun a lecture on defense needs when Shultz rose and started walking out. But first he turned toward Weinberger and said: "You know it's pointless to try to do business with you, Cap. You don't analyze things. You take stances. If you are going to govern, you have to listen and analyze to figure out the right thing to do. But you don't ever do that, Cap."[14]

As we noted previously, President Reagan had a better record in policy affairs than GW Bush. One major reason is because of Shultz and James Baker, who served as chief of staff and Treasury secretary, had the president's ear, and were willing to give him the facts (and he listened). So in the case of the two presidents, who both had little knowledge or capacity to analyze policy issues, one simply was more receptive to good advice than the other.

---

[14]Richard Reeves, *President Reagan.* New York: Simon and Schuster, 2005, p. 295.

Some Misunderstandings

A key assumption commonly made about neutral and responsive competence is that budget and policy analysts practicing neutral competence are not willing to be responsive to the other needs of their political superiors.[15] Do the careerists have different political goals than the president so that their particular skills and professional orientation may ill serve the chief executive? Using career staff at such a high level in the presidential decision process raised the question of political control. Were political leaders controlling the government bureaucrats, as the theory of democratic accountability would require, or were the careerists so strong that they effectively controlled the political appointees.

The early history of the Bureau of the Budget indicates that in fact civil service personnel can be quite sensitive to the political needs of the chief executive, their boss. Historically, careerists, who engaged in neutral competence as budget and policy analysts, understood that their political superiors had the authority to tell them to carry out a variety of tasks that could have a political component. For example, policy analysts might be asked to spell out the political implications of program alternatives set out in their analyses. Or budget and policy analysts might work on requests about proposed programs by members of Congress and their staffs from either political party.

In one of the few data-based studies of these theories, political scientists Matthew Dickinson and Andrew Rudalevige went back to what is considered the "golden age" at the Bureau of the

---

[15]For a comparative analysis of these concepts, see Joel Aberbach and Bert A. Rockman, "Civil Servants and Policymakers: Neutral or Responsive Competence," *Governance*, 7, 1994, pp. 461–478.

Budget (1945–1950 in Harry Truman's presidency) to examine archival and historical material. They found that the budget analysts were responsive to Truman's political needs.

Recognizing this responsiveness, however, did not mean that these Truman-era analysts were unrestricted in what they would do. When career policy analysts engaged in developing and analyzing relevant policy information for the internal decision-making process, they were committed to providing sound information and nonpartisan analyses. They refused to spin their analyses to tell their political superiors what they wanted to hear. Nor were their superiors likely to ask them to do so.

This made sense in terms of comparative advantages, because policy specialists generally did not have the same set of tools as political advisors. Putting policy issues in partisan terms fit the comparative advantage of the latter. The view that presidents and cabinet secretaries should want unvarnished numbers and analyses to check whether the political advice they received is sound had broad support until the Reagan administration that fostered the concept of responsive competence. About that time, a number of political scientists argued that neutral competence had become obsolete in the modern presidency. Dickinson and Rudalevige in their 2004 essay summed up this view: "Presidents see virtues in an OMB organized to facilitate 'top-down' control over policy making and implementation. The change to a political agenda dominated by budget deficits, deregulation, and government retrenchment beginning in the early 1970s altered presidents' administrative needs in ways that made the traditional qualities of neutral competence—continuity, professionalism, and the substantive analysis of policy—less important to presidents than the ability to exercise 'top down' budgeting and regulatory control."[16]

This view misses the key point that reasoned presidential decisions about the appropriate size of the budget deficit including the levels of expenditures and tax revenues, the dimensions of the regulatory control process, and cutting federal programs require as much sound data and analyses as any other critical policy decisions. It can be debated whether top-down budgeting, with the president imposing spending priorities (contrasted with bottom-up budgeting, in which agencies make their case to the president) is a sound strategy. But this approach only works when budget choices are framed with a sound empirical base.

Advocates of responsive competence trace the focus on control to Richard Nixon's 1970 reorganization that established the Office of Management and Budgeting. The reorganization created a new group of political appointees—the Program Associate Directors, or PADs. They took over OMB's examining divisions that had previously been headed by careerists who had responsibility for the executive budget. The change strengthening the president's political advisors relative to the OMB civil servants by shielding the generalist White House staff from challenges from the careerists with their greater policy expertise, experience, and institutional memory. This meant that the

---

[16]Matthew J. Dickinson and Andrew Rudalevige, "Presidents, Responsiveness, and Competence: Revisiting the Golden Age at the Bureau of the Budget, *Political Science Quarterly*, 119, 2004, pp 633–654.

top White House staff had unchallenged control of the EOP.[17] Replacing BoB with OMB was not a mere reshuffling of boxes on the organization chart, but rather it was a pronounced shift away from the direct role for neutrally-competent career staff in the decision-making process.

After Dickinson and Rudalevige delved into the golden age of BoB and found the budget analysts were responsive to President Truman's political needs, they observed: "The BoB exhibited 'responsive competence' long before political scientists coined the term. . . . However, its responsiveness embodied many of the virtues extolled by advocates of neutral competence: continuity, input from career employees, and a desire to protect the presidency as an institution."[18]

These virtues of neutral competence, however, can become barriers to responsive competence because they may be used to block questionable information and analyses that fit the ideological predilections of the president. Those Truman era civil servant advisors were responsive, but to a totally different kind of president and offered him different skills, experience, and professional codes from today's political advisors. The latter and BoB staffs are, as the British might remark, "like chalk and cheese." Earlier presidents demanded sound information, whereas George W. Bush demands ideological confirmation and information that will allow him to argue his case. Responsive competence so often produces failed policies because it enables bad ideas to flourish rather than winnowing them through sound information and analysis.

---

[17]John Hart, *The Presidential Branch*. New York: Pergamon, 1987, pp. 193–197.
[18]Dickinson and Rudalevige, "Presidents," p. 635.

Responsive Competence and the Executive Function

Responsive competence is not just some arcane theory of public administration confined to the academy. Its tenets have been used to damage the institutions of governance. During much of George W. Bush's presidency, this political bad idea has undermined our constitutional balance. At issue are the responsibilities of the three branches of government as set forth in the 1789 Constitution. Those who crafted the new Constitution thought of government as filling three separate functions, and they assigned each function to a different branch of government. Article I assigned Congress the legislative function. The Founders considered the legislative branch as first among equals, and Article I is much longer and more specific than the articles for the other two functions. Article III vested the judiciary power in the Supreme Court and lesser courts established by Congress. Article II, Section 1 addressed the presidency: "The executive power shall be vested in a President of the United States of America."

In *The New Oxford American Dictionary*, the term *executive* is defined as "having the power to put plans, actions, or laws into effect, [that is,] managing an organization or political administration."[19] The president is the nation's chief executive officer with the constitutional mandate to implement and manage the laws enacted by Congress. Part of this responsibility may be delegated to executive branch subordinates, such as the cabinet secretaries, but no delegation can relieve a president of this constitutional

---

[19]Elizabeth J. Jewell and Frank Abate (eds.), *The New Oxford American Dictionary*. New York: Oxford University Press, 2001, p. 594.

charge. Delegation is a means of carrying out his responsibilities, not a way to be absolved of them.

The notion of responsive competence is in substantial conflict with Article II, Section 1. Political scientist Terry Moe set out his image of a president: "He is not interested in efficiency or effectiveness or coordination, per se, and does not give preeminence to the 'neutral competence' these properties may seem to require."[20] But efficiency, effectiveness, and coordination are central elements of the executive function. The Constitution requires that the president act as the nation's chief executive, responsible for executing—that is, implementing and managing—the policies Congress has enacted to achieve the specified policy objectives at a reasonable cost.

The president is, of course, no simple agent of Congress—the Constitution assigned dual functions to him. The president was to participate in the policy-making process, but he was also assigned the duty of executing the laws. Proponents of the concept of responsive competence cast presidents as the nation's political leaders, while relieving them of their responsibilities as chief executives. Moe made his president "a politician fundamentally concerned with political leadership."[21] The Constitution requires more. Good political advice is essential, but it is insufficient for governing the nation. As Bert Rockman astutely observed more than 20 years ago, "A president whose only skill is policy analysis is not apt to be a president for very long. On the other hand, statecraft without policy analysis is government by pure instinct."[22]

---

[20]Moe, "The Politicized Presidency," p. 239.
[21]Ibid.
[22]Bert A. Rockman, *The Leadership Question*. New York: Praeger, 1984, p. 14.

The political advisors who provide responsive competence differ markedly from the civil servant budget and policy analysts of an earlier era who crunched and analyzed the policy numbers without political spin. But it is reasonable to ask whether those responding to the president's political concerns have policy skills in their kit of tools too. After all, presidential decisions are still made about policies, even if the main concern is with gaining political support and political payoffs. Bad policies hardly qualify as good political strategy. And sound information should help in crafting a winning one.

Presidents have had no shortage of political advisors in the past. Exactly what are the special skills of this new brand of advisors that the earlier ones apparently lacked? Without an answer, responsiveness may simply come down to presidents being told that which they want to hear about proposed or ongoing policies—even if the desired answers do not mesh with reality. "Speaking truth to power," the motto of the champions of neutral competence, has fallen out of favor in the current polarized environment. In such a setting where political information, however questionable, trumps hard facts, the president may be fulfilling his responsibility as the chief political leader, but he is failing to carry out his duty as chief executive. Neither of the authors is a lawyer, but it seems to us that the concept of responsive competence not only is a bad political idea but a constitutionally questionable one.

SELLING BAD POLICIES

The term *propagandize* is chiefly derogatory. Spreading propaganda describes an effort to deceive that can include a number of means such as misinformation, biased commentary or interpretation, and the hiding of evidence. Repetition has long been a successful propaganda tactic in that making a misleading or false statement over and over seemingly raises the likelihood it will gain credibility. This became a favored means of the Bush administration.

We noted earlier that tax revenues "surged" in 2006, but the administration's real per-capita revenue growth in the five plus years following the peak of the previous business cycle had been slower than the average revenue growth in the previous postwar business cycles. However, the failure of the growth of tax revenues in the earlier Bush years to increase nearly as fast as all the other presidencies since World War II did not deter President Bush from taking the fact of the one year surge out of context to tout his tax policies.

In a speech in New Hampshire following the introduction of his 2007 budget proposals, President Bush turned once again to the discredited supply-side arguments, claiming that "Tax relief not only has helped our economy, but it's helped the federal budget. In 2004, tax revenues to the Treasury grew about 5.5 percent. That's kind of counter-intuitive, isn't it? At least it is for some in Washington. You cut taxes and the tax revenues increase."[23]

The New Hampshire speech was not a one-time comment, but rather part of campaign to gain acceptance for continuing the tax reductions that are set to expire at the end of 2010. On

[23]The White House, "President Discusses 2007 Budget and Deficit Reduction in New Hampshire." The White House, February 8, 2006.

January 16, the president said, "You hear a lot of debate about the deficit, and it's an important debate, don't get me wrong. But in my judgment the best way to solve the deficit is to grow the economy, not run up your taxes. There is a myth in Washington, they say all we've got to do is just raise the taxes a little bit and we'll solve the deficit. No, that's not how it works. . . . The best way, it seems like to me, to solve the deficit is to keep pro-growth tax policies in place and do something on the spending side."

Yet the president's own FY2007 budget proposals show revenue *decreases* associated with each of the tax cuts he proposes.[24] The president either doesn't believe his own analysts, or he ignores them, or he is just misleading the public. It is true that tax cuts can yield increased economic growth, and hence may replace some of the revenues lost, but never all of it as the miracle supply-side thesis claims. So tax cuts can never "solve the deficit." This level of presidential disinformation on tax cuts has been unprecedented.

At the same time as Bush's New Hampshire speech, Vice President Dick Cheney was hawking a more sophisticated version of the supply-side myth. In a speech to the Conservative Political Action Committee in February 2006, he told the faithful that a new administration proposal for a Treasury Department tax analysis division would support the old, surely discredited supply-side arguments. "The president's tax policies have strengthened the economy, as we knew they would," Cheney told the conference, according to a text posted on the White House's website:

---

[24]The Center for American Progress points out that "Page 324 (Table S-7) of his budget gives cost estimates for extending various tax changes . . . all of which show revenue decreases."

"And despite forecasts to the contrary, the tax cuts have translated into higher federal revenues. . . . The evidence is in, it's time for everyone to admit that sensible tax cuts increase economic growth and add to the federal treasury."[25]

At issue is the so-called "dynamic analysis," the idea that tax cuts initially decrease revenues and raise deficits, but over time they so change the incentives that businesses face that they produce enough new tax receipts to eliminate the deficit. The use of dynamic analysis in budget estimates is termed *dynamic scoring*. Some economists, including former CBO director Douglas Holtz-Eakin, are in favor of such methods, but they worry that the effects are too indirect to estimate and in any case may well not lead to the results desired by the tax-cut crowd. Indeed, a dynamic analysis done by CBO fails to eliminate the long-run deficit estimates.

Dynamic analysis is not going to change the facts on the ground: structural budget deficits will not end with a magic bullet, whether that bullet be supply-side economics, starving the beast, or dynamic scoring. The president's own former chief economic advisor, Gregory Mankiw, said on November 4, 2003 to the National Press Club: "Let me be perfectly clear here. Tax reductions are generally not self-financing . . . the behavioral responses to changes in tax rates are just not high enough to yield that result."[26]

---

[25]Neil Henderson, "Cheney Says New Unit Will Prove Tax Cuts Boost Revenue," *Washington Post*, February 11, 2006, p. A11.
[26]Remarks by Dr. N. Gregory Mankiw, Chairman Council of Economic Advisers at the National Bureau of Economic Research Tax Policy and the Economy Meeting, National Press Club, November 4, 2003.

RESPONSIVE COMPETENCE AND SELLING POLICIES

Demands made by a president pursuing political ends and willing to use propaganda to justify them have resulted in the corruption of the policy analytic process. Responsive competence is undermining good government.

A major example of this corruption stems from the attempts of Republicans to justify their tax cuts. This matters more than might be the case otherwise because the tax cuts of the first term of the Bush presidency were made temporary. They were subject to special budget rules that forbade legislation from being adopted for more than ten years; otherwise, the legislation would have been held hostage by a Democratic filibuster in the Senate. To avoid this possibility, the Bush administration urged Congress in 2001, 2002, and 2003 to "sunset" the provisions—that is, end them on a particular date—and Congress did so. Most of the tax reductions were scheduled to expire on December 31, 2010. Sunset provisions had been used before in the tax code, but the Bush administration used them much more aggressively.

In 2003, the Office of Management and Budget changed from ten-year to five-year projections. This avoided the problem of projecting the much higher revenue losses from the tax cuts in the later years. But the OMB director at the time, Mitch Daniels, claimed that the change had been made for the practical reasons of prediction difficulties over the longer time period. But now we can see the predictions made by the professional budget analysts at OMB, because for Fiscal 2007, the required five-year projections included an estimate of what would happen if these cuts are extended through September 2011.

This analysis enables anyone, including the president of the United States and the director of the Office of Management and Budget—who signed the budget—to see exactly what the budget they signed says about the revenue effects of tax cuts. The budget shows that these cuts will cost approximately $119 billion in 2011 alone, and it estimates a total of $1.35 trillion of revenue losses for the period 2007–2016. Nor is this the only study to conclude that tax cuts cut revenue. A recent Treasury Department study concluded that economic growth stimulated by tax cuts would pay at most 10 percent of their costs.[27]

We have reproduced Table S-7 from the U.S. Budget for the disbelievers. That table estimates the cost to "Make Permanent Certain Tax Cuts Enacted in 2001 and 2003." The estimates are for extending the president's tax cuts beyond their expiration point, December 31, 2010. The relevant data are for 2011. Notice that every number in the column for 2011 is negative, reflecting the budget's assumption that revenue losses will occur even years after the tax cuts were implemented.

OMB director Joshua Bolten, who is now White House chief of staff, in his press briefing on the Fiscal 2007 budget, said, "Many of the administration's critics will argue that we should let the tax relief expire. A tax increase is the wrong prescription, not only for the nation's economic health, but also for the government's fiscal health."[28] Yet his own budget denies this statement. The

---

[27]Cited in "Tax Cuts: Myths and Realities," Washington DC: Center for Budget and Policy Priorities, October 12, 2006.

[28]Joshua B. Bolten, "Press Briefing on the President's Fiscal Year 2007 Budget by Office of Management and Budget Director." The White House, February 6, 2006.

TABLE S-7
Budget of the United States Government, FY2007

							TOTAL	
	2006	2007	2008	2009	2010	2011	2007–2011	2007–2016
Make Permanent Certain Tax Cuts Enacted in 2001 and 2003 (assumed in the baseline):								
Dividends tax rate structure	288	571	−1,329	−14,161	−537	−6,545	−22,001	−128,050
Capital gains tax rate structure	—	—	—	14,183	−5,519	−6,606	−26,308	−74,931
Expensing for small business	—	—	−4,679	−6,498	−4,872	−3,853	−19,902	−32,620
Marginal individual income tax rate reductions	—	—	—	—	—	−66,918	−66,918	−605,961
Child tax credit	—	—	—	—	—	−5,452	−5,452	−116,691
Marriage penalty relief	—	—	—	—	—	−4,968	−4,968	−37,678
Education incentives	—	—	—	—	3	−1,098	1,095	−10,960
Repeal of estate and generation-skipping transfer taxes, and modification of gift taxes	−205	−1,102	−1,728	−2,181	−2,676	−23,758	−31,445	−339,022
Modifications of pension plans	—	—	—	—	—	−346	−346	−2,858
Other incentives for families and children	—	—	—	—	5	−170	−165	−4,362
Total make permanent certain tax cuts enacted in 2001 and 2003	83	−531	−7,736.	−37,023	−13,596	−119,714	−178,600	−1,353,033

government's fiscal balance sheet deteriorates with tax cuts, and the president's own budget, prepared by Bolten, estimates how this will occur. That the chief budget officer of the United States government would tell such an obvious untruth may be deeply disturbing, but at least we can go and get the honest numbers from the budget prepared by professional analysts.

In the past, vigorous congressional oversight would have counteracted such blatant propaganda. But Republican members of Congress, even those heading oversight committees until January 2007, squawked for tax cuts without paying attention to their actual effects on the revenue stream. Congressman Jim Nussle of Iowa, chairman of the House Budget Committee, is a case in point. In 2004 he claimed that "Tax cuts don't need to be paid for [with spending offsets]—they pay for themselves."[29] Bush rewarded this claptrap by appointing Nussle as director of OMB in June of 2007.

Senate Budget Committee chair Judd Gregg chimed in on March 9, 2006: "You have to pay for these tax cuts twice under these pay-go rules if you apply them, because these tax cuts pay for themselves."[30] It is striking testimony to the continuing power over time of bad economic ideas when roughly 25 years after it became clear in the early years of the Reagan presidency that the miracle version of supply-side economics was a bad idea of world-class dimensions, the chairs of both budget committees during the latter years of the Republican controlled Congress either still believed in that miracle thesis or else thought it still salable to the public.

---

[29]Bud Newman and Nancy Ognanaovich, "Nussle's New Budget Enforcement Bill to Apply to Spending, Not to Tax Cuts," *Bureau of National Affairs Daily Tax Report*, March 17, 2004.
[30]Quoted in "Tax Cuts: Myths and Realities."

THE MEDICARE PRESCRIPTION
DRUG BILL

It is certainly not true that agencies have stopped performing good analysis; indeed, in many cases, they are required to do so by law. The issue is the extent to which sound analysis is ignored or dismissed at the top levels of decision making, and the subsequent lack of truthfulness when characterizing the policy in public. In important instances, Bush administrators have gone beyond their internal distaste for hard facts to suppress or distort critical policy-making information.

Efforts by the Bush presidency to pass legislation that provided prescription drug insurance under Medicare offer a pristine example of such behavior. In selling the proposed policy, the administration gave Congress a low-ball number on cost and blocked it from receiving a more accurate one that indicated costs nearly 40 percent higher than the White House claimed. Bush administration efforts made reasoned governance much more difficult for Congress.

To pass the Medicare prescription drug bill, the administration promised reluctant Republican conservatives that the legislation would cost less than $400 billion over ten years. However, Medicare's chief actuary Richard Foster, a career civil servant, had earlier projected the cost at around $550 billion. After Congress requested the actuary's numbers, Thomas Scully, then the head of the Medicare and Medicaid agency, threatened to fire Foster if he met Congress' request for his cost projection. Less than two months after enactment, the administration admitted that Medicare would cost $530 billion for ten years.

Scully's action was ruled illegal "in a formal legal opinion" by the General Accountability Office because he had threatened a federal government employee to keep him "from communicating with Congress."[31] After pointing out that similar laws concerning such intimidation go back to 1912, Robert Pear of the *New York Times* wrote: "Scully's threats to the actuary were 'a prime example of what Congress was attempting to prohibit' when it outlawed 'gag rules.'"[32] Lawmakers in both parties indicated they would not have voted for the bill if the higher cost projection had been known.

The suppression of information from the legislative branch helped pass one of the most costly pieces of legislation in history, with the creation of more than $8 trillion in unfunded liabilities over 75 years. This huge increase came at a time of big deficits as well as the impending arrival of the first wave of the Social Security- and Medicare-eligible baby-boomer generation. In the polarization-poisoned environment of the early 21st century, it is not clear that the Republican-controlled Congress would have voted down the budget-busting legislation. But it did not have the chance. Keeping federal employees from communicating information requested by Congress that it needs to exercise informed policy choices can undermine the checks and balances that are central to the constitutional process.

---

[31]Robert Pear, "Inquiry Proposes Penalties fot Hiding Medicare Data," *New York Times*, September 8, 2004, p. A16. The material in this and the next paragraph, including Pear's quoted statement, is drawn from this article.
[32]Pear, "Inquiry," p. A16.

THE CONSEQUENCES OF
RESPONSIVE COMPETENCE

Though the intransigence of the Bush administration in refusing to engage fact-based analysis is extreme, such behavior is not unusual. Indeed, resistance to information that conflicts with one's prior assumptions about how the world works is just part of human nature. Unfortunately refusal to deal with honest analysis will undermine the incentives for its supply; political leaders will get less of it if they corrupt the conditions of its supply. On the other hand, it is also undeniable that bureaucrats themselves can develop world views that are at odds with what policy makers desire, and these views have the potential to influence sound analysis. So the issue is complex, made more so by the entire question of how factual analysis jibes with democratic accountability.

The aggressiveness in the executive branch in demanding conformity to its policies, and the failure of Congress to provide offsetting investigatory and informational critiques, has led to the institutional crisis that we document in this chapter. Institutions change when they incorporate new rules for structuring the behaviors of actors in the institutions. This happened during the Bush administration. The rules prescribing fact-based analysis and tension between the branches were replaced by a struggle for partisan advantage and demands for an all-powerful chief executive, at least in the very amorphous arena of "foreign affairs." The process has politicized the information and the policy analytic capacities of the executive branch and led to tensions between the branches only when they are controlled by different parties. New theories from the academic world have justified the sacrifice of factual analyses on the alter of responsiveness. Top-down administrative control, which enabled the president to dominate the diverse and at times recalcitrant bureaucracy, became instituted to such an extent that it corroded the information-processing capacity of government.

In six years of Republican control of both the executive and legislative branches, neutral competence became a victim of virulent ideology imposed by the White House. When divided government returned in January 2007, the Democratically-controlled Congress moved quickly to reestablish legislative branch independence from the president. Such a change, however, does not restore full health to the institutions of governance. After all, the executive and legislative branches had suffered much deterioration prior to the presidency of George W. Bush when there was divided government with a Democrat as president and a Republican-controlled House. The excessive polarization that marked Clinton's last six years and the Bush presidency has not disappeared. Nor did the November 2006 mid-term election results eliminate extreme White House control of the executive branch, its propaganda operation, or its disdain for honest numbers and analyses. The federal government institutional problems have not been solved and are unlikely to be without recognizing the damage and working to repair it.

CHAPTER 11

Why Do Bad Ideas Persist?

There should no longer be any doubt that all versions of supply-side economics and starve-the-beast used during the presidencies of Ronald Reagan and George W. Bush are bad economic ideas that can bring long-run fiscal insolvency to the federal government and a lower standard of living to the bulk of the population. The ends-means thinking that is supposed to characterize policy debates has been replaced with a deep love for the means. Tax cuts are no longer a method to achieve a better society, but a matter of deep core belief.[1] The financial and fiscal problems almost certainly will worsen unless the continuing damage from the tax and budget policies is stopped. This is difficult to do as long as the ideas remain unchallengeable myths.

We have shown in earlier chapters just how bad these ideas are, and how they were once kept in check by a firm commitment to factual analysis and the construction of an institutional framework that made it costly to ignore the evidence. This is most clearly exemplified by the pay-go budget rules in force for

---

[1] Paul Sabbatier and Hank Jenkins Smith show how difficult change is when it affects the core belief structure of a political coalition. See in Paul Sabbatier (ed.), *Theories of the Policy Process*. Boulder, CO. Westview Press, 1999.

most of the 1990s, but the same kind of thinking can be found in the compromise to put Social Security on a sound basis in 1983.

Today, all this has collapsed. In the executive branch, the demand for sound analysis exemplified by Paul O'Neill's 1988 "guiding light" principle has been replaced with the demand for confirmatory evidence. In area after area during the Bush administration, from foreign policy to Medicare reform to tax policies, that demand has been met. Sound analysis may still be performed by career civil servants, but it is too often supplanted by "reality-creators"—political appointees whose job is not to provide factual analysis, but who are supposed to provide a "different reality" that favors preferred policies. In Congress, sound analysis by the independent agencies is still nonpartisan, but it has been blithely ignored in the polarized warfare spawned by "Harsh Reaganism." During the first six years of the Bush presidency, congressional oversight hearings were minimal, and when they occurred they sometimes took the form of partisan screeds rather than the careful analytical studies of the past.[2]

In the ideal world concocted by many political scientists, none of this matters very much, because elections and the free exchange of ideas will magically produce the proper results. In the theories of electoral accountability, it is more important to allow leaders to govern and to be held accountable at a later election than to subject them to neutral competence. Yet politics and three elections—two presidential, one mid-term—failed to

---

[2] A case in point is the House Permanent Select Committee on Intelligence Report, *Iran as a Strategic Threat*, so inflammatory that the UN nuclear inspectors for Iran sent the committee chairman, Peter Hoekstra, a letter objecting to the report as "dishonest." Dafna Linzer, "UN Inspectors Dispute Iran Report by House Panel," *Washington Post*, September 14, 2006, p. A17.

correct years of disastrous policies in both foreign and domestic affairs. Even though Democrats won both houses of Congress in the 2006 mid-term elections, the underlying fundamentals are unchanged. The damage to the public policy process is wide and deep, and even the minority Republicans have means to protect the policies they have enacted. Certainly Republican leaders continue to adhere to their strategy of tax cuts first with little concern for the fiscal results. Nor is it guaranteed by any stretch of the imagination that Democrats will cast off the Republican style of governing.

Finally, Democrats will face strong pressures that act against fiscal responsibility. Though Democrats have pledged to restore the pay-go rules that dictated budget limitations until they were breached in 2001 and disavowed by Republicans in 2002, they fear a repeat of the Republican spending/tax cutting binge that was partially enabled by the large late Clinton-era surpluses. Moreover, they have their own tax cutting agenda—dealing with the Alternative Minimum Tax (AMT), which was passed in 1970 to ensure that millionaires paid at least some taxes. The tax has never been adjusted for inflation, and as a consequence is being paid today by millions of middle-income Americans. It will affect millions more in the future, but it is very expensive (in terms of revenue losses) to fix. And Democrats have an ambitious domestic agenda that could cost billions.

As Republicans faced increasingly obvious problems in the 2006 campaign, the party strategy degenerated into a "Democrats will raise your taxes" mantra. It was a parody of the old conservative Republican ideals of limited government, in which small, effective government and balanced budgets led to more liberty and lower taxes. Today's Republican ideology stresses tax cuts first and foremost, and cares much less about the size of government or its intrusiveness. The bad ideas that underpin these policies, especially tax policies, continue to drive modern Republican ideology, and the defeated congressional Republicans show no signs of giving up what has become their major principle.

The extreme difficulty that the American political system has had in shedding the obviously bad economic ideas that underpin today's fiscal policies ought to make us all pause when we glibly repeat Justice Oliver Wendell Holmes's dictate equating democracy with the marketplace of ideas. Holmes' may have been right in the abstract that "the ultimate good is better reached by free trade in ideas," but that does not mean that in practice the "ultimate good" will actually be reached before catastrophic results engulf the nation.[3] In practice, the appeal of bad ideas can be strong indeed.

To change the course of public finance we will need to understand the reasons for the continued vitality of these ideas. This chapter examines several reasons for the persistence of the tax cut delusion in American politics today. We line up all of the usual suspects: self-centered voters, partisan advantage, interest groups and lobbyists, and right wing activists. Though in each case some blame is due, in the end these ideas seem to have taken on a life of their own, even when benefiting a few (usually rich) people while harming far more. They *are* myths, but dangerous ones, because they enable politicians to pursue dangerous fiscal policies all the

---

[3]In his dissenting opinion in *Abrams v. United States* (1919).

while undermining government's ability to process information and conduct sound analysis.

REASON I: THE PUBLIC IS "MYOPIC," WANTING LOWER TAXES AND MORE GOVERNMENT PROGRAMS

One possible reason for the persistence of bad economic ideas involves public attitudes on both taxes and spending. Are irresponsible fiscal policies just a result of demands by self-centered voters?

Taxes

It is certainly true that people don't like taxes. Or more accurately, they don't like *their* taxes. Figure 11.1 shows Gallup Poll data on the percentage of people who think their taxes are too high versus those who think they are too low. Only twice in the series has the number of "about right" respondents exceeded the "too high" percentage. One of those times came during the GW Bush presidency. Of course, you might be quite happy to see someone else taxed; Senator Russell Long, Democrat of Louisiana from 1948 to 1986, was fond of commenting: "Don't tax you; don't tax me; tax that guy behind that tree."

On the other hand, public opinion polls suggest that citizens are sensitive to increases and decreases in the tax rate, but the relationship is complex. For example, whether people feel their taxes are too high depends on their particular tax obligations as well as what programs government is pursuing at the time. Although

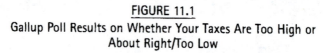

FIGURE 11.1

Gallup Poll Results on Whether Your Taxes Are Too High or
About Right/Too Low

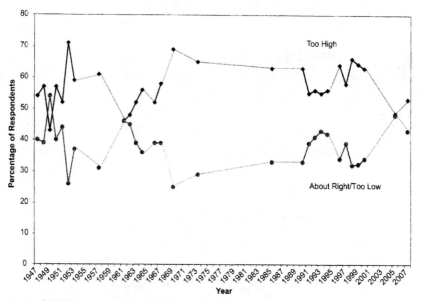

Source: Pollingreport.com. About Right and Too Low categories combined; very few
respondents answered "Too Low."

Gallup didn't ask the same question on taxes every year, gross trends can be detected:

- Between 1952 and 1966, the top tax rate was cut from 92 to 70 percent. The percentage of the public feeling taxes were too high declined from 71 to 52 percent.
- When President Johnson's 1969 Income Tax Surcharge raised the top rate to pay for the Vietnam War, 69 percent of the public responded by saying that taxes were too high. That percentage declined when the 1968 rates were restored.

- By 1991, when the Reagan tax revolution had dropped the top tax rate to 31 percent, a bare majority of 55 percent said their taxes were too high.
- But after several tax increases during the late Reagan, GHW Bush, and Clinton administrations, many more Americans felt the tax pain.
- The GW Bush tax cuts resulted in a dramatic fall in the proportion of Americans saying their taxes were too high, and a bare majority said their taxes were about right in 2005 and 2006, for the first time since 1949.

These trends are rough, but they suggest a general responsiveness on the part of public opinion to tax policies. In general, people don't like to pay taxes, but this kind of abstract question probably leads to a considerable overestimation of potential tax resistance, at least on the part of the general public. More interesting is the changes we detect when taxes are raised or lowered; more people say their taxes are too high when tax rates are raised, and fewer respond this way when rates are reduced.

Finally, in an NBC News-*Wall Street Journal* poll taken in June 2006, 35 percent said that the Democratic Party would do better "in dealing with taxes," with 29 percent choosing the Republicans and 18 percent saying that the parties were about the same.[4] A year later, the same question showed a similar Democratic advantage. If the poll is to be believed, the Republican Party does not necessarily enjoy an advantage on the tax issue, even though tax reductions have been the party's signature policy for years. Can the same be said of spending priorities?

---

[4]PollingReport.com (http://www.pollingreport.com/).

Spending

Mostly people like government programs and think they are worthy. Tom Smith of the National Opinion Research Center at the University of Chicago wrote as President Bush was being inaugurated for his first term:

> *Despite a dislike of taxes, more people have always favored increases in spending than cuts. In 2000, as in most years since the 1970s, people have backed more spending in three-quarters of the areas and less spending in only the bottom quarter. . . . In 2000, the largest negative score (-50.2 for Foreign Aid) was bested by seven positive scores (Health +68.9, Education +66.4, Social Security +55.2, Halting Crime +55.1, the Environment +54.4, Dealing with Drug Addiction +53.3, and Assistance to the Poor +52.8).*[5]

Evidence both from the United States and other democracies suggests that nothing in the past several years has reversed this trend.[6] In the United States, during the period 1976 through 2002, only spending for welfare consistently received suggested cuts by the public; education, health, the environment, and big cities all were rated as deserving increases every year. Defense was variable, receiving recommended cuts in some years and increases in others.[7]

Some recent polls indicate that people like tax cuts, but they like government programs more. In January 2006, the Pew Foundation asked simply whether people approved of the tax cuts made by President Bush and Congress in the past several years.

---

[5]Tom Smith, "Trends in National Spending Priorities," Chicago: the National Opinion Research Center, University of Chicago, 2001.
[6]Stuart Soroka and Christopher Wlezien, "Opinion Representation and Policy Feedback," *Canadian Journal of Political Science*, 37: 2004, pp. 531-559.
[7]Soroka and Wlezien, "Degrees of Democracy," Madrid: Juan March Institute, 2004.

Fifty percent approved, with 38 percent expressing disapproval. Around the same time (October 2005) in an NBC/*Wall Street Journal* poll, people were asked whether the cuts were worth it (because they strengthened the economy and let people keep more of their earnings) or not (because they resulted in program cuts and increased deficits). The researchers reported that 53 percent said the cuts were not worth the cost, only 38 percent said they were. Interestingly, in similar NBC/WSJ polls more voters chose the Democrats as the party best able to reduce the deficit beginning in 2005 and continuing to the present. Republicans were losing their reputation as fiscal conservatives.

Can people make trade-offs? Or do they want lower taxes and more government benefits regardless? Cynics would claim that they do want it all. *Washington Post* columnist Sebastian Mallaby gives voters a hefty dose of the blame, writing that "Voters like big government. . . . Voters' appetite for public goods always existed as a check on small-government crusaders; but, it has grown more powerful lately."[8]

Has it? In 2003, the Pew Research Center asked a sample of Americans how best to pay for increased defense and homeland security costs. Forty percent would have delayed the Bush tax cuts; 21 percent would cut domestic spending; and only 23 percent would increase the deficit, the route taken by the administration.

Moreover, people will reallocate priorities set by political leaders in a reasonably consistent fashion. The Program on International Policy Attitudes (PIPA) at the University of Maryland occasionally sets forth the broad outlines of the federal budget before a sample of the public and asks them if they thought items should be rearranged.

---

[8]Sebastian Mallaby, "Big Government Again," *Washington Post*, June 14, 2004, p. A17.

They usually do. In the poll taken in March 2005, respondents were given the opportunity to rearrange federal budget categories. Sixty-one percent redirected money toward reducing the deficit, 65 percent reduced defense expenses (by an average amount of 31%), 63 percent suggested eliminating tax cuts for the well-off, and education and job training received healthy increases from most respondents.[9] Comparisons with earlier PIPA polls indicate that Mallaby is also wrong when he claims that the public urge for more government has increased recently.

Additionally, when people are surveyed, they show concern about the government's budget priorities. In past surveys, PIPA researchers have given respondents 17 budgetary areas (excluding the mandatory entitlement programs that cannot be adjusted year-to-year) and have included the possibility of deficit reduction. Respondents were given percentages the president's budget allocated to each category and were asked to adjust them according to their own priorities. In the 2005 exercise, the biggest target for increased allocation of resources was deficit reduction. Respondents indicated a willingness to forgo tax cuts or even raise taxes when deficits are a problem. Generally the public seems able to steer a centrist course, cutting programs (especially defense) and raising taxes to protect positive government.

The PIPA, Pew, and many other polls that ask about direct tradeoffs indicate that federal fiscal problems are not the fault of an inconsistent public. Most people resist a large deficit and can reallocate (at least hypothetically) accordingly. In general, the public seems to have a sense of priorities and is able to relate them to what

---

[9]The poll was conducted by Knowledge Networks, a firm that maintains a panel of respondents who interact via the Internet.

government is doing. This does not mean that people generally have a very good idea of what government costs; other polls show that they make sizable mistakes, for example, they consistently overestimate what foreign aid costs the country. But the results of the PIPA polls are not nearly as dismal concerning the public's ability to make reasonable budget choices as the cynics claim. Indeed, compared to their political leaders, the American public seems to be a paragon of virtue on the finance issue. And voters are taking notice that the Republicans are no longer the party of fiscal responsibility.

Political scientists studying public opinion have put forward the thesis that the public reacts to policies initiated by political leaders in a manner something like a thermostat. When policy makers increase program spending, they often commit more than the public wants. People at some point respond by telling pollsters that they disapprove of the priorities set by the politicians.[10] This pattern is particularly in evidence in defense. One might say that the public corrects the errors that politicians make, bringing them back into line with broad public preferences (indeed, much like what are technically called "error correction" models).[11]

Of course this pattern can stay out of correspondence for a very long time, because political leaders don't respond simply to general public preferences. Even if the public has a distaste for the GOP's fiscal policies, they may not enforce this distaste in elections, and even if they do, great damage may be done to the financial stability of the country before an election occurs. Two political scientists even claim that we'd be better off if they

[10]Christopher Wlezien, "The Public as Thermostat," *American Journal of Political Science* 39: 1995, pp. 981-1000; Soroka and Wlezien, "Opinion Representation."
[11]Robert S. Erikson, Michael MacKuen, and James A. Stimson, *The Macro Polity*. New York: Cambridge University Press, 2002.

responded to these preferences more intensely—something pundits might dismiss as "pandering."[12]

Finally, it is perhaps unrealistic to blame the public for falling for the fiscal illusion that tax cuts offer something for nothing when politicians and some renowned economists are in the business of encouraging it. We've shown that tax cuts encourage the public to demand more programs. After President Bush justified tax cuts through poor economic theories and ran up huge budget deficits instead, can we blame the public for the sorry state of affairs that has transpired?

Moreover, the abrupt transition from fiscal responsibility to fiscal mismanagement in 2001 shows that voters cannot be blamed unless their attitudes toward funding government programs all of a sudden shifted at exactly that point. There is no evidence that this happened, and it defies common sense even to suggest it.

The out-of-balance fiscal system that the United States currently runs cannot be blamed on short-sighted voters. They can at best respond to what political leaders are doing. While it is true that they can be fooled, there is scant evidence that American voters are insufficiently supportive of sound public finances when they have the choice. If they are confused by propaganda blame leaders, not followers.

REASON 2: OUTSIDE FORCES

Although the Republican-controlled government could hardly deny the increases in yearly budget outlays and deficits, they could place the blame on forces beyond their control. That is, the problem

---

[12]Lawrence R. Jacobs and Robert Y. Shapiro, *Politicians Don't Pander*. Chicago: University of Chicago Press, 2000.

is not with the administration's ideas, but with external forces. Most emphasis has been placed on surprises, two of which have been repeatedly cited—(1) "the war on terrorism" with vast new expenditures arising from the invasion and occupation of Iraq and Afghanistan, and the build-up in homeland security measures and (2) the unexpected outlays in response to the devastation of New Orleans and other areas, and the ensuing disruption of the lives of their inhabitants after Hurricane Katrina.

The administration argued that the staggering costs stemming from necessity, not any lack of budgetary control on its part, simply overwhelmed the gains from the tax cuts. However, administration officials go on to say, over time the incentives from the lower taxes will generate much stronger economic growth and a subsequent material rise in tax receipts. This explanation does not fit the facts. As we saw in Chapter 6, expenditures burgeoned in many budget categories. The budget discipline of the three presidents preceding George W. Bush vanished in his presidency. Moreover, most defense analysts, as well as most Americans, saw the Afghan war as an utter necessity, but its costs paled in comparison to the Iraq invasion and occupation, a classic war of choice. It is not honest to choose a course of action and claim necessity when the costs ballooned beyond the wildest estimates of the administration.

A report from the Center for Budget and Policy Priorities (CBPP) based on Congressional Budget Office data indicates that the tax cuts bear the primary responsibility for the yearly budget deficits. As discussed in Chapter 8, 33 percent of the increased costs in the period 2001–2006 are attributable to defense and homeland security; and 51 percent to the tax cuts; without the tax cuts, the 2007 budget would show nearly a $100 billion surplus.[13] But this is an apportionment exercise and does not represent long-run economic equilibrium. Gregory Mankiw, formerly chair of GW Bush's Council of Economic Advisers, performed a simulation of the economic long-run results of tax cuts. He estimates that around 25 percent of the lost revenue will be replaced.[14] As Shakespeare's Cassius tells his co-conspirator, "The fault, dear Brutus, is not in our stars, but in ourselves."

REASON 3: THE LOBBYISTS DID IT

By the middle of the opening decade of the 21st century, the number of registered lobbyists in Washington had ballooned to almost 35,000.[15] Lobbyists have been the favored whipping boy for anti-corruption advocates for as long as legislators have been approached by supplicants. Many lobbyists are paid to garner benefits from government spending or reduce the tax liability for the firms that employ them without regard to the potential cost to taxpayers. The United States today has many public interest groups, and these groups may also want programs, increased regulation of business, and the like that also drive up the costs of government. So lobbying can be seen as part of the problem.

But it is wrong to over-allocate blame for our current out-of-kilter national balance sheet to the lobbyists. There is evidence

[13]Center for Budget and Policy Priorities, "Tax Cuts: Myths and Realities," October 12, 2006, p. 1-2; James Horney, "Smaller Deficit Estimate No surprise: New OMB Estimates Do Not Support Claims About Tax Cuts," Center on Budget and Policy Priorities, Revised July 13, 2007, p. 7.
[14]N. Gregory Mankiw, "Mankiw versus Bush." Greg Mankiw's Blog, January 6, 2007. The full results suggest a large effect for capital gains tax reductions—50%—but a much smaller result for income tax on labor—only 17%. See Mankiw and Weinzierl, "Dynamic Scoring: A Back of the Envelope Guide," Harvard University, December 2005.
[15]Birnbaum, Jeffrey. "The Road to Riches is Through K Street," *Washington Post*, June 22,2005, A01.

that expansions in government programs and increases in the number of lobbyists are intertwined. Moreover, it is highly likely that expanding government precedes increases in the number of lobbyists. We might call it the "honeypot theory of lobbying."[16] When government grows robustly, you can be sure that businesses and interest groups will be attracted to the spoils as contracts are let; consulting firms are hired; and money is to be made in the appropriations, taxation, and conference committees of Congress by getting favorable provisions inserted into bills.

"The lobbyists did it" is much like "outside forces" as an excuse for excessive spending. That is, there is some truth in the explanation—and it has the ring of plausibility—but does not hold up upon inspection. Lobbyists are the specialists hired by corporations and interest groups to help them increase their revenues from government programs or decrease their tax burden. Overall, lobbyists may increase the amount of appropriations or tax write-offs over what that amount would have been without their effort (surely, those paying for their services must think so). Even so, members of Congress make the spending decisions that become the law only after Congress votes favorably on them and the president does not veto the legislation. In the first six years of the GW Bush presidency, with a tightly controlled Republican Congress following the lead of an active president, the claim that the lobbyists were the culprits in excessive government spending is even less credible than in previous presidencies.

In any case, it is unlikely that the abrupt spending burst after 2000 was caused by lobbyists, although once the government—

[16]Thanks to Valerie Hunt for this.

under Republican control—undertook vigorous new spending, plenty of new lobbyists were attracted to the spoils. Moreover, Republicans, being distrustful of professional government bureaucrats, have been far more likely than Democrats to contract out government functions. As a consequence, contracts for government services became much more lucrative to private businesses than when Democrats were in control of government. The relationships between lobbyists and Republicans have been cemented both by the explosive growth in government and by heavier reliance on contracting. The question now is whether Democrats, as they hold control of Congress, will back away from contracting out that has reached such a high level.

The current fiscal insanity has been aided and abetted by certain interest groups pushing tax cuts without regard to their fiscal effects. As is the case with public opinion, however, it is hard to blame lobbyists for the state of financial affairs we now face.

REASON 4: THE IDEAS OF THE "INTELLECTUAL RIGHT" HAVE DOMINATED MODERN DISCOURSE ON GOVERNMENT FISCAL POLICY

This book began with Lord Keynes' reference to the importance of ideas, even bad ones. And the notion that tax cuts can be pursued without detrimental fiscal consequences is a very bad idea. But an entire industry of think tanks, professional economists, politicians, and citizen intellectuals has developed around these ideas.[17] The

---

[17]Andrew Rich, *Think Tanks, Public Policy, and the Politics of Expertise.* Cambridge: Cambridge University Press, 2004.

frenetic outpouring of arguments, justifications, and supposed analyses in support of tax cuts swirled around in the editorial pages of the *Wall Street Journal* and became the received word of the pro-tax cut true believers.

Our University of Washington colleague Mark Smith has shown that the activities of the intellectual right since the 1960s shifted from stressing the illegitimacy of government's redistributive policies to an emphasis on the role of free market policies in ensuring economic success.[18] During this period, the Republicans were rewarded with public approval of the party's economic program—the "party of business" came to be seen as much more capable than the Democrats to run the nation's economic policies from the 1980s to 2004. An emphasis on free market policies as both individually empowering and economically successful helped to bring about the mass public's more positive view toward the Republicans. This public approval has now disappeared, however, and polls now show substantial pluralities think that the Democrats would do a better job in handling the economy (41% to 26% in a July 2007 NBC/WSJ poll).

The successful selling of free market ideas was aided immeasurably by the advocacy of President Ronald Reagan. His straightforward, simple, and sunny view of private markets mobilized a generation and more of Republican activists. Further, his adoption of Laffer-style supply-side economics gave his view an undeserved legitimacy that helped make it resistant to attacks, even those based on sound policy analysis. It also undermined the ability of

---

[18]Mark Smith, *It's the Economy, Stupid: Rhetorical Innovation in the Conservative Ascendancy.* Princeton: Princeton University Press, 2007.

fiscal conservatives, such as Reagan's budget director David Stockman, to materially reduce the size of government in conjunction with tax cuts. Nevertheless, the system was kept in some balance by sound budget rules, resulting in the slower growth of government throughout the entire period—until the system was rejected by President Bush in 2001.

Once Bush's popularity and power slipped, the intellectual right developed severe splits over the course of Big Government Republicanism. Particularly bothersome to some fiscal conservatives has been the adoption of so many large programs that they believe either smack of socialism, such as the prescription drug benefit for the elderly, or are market-distorting subsidies, such as the massive farm bill of 2002. In his recent book, former Reagan Treasury official and avowed conservative Republican Bruce Bartlett documents the conservative intellectual discontent with Bush and Big Government Conservatism.[19] Bartlett's criticisms go not just to the big new programs, but also to the aggressive foreign policy and even the tax cuts, which he views as inefficient and not policy focused, "simple giveaways, little different, economically, from government spending."[20]

Bartlett's diagnosis of the causes of the difficulties is just as searing. He saw, as do we, a complete collapse of sound policy analysis and motivation based on partisanship rather than conservative ideas. The free-market ideas had been corrupted toward helping major corporations instead of promoting market solutions. In particular, he pointed to a lack of appreciation of the difference between tax policies based on economic analysis and those designed to shovel benefits onto big business. Echoing the respect

---

[19]Bruce Bartlett, *Impostor*. New York: Doubleday, 2006.
[20]Bartlett, p. 156.

of Reagan Secretary of State George Shultz for his career bureaucrats, Bartlett decries the reliance on private think tanks rather than Treasury experts for analyses of tax laws. The Republican shift to protecting business from the free market resembles a classic political machine, in which favors are provided to supporters in return for political support in the form of campaign finances and other benefits.

REASON 5: A POLITICAL MACHINE

In the winter of 2005–2006, a major scandal broke in Washington, connecting lobbyist Jack Abramoff with several important Republican congressional leaders. Scandal was the bitter fruit of House Majority Leader Tom Delay's "K-Street Project," which demanded Republican loyalties from lobbyists and in return brought them directly into the legislative process. As Mann and Ornstein observed: "The desire to hold power and advance their ideological vision required a formidable political machine, one greased by money, staffed by loyalists in lobbying shops, and unabashedly adept at smash-mouth politics. . . . The anything-goes atmosphere also led to the rise and fall of Jack Abramoff."[21]

Many of today's corruption scandals involve high-paid lobbyists in intimate (financial) relationships with powerful politicians. But as the K-Street Project indicates, politicians exploit lobbyists as much as the other way around. Garnering re-election funds or other favors can be motive enough to engage in what more than one lobbyist has quietly decried as "not bribery, but extortion."

---

[21]Thomas Mann and Norman J. Ornstein, *The Broken Brach*. New York: Oxford University Press, 2006, p. 214.

There isn't any doubt that congressional Republicans, collaborating with the White House, constructed a political machine. It has somewhat different characteristics than the classic machine form that dominated many American city governments during the era of industrialization and immigration from the end of the Civil War through the 1920s. These earlier political machines served their purposes, integrating waves of immigrants into public life and boosting employment in an economy that discriminated against them. Politicians provided public sector jobs and particular favors for voters. They also provided lucrative traction (rail) and utility contracts for private firms in the great era of city-building. In return the citizenry provided votes for the machine politicians.

Municipal machines essentially delivered two benefits: patronage jobs and contracts to business. Although fundamentally nonideological, they did need big city governments to operate at their peaks. The bigger the government, the more the jobs and contracts, and the more important the political leader. Machines withered as the demands of the Progressive movement—a reform-oriented movement consisting of civic reformers, newspaper editors, protestant church leaders, and concerned businessmen—escalated. The strategy of the municipal reformers was to deny the machines their lifeblood; patronage jobs were moved onto civil service lines, and rigorous rules for the letting of contracts were established. Machine politicians worked to avoid the inevitable by such tactics as keeping permanent civil service job positions on "temporary" status and filled by patronage employees. In Chicago in the mid-1970s, one analysis showed that some 15,000 of the 45,000 regular civil service positions were filled by some form of temporary employee, but this varied from very few in the police department to almost half in the traditional patronage haunts of the departments of buildings and streets and sanitation.[22] By the 1980s, even the vaunted Chicago machine was about done as court decisions and crusading newspapers pushed machine politicians into a complete civil service system.

During the first six years of the GW Bush presidency, congressional Republicans, and in particular former House Republican Majority Leader Tom DeLay, constructed a new form of political machine in American life, and this is no trivial accomplishment. The K Street Project may be broadly viewed as providing private firms access to the halls of power, but only on the terms of the Republican Party. That is, lobbyists were allowed inside but only if they swore absolute fealty to the party and its program. This meant hiring only Republicans and donating only to Republican candidates.

DeLay was known in the House as "The Hammer" but his touch was pure velvet green. He used his political action committee, Americans for a Republican Majority (ARMPAC), to fund the campaigns of fellow Republicans; ARMPAC raised more than $13 million from 1999 to 2005, much of it from businesses and individuals interested in government benefits.[23] Rather than hammer his colleagues, like a classic political boss he enticed them.

DeLay had no access to the most important pillar of the classic municipal machine, patronage jobs. As a substitute, he and the Republican Party relied on ideas—ideology for the raw patronage of years past. The pay-off for fellow representatives and party activists included a heady dose of committed ideological fervor in support of the free market and the private sector. DeLay of course did not construct this, but he did harness it to his machine.

[22]Bryan D. Jones, *Governing Buildings, Building Government*. University AL: University of Alabama Press, 1985.
[23]R. Jeffrey Smith and Derek Willis, "Amid Audit, DeLay PAC Revises SEC Filing," *Washington Post*, May 20, 2005, p. A06.

Like the machines of yore, however, this type of machine works best when government is big and growing. Congress increasingly used legislative mark-up committee sessions and conference committees, where Republicans refused to allow participation by Democrats, to write special provisions for particular companies or industries in law. Similarly, there was a virtual explosion of "earmarking" in appropriations bills. This is the practice of designating specific funds for projects that are designed by individual Congress members rather than leaving the process up to administering agencies. Congress under the Republicans used earmarking to designate particular projects for particular districts, as in the past, but it went further to write provisions in a manner that favors specific companies for government contracts. The result was a large number of abuses, including special provisions for campaign contributors. When they assumed control of Congress in 2007, Democrats continued the practice of earmarking, but they made the process more transparent by requiring notice of the sponsor of the earmark. Whether this will result in a decline in the number of them remains to be seen.

The weighting down of systematic legislative appropriations procedures in Congress by earmarking and special provisions results in an ad hoc legislative process by which the politically connected gain considerable influence. Moreover, a second trend has added to the resources of the Republican Machine. This involves demands by proponents of the "New Public Management" for increased flexibility on the part of public sector managers to write contracts unburdened by the strictures of the Progressive Era. These rules, so the argument goes, add to red tape and inefficiency in government, and, anyway, these rules were designed in an era when corruption and favoritism was more of a problem than today. But no-bid contracts by the Pentagon in Iraq and by FEMA in the wake of Hurricane Katrina look both inefficient and subject to political influence. Contract monitoring is so sporadic and so inefficient (partly because Republicans in Congress and at the White House failed to provide enough auditors to do the job) that scandals involving misspending and corruption have begun to emerge.

The Republican political machine in the early 21st century took corruption in the federal government to a level not seen in the postwar era, and probably not in the past 100 years. In the period from 9/11 2001 to January 2007, some major legislation had two targets: the group designated to receive the benefits and the supposed implementers of the program. The Medicare Reform Act of 2004 was designed to provide prescription drug benefits for the elderly, but it did so in an indirect and inefficient manner to keep prices high for drug manufacturers and to involve private insurance companies in the process of delivery. The act could have allowed government to negotiate prices with drug companies and provide the benefits directly, a strategy that would have yielded at much less cost than the indirect arrangement favored by the administration. But that would have defeated the second purpose of the act: to shower benefits on drug manufacturers and insurance companies. The strategy adds substantial costs to the program.

There is no doubt that the Republicans created a modern political machine in Washington, characterized by more or less direct exchange of favors for election finance and personal gain. That alone is not enough to explain the problematic tax behavior, however. Indeed, the machine explanation may account for spending such as earmarking and the structure of the Medicare reform legislation, and it can even explain specific changes in the tax code, but it cannot account for the broad-swath tax reductions pursued with such vigor by the Republicans. It is only a piece of the puzzle.

REASON 6: POLITICAL POLARIZATION AND THE POLITICS OF CLASS

Chapter 9 showed how the analytic capacity of the federal government began to decline under the increasingly ideological stance taken by political officials in the Reagan presidency. That polarization has also affected Congress. In Congress, parties today are polarized around class in a manner not seen since the 1920s, prior to the Great Depression and Roosevelt Coalition. A unified Republican Party does political battle with a unified Democratic one.[24]

Polarization and Governing

Debilitating political polarization is an increasingly critical factor in the decline of the American political system. After the 1994 midterm election in which the Republicans won control of Congress for the first time since the Eisenhower administration, the harsher version of Reaganism dominated the political environment. In particular, the failed Republican effort to impeach Bill Clinton poisoned the atmosphere as congressional Republicans and Democrats engaged in

---

[24]Nolan McCarty, Keith T. Poole, and Howard Rosenthal, *Polarized America*. Cambridge, MA: MIT Press, 2006.

all-out warfare. Comity between the political parties that had been central to bipartisan cooperation in Congress evaporated.

The extreme polarization between the Democrats and Republicans helped the Bush administration push a number of its policies through Congress as the Republican leadership in both houses displayed extraordinary party unity while many Democrats broke ranks to support elements of the Bush agenda, particularly on terrorism and taxes. Strong party control in Congress, in political science lore, was supposed to help Congress challenge the demands of an increasingly powerful presidency, but it didn't work out that way. This strong control over Congress by its Republican leaders had the surprising result of helping President Bush make both the Republican House and Senate extensions of the White House.

Partisan animosity provided Bush's trump card for pressing party leaders not to let the hated Democrats defeat one of his major programs. As Jacob Hacker and Paul Pierson indicate in their 2005 book *Off Center*, it is "unequal polarization" between the Democrats and the Republicans that is critical: "Over the same era in which the conservatives have risen to power, they have moved further and further from the political center. Nothing remotely close to the massive shift has happened on the other side of the spectrum, much less among the great bulk of ordinary voters."[25] Unequal polarization had been developing since Reagan, but it took George W. Bush's election that brought Republican control of the presidency and Congress to let it out of the bottle in full force. Indeed, the 2006 electoral successes for the Democrats can in part be attributed to their centrist strategy—capturing three seats in the strongly

[25]Jacob S. Hacker and Paul Pierson, *Off Center*. New Haven: Yale University Press, 2005, pp. 5–6.

Republican state of Indiana is testimony to the power of a centrist party contesting a right-wing one. Whether this centrism can be maintained in the face of strong demands from party activists, who are more liberal than the typical American voter, remains to be seen. If Democratic control of Congress pulls the Democrats leftward but leaves the Republicans still far to the right, polarization will worsen.

Causes of Polarization

What accounts for this increasing partisan rancor? Three political scientists—Nolan McCarty, Keith T. Poole, and Howard Rosenthal—investigated in depth the relationship between polarization and income inequality in their 2006 book *Polarized America*. Using a polarization index based on roll call votes in Congress, they found a strong positive correlation between that variable and inequality for much of the 20th century, noting that "causality can run both ways."[26] Their analysis of Congress shows two periods of high polarization, one beginning in the early 1880s and ending in the early 1900s, and the other commencing in the late 1970s that is still continuing.[27] The first corresponds to the Gilded Age; the second, to the rise of Reaganism. In both eras, the richest of the rich gained at the expense of most other citizens.

They point out that income inequality rose with a couple of "slight interruptions" after 1969, but "polarization bounce[d] at a low level until 1977" and then shot up. Polarization occurred after the rise in inequality. They argued: "We stress an important aspect of the timing of the reversal in inequality and polarization.

---

[26]McCarty, Poole, and Rosenthal, *Polarized America*.
[27]Ibid., p. 9.

In some circles, both of these phenomena are viewed as a consequence of Ronald Reagan's victory in the 1980 elections. Both reversals, however, clearly predate Reagan and Reaganomics. Reagan conservatism was a product sitting on a shelf in the political supermarket. In 1980, customers switched brands, arguably the result of a preference shift marked by rising inequality and party polarization."[28]

Political shifts seldom can be so precisely pinpointed but rather have pressures, including new ideas that build up over time. Reagan came to national attention with his speech in support of Barry Goldwater at the 1964 Republican National Convention, served as governor of California from 1967 to 1974, and tried for the Republican presidential nomination in 1976. From 1964 on, he was espousing Reaganism on the national stage. Conservative philosophers, economists, and think tanks were also making related arguments.

These ideas became prominent in the marketplace of ideas and gained increasing strength after the 1973 and 1979 OPEC-induced gasoline price hikes, the latter bringing double-digit inflation. Polarization did not begin when Ronald Reagan took office. However, Reaganism as preached by the new president, including tax cuts at the top, was critical to why the link between income inequality and polarization emerged at the start of the Reagan presidency and will run at least to the end of George W. Bush's presidency.[29] The big unanswered question is what forces might materially alter the income inequality–polarization linkage.

---

[28]Ibid., p. 7.
[29]Walter Williams, *Reaganism and the Death of Representative Democracy*. Washington DC: Georgetown University Press, 2003, pp. 51–62.

The authors of *Polarized America* argued that only the increasing disparity of income in the United States can account for the harsh partisan climate we endure today. This may be surprising to some, because Republicans do well in the so-called Red States, which are on average poorer than the Blue State Democratic Party bastion. Cultural issues are indeed a part of the story, and these issues that have been championed by the Republicans to extend the party base down further into the middle and working classes than in the past. But within each state, the class basis of politics holds; that is, in both the Red States and the Blue States, the richest are more Republican than are less well-off citizens.

Inequality in America

Income inequality in America has increased swiftly in the years since 1979, according to a new study from the Internal Revenue Service. Then, the 80 percent of Americans who were the least well-off held a 50 percent share of the total income earned in the United States, but in 2002 they held only about a 40 percent share. This difference was basically shifted to the very wealthy: in 1979, the top 1 percent held a 9.58 percent income share, but by 2002 they held fully a 21.55 percent share. The data further indicate the creation of a hyper-rich class in the United States: the top one-tenth of one percent of the population in 2002 held 7.10 percent of the total income generated in the United States.[30] Some analysts maintain that out-of-control pay for corporate executives is the major reason for the change.[31]

---

[30]Michael Strudler, Tom Petska and Ryan Petska, *Further Analysis of the Distribution of Income and Taxes, 1979–2002*. Washington DC: Internal Revenue Service, 2005.
[31]Robert Boyer, "Contemporary Corporate Governance in Light of CEO's Remuneration Boom," Paper presented at the Opening Up Governance Conference, Manchester University, March 16–7, 2006.

In the rising polarization of today, the top of the income distribution is taking an increasing share of national income. That would be mitigated to some extent if the members of the broad American middle class were experiencing significant growth in real income, but they are not. Whatever the rationale given for continued tax cuts for the wealthiest, the result is that the big gains go to the upper 5 percent and increasingly to those at the 1 percent level or even higher. In the 2003 tax cut for capital gains and taxable dividends, more than 50 percent of the total benefits went to the top 0.1 percent.

This wealth disparity has great consequences for politics and is corrosive of the conduct of democracy, as Kevin Phillips has shown.[32] The decline of the political center associated with political polarization, especially among the politically active, has made it far more difficult to construct centrist governing coalitions. As parties have increasingly become polarized around class, money has poured into politics, with heavy support from conservatives and business groups. As the traditional Democratic Party allies—particularly labor unions—have weakened, conservative groups have proliferated. Moreover, organizing on the left has been far more successful on issues of environmentalism and even cultural issues than on class issues. These issues resonate with middle income voters in a way that class-based issues have not. The failure of the president's Social Security privatization initiative suggests the limits to this and the possibility of class politics, but with the low turnout of working class Americans and the incarceration of such a high proportion of poor and minorities, this is better explained as a "revolt of the elderly."

---

[32]Kevin Phillips, *Wealth and Democracy*. New York: Broadway Books, 2002.

In *Polarized America*, McCarty and his co-authors showed a strong positive correlation between income inequality and polarization and indicated that the Gilded Age and the modern period that began in the late 1970s show the highest polarization. Both periods experienced increasing inequality and the rise of a super rich class. Although Americans have long claimed that this country has no classes and have spurned the notion of class warfare, federal tax policies act now as a mechanism for the upward redistribution of income from most of the population to the richest citizens of the nation and particularly the very richest percent top 1 percent.

The upward redistribution and the consequent rising inequality have no justification in public finance, and very, very little in economics. This is the inescapable conclusion of our analysis of the great tax cut delusion. The tax cuts, properly unmasked, are redistributive from poor to rich. Juxtaposing the fact that the 2001 and 2003 tax cuts disproportionately enriched the top 1 percent of families at the expense of a deleterious impact on nation's fiscal strength and the middle classes' financial security, it well may be that the redistribution upward to the super rich had been the well-hidden rationale of these tax cuts. All else may have been a propaganda smoke screen to mask the real reason for the tax cut.

REASON 7: PROPAGANDA

No administration in the postwar era has been nearly so adroit in selling and defending its policies through deception, secrecy, and misinformation as has Bush's. And no success has been any greater than in creating the myth that tax cuts are good and increases are bad. It is most unlikely that without the propaganda operation, all the muscle and the money used by its Republican political machine could have sold the bad economic ideas on fiscal policy and kept the tax cuts on the books in the face of massive deficits. The power of myth and ideology, sustained by modern propaganda techniques are critical suspects in the resilience of bad ideas in modern American politics. Once party activists and intellectuals on the right adopted the "tax cut first" strategies, the public supported the Republican Party in part because of these ideas, and Democrats offered enough support to pass the program (both the 1981 and in 2001 tax reductions were passed when Democrats controlled at least one house of Congress).

AN EVALUATION

To understand the resonance of the great American tax cut delusion today, we have to see it as a mix of political cover and political myth. Calling the bad economic ideas myths should not imply that these ideas are not powerful or that they can be easily discarded. Just the opposite. The problem is that people tend to adopt the ideas so strongly that they become ends in themselves—people in effect "identify with the means" rather than using means to achieve an end.[33] Because people identify emotionally as well as cognitively with ideas, it can be very hard to dissuade them with mere facts. When these ideas are passed along as truths, complete with stories which, on first telling, seem to support the idea, we have something very powerful.

---

[33]This term was developed by Herbert Simon, who claimed that was one of the two most important ideas that he developed in his long and robust scholarly career. See Simon, *Models of My Life.* Cambridge, MA: MIT Press, 1996.

The tax cut delusion has been propagated by a powerful set of political actors—the president, the vice president, numerous Republican politicians, right wing think tanks, and editorial opinion-makers. When political myths justify a governing regime, their retention and vitality will be supported by all sorts of people who see short-term advantage—or, perhaps more correctly, allow their good judgment to be colored by short-term advantage, themselves falling prey to identification with the means.

The puzzle posed in the first pages of this book as to why the bad ideas justifying tax cuts without associated spending limits have been so powerful in modern American politics has a clear answer: They are convenient devices for governing—or what passes for it in Washington today. There is the seductive promise of gain without paying the piper. But if the ideas are as wrong as we think they are, the consequences are frightening. The wrong-headed economic theories of supply side and starve-the-beast are but postponing a reckoning that is likely to be catastrophic.

The real tragedy of the modern Republican political machine is that it has undermined half a century of a grand political bargain between the parties. After the Second World War, both political parties accepted that policy would not rely on bad numbers. Rather, policy making was moving toward an increasing consensus that we would debate vigorously what government should do, but we would leave it to professionals to estimate the effects of proposed policies (including tax cuts). Institutional arrangements, such as the pay-go budget rules, were put in place to enforce the bargain. The Reagan administration undermined the tax side of the equation, generating large deficits, but kept the budget side rules. George W. Bush went the next step by making more excessive tax cuts and abandoning the budget rules and left Americans with increasingly poor government.

Perhaps the greatest irony of all for small government Republicans is that they forgot (or never learned) something very important. A long period of fiscal restraint will lower the size of government relative to the economy. From 1983 through 2000, the size of the federal government relative to the economy fell from 23.5 percent to 18.4 percent, only to rise to 20.8 percent by 2006. The GHW Bush and Clinton presidencies raised taxes and eliminated the deficit, which burgeoned as taxes were cut by GW Bush. Fiscal conservatives got both big government and red ink. Staying the course would have been far better fiscal policy for American conservatives than the reckless strategy of the Bush administration that conservatives supported.

TENSIONS IN THE MACHINE

The Republican machine needs big government, but traditional Republican ideology stresses small government. And this conflict may be the Achilles heel of the Republican coalition. It is increasingly difficult to paper over the problem that the big money demands clash fundamentally with the basic limited government ideology of the Republican Party.

The role of the intellectual right has been important in the ascendancy of the Republican Party. But serious tensions emerged as conservative ideas were harnessed to the tasks of building a governing coalition. The intellectual right came to believe that the ideas of limited government and fiscal responsibility once championed by the Republican Party never led to the opportunity to govern. In this line of thinking, only with Big-Government Republicanism—perhaps we should call it K Street Republicanism—can Republicans govern. When tax cuts are accompanied by increases in public programs, three separate constituencies are served: taxpayers, and in particular wealthy taxpayers; consumers of government programs, such as the elderly; and businesses contracting with government. Going back to the notions of limited government in a serious way would undermine these relationships.

The current conception of governance that has driven the Bush administration ripped the fabric of both intellectual conservativism and the Republican Party. Libertarian think tanks such as the Cato Institute have rejected the starve-the-beast philosophy, instead returning to the fiscal responsibility doctrines of the past. The fiscal conservative wing of the Republican Party was barely contained by the House leadership on such bills as the Medicare Reform Act of 2004. It is now in open revolt. Former House Speaker Newt Gingrich, whose vision for the Republican Party centered on limited government and grassroots party development, has been highly critical of K-Street Republicanism and its associated corruption. Yet all wings of the party have failed to recognize the extent to which their tax cut first philosophy has eroded the very foundations of conservatism in America, dragging the Republican Party with it.

CHAPTER 12

Escaping the Dead Weight of Bad Ideas

Bad ideas persist in politics because they have value to some people, hence motivating them to political action. But ideas in politics, just like stocks or housing, can experience "booms" of overinvestment. It accounts for the persistence of bad ideas far beyond their utility, even in democratic societies where they can be tested and criticized. People come to identify emotionally with a policy idea—supposedly a means to an end—and value it in itself rather than appreciating it for its utility in achieving goals.

Like an overpriced Internet stock during the late 1990s boom, the tax cut program of Republicans has become disconnected from its underlying value. In the right situation, tax cuts can make great sense. In the wrong situation, tax cuts can harm the solvency of the nation and damage the economy. That is the case today. So the essential issue for us here is how to bring the idea of tax reductions back down to a sensible valuation.

THREE INTERTWINED THEMES

We have developed three major themes in this book. First, the tax-cut justifying theories of miracle supply-side economics and starve-the-beast-are wrong. They are political ideology masquerading as economic ideas. In contrast, academic supply-side economics did have theoretical validity, but the 2001 and 2003 tax cuts based on this version did not yield the expected results. These two tax reductions were policy failures yet were still justified by the bad ideas that Republicans have propagated. As was the case for all tax cuts since 1981, they were funded by borrowing, harmed the public balance sheet, and facilitated growth in the size of government. Any economic growth seems more a function of the stimulative effects of deficit financing than any supply-side effects.

In market booms, the language used to sell stocks becomes increasingly frenetic and detached from sensible assessments of underlying value. Similarly, the language used by Republicans to sell tax cuts has become increasingly dissociated from a hard-headed, honest numbers assessment of their utility in achieving goals. Supply-side arguments have morphed into advertisements promising the curative powers of tax cuts on investment income for all sorts of economic ills, much like an old-time patent medicine that claims the power to rid the buyer of a host of aliments. Starve-the-beast is rolled out for the party faithful, even as government grows faster than at any time since the Great Society. "Giving the people back their money" survived long past the rapid spending of the federal surplus during the first year of the GW Bush administration.

Instead, in a public sector version of a Ponzi scheme, Bush was offering cash borrowed from future generations. Because of the integrity of the analysts at OMB, the books are not "cooked."

However, the Chief Executive Officer (President George W. Bush) and the Chief Financial Officer (former OMB director Joshua Bolton) have been untruthful about the tax cuts proclaiming their wonders despite the hard facts to the contrary produced by the OMB analysts. With former House Budget Committee Chair Jim Nussle assuming the position of Director of OMB, the nation will be treated to more of the same.

Our second theme is that it is entirely possible to establish a fiscal regime in government that properly evaluates the costs and benefits of government spending. Indeed, for much of the postwar era, the Federal government did so, and used the analyses as a guide for controlling budget outlays. Though that regime experienced extreme stress during the early Reagan years, it was robust enough to endure until 2001. However, maintaining a viable system demands a basic understanding among political antagonists that a responsible fiscal policy is, in the long run, in the best interests of the nation. And it requires a set of institutional rules and procedures that reinforces the consensus, making sure that violations of the understanding are sanctioned.

Third, the system for producing honest numbers—and making and executing policy according to them—has been badly eroded by attacks from those in power, beginning in the Reagan presidency and reaching a frenetic pace in the current Bush administration. We have unfortunately elected political leaders who did not really want honest numbers and too often ignored them, suppressed them, or made it clear that they should not be produced in the first place. The guiding principle of honest numbers has been replaced with the demand for bad evidence.

This system has its justifications in academic political science and public administration through the twin notions of electoral accountability and responsive competence. In this thinking, if citizens don't like the policies pursued by government, they can simply replace them in elections. We've shown that the damage from bad policies can cumulate and become extensive before the rascals are thrown out. Moreover, elections are blunt instruments; if Iraq had been going better, it is probable that the Republicans would still control Congress.

Fiscal Damage

Motivated by Lord Keynes' great insight about the importance of good and bad economic and political ideas, we have examined the impact of bad ideas on the nation's major fiscal policies in recent years. The available evidence is unambiguous in showing the extent to which misguided concepts led to bad policies and governance practices that caused damage to the nation.

Since 1981 (except for 1995–2000), bad economic ideas and incompetent implementation have produced big yearly budget deficits; a rising debt/GDP ratio, and sharply rising federal interest payments. Since 2001 these policies have yielded massive new unfunded liabilities and a tax structure that disproportionately benefits the richest citizens. Bad political ideas aided and abetted extreme political polarization in Washington, a presidential decision-making approach that lacked sound information and analyses, and a weakened system of governance. Bad policy information and analyses increased the deleterious impact of bad economic and political ideas.

Reaganism has proved to be a poor guide for fiscal policy. Supply-side economics, starving the beast, and the conviction that the market will always outperform the government blighted policy-making in recent years. Since 1981 anti-governmentism and free market fundamentalism have combined to bring fiscal policies that have contributed both to rising national debt and overall slow economic growth during the last 25 years. In the early 21st century, Reaganism, as employed by the Bush administration, has brought serious threats to the long-run solvency of the federal government and the living standard of the broad American middle class.

The "Demographic Tsunami"

How serious are these threats? The U.S. comptroller general David Walker is "committed to touring the nation through the 2008 elections, talking about the 'demographic tsunami' that will come when the baby-boom generation begins retiring."[1] Walker is leading the Fiscal Wake-up Tour that seeks to force the presidential candidates in the 2008 election to treat the fiscal consequences of the growing debt seriously in the campaign.

In his article in the *Seattle Times* on October 26, 2006, Associated Press reporter Matt Crenson wrote: "The basic message of the Fiscal Wake-Up Tour is this: If the U.S. government conducts business as usual over the next few decades, a national debt that is already $8.5 trillion could reach $46 trillion or more, adjusted for inflation. . . . According to some projections, just the interest payments would be as much as all the taxes the government collects today. And every year that nothing is done about it, Walker says, the problem grows by $2 to $3 trillion."[2]

Walker is right to stress that the nation is marching toward fiscal calamity unless there are major policy changes. But there is a huge hurdle in selling the problem to the public because the rise in the national debt is projected to increase relatively slowly in the next few years before growth takes off. A General Accountancy

---

[1]Matt Crenson, "Economists Warn of Nation's Coming Fiscal Meltdown," *Seattle Times*, October 29, 2006, p. 2. Crenson's first sentence was previously quoted in Chapter 8.
[2]Ibid.

Office simulation shows that spending as a percentage of GDP will grow from 20 to 22 percent from 2006 through 2015, but it will reach nearly 50 percent by 2045 with net interest at 20 percent of GDP.[3]

The warning of doom years in the future does not exactly strike terror in the hearts of the broad middle class struggling just to stay afloat. As *New York Times* columnist Bob Herbert observed: "A two-tiered economy has been put in place in which a small percentage of the population does extremely well while a majority of working Americans are in an all-but-permanent state of anxiety about job security, pensions, the economic impact of globalization, the cost of health care, college tuition, and so on."[4] Convincing people that quick action must be taken on a $46 trillion national debt 40 or 50 years down the road is a very hard sell. The financial problem, in contrast, has become more urgent because the administration's fiscal policies have increased the immediate strains on the middle class as it tries to maintain its standard of living and have raised moral concerns about the rise in the maldistribution of income.

New York Times reporter Louis Uchitelle reported on a conversation he had in November 2006 with Mark M. Zandi, one of the founders of the highly successful Economy.com, a data gathering and forecasting company: "'Our tax policies should be redesigned through the prism that wealth is being increasingly skewed,' Mr. Zandi said, arguing that *higher taxes on the rich could help restore a sense of fairness to the system and blunt a*

[3]"Better Transparency, Controls, Triggers, and Default Mechanisms Would Help Address Our Large and Growing Long-term Fiscal Challenge," GAO-06-761T, May 25,2006. www. gao. gov/ htext/ d06761t. html.
[4]Bob Herbert, "The Fading Dream," *New York Times*, November 13, 2006, p. A27.

backlash from a middle class that feels increasingly squeezed by the costs of health care, education, and a secure retirement."[5] The tactical implication is that both the fiscal and financial problems are best addressed by a strong focus on the plight of the middle class.

Can the public be sold on rejecting dangerous fiscal policies? The 2006 mid-term elections that restored Democratic control in the Senate and the House present the latest and perhaps the greatest challenge to Reaganism. Even before the election, *New York Times* columnist David Brooks stated without reservation: "It is clear that this upcoming mid-term election will mark the end of conservative dominance. This election is a period, not a comma, in political history."[6] That political judgment may be true, but it remains to be seen whether this change will influence fiscal policy. Neither the public nor either political party made tax increases or strengthening the federal government to attack the nation's huge fiscal and financial problems key issues in the mid-term election.

The November election may have rejected the Republican-controlled government, but it did not repudiate Ronald Reagan and Reaganism's two pillars—anti-governmentism and free-market capitalism. Reagan remains the towering political figure of the postwar era. In its December 2006 issue, the *Atlantic* reported on the results from ten prominent historians whom the magazine had asked to rank the 100 most influential people in American history based on "a person's impact, for good or ill, both on his or her era and on the way we live now."[7] Among post–World War II figures

---

[5]Louis Uchitelle,"Very Rich Are Leaving the Merely Rich Behind," *New York Times,* November 27, 2006, p. A1.
[6]David Brooks, "The Era of What's Next," *Herald Tribune,* October 27, 2006, p. 7.
[7]Ross Douthat, "They Made America,"*Atlantic,* December 2006, p. 60.

Reagan, at seventieth on the list, trailed only Martin Luther King, Jr., who ranked eighth. Even if, as we have argued, the influence is for ill, Reaganism's influence continues without any indication that the public has turned away from the man and his tenets.

The 2006 mid-term election ended Republican unified government and the system that limited congressional oversight of the executive branch. At the same time, polarization and big-money politics have not been eliminated. Corporate America and the wealthiest citizens remain central in politics, and the American political system continues to allow huge and potentially corrupting money flows into both electoral politics and the post-election influence process.

Whether 2006, like 1980 and 1994, will turn out to have been a critical election is unclear. If a shift away from Reaganism is to occur, the public must reject Bush's fiscal policies—particularly the mantra that all tax cuts are good, and any tax increases are bad. This will be difficult in part because Republicans have been busy sending the message that any tax increases, including not making the earlier tax cuts permanent, will limit economic growth. This claim plays on the psychological tendency of people to dread losses more than they welcome gains.[8] Although it is factually in error, if the past is any guide, the claim remains a powerful one.

The public may be worried about its financial plight, but most people appear to have kept up their standard of living through borrowing more and abandoning saving. That is a dangerous game,

---

[8]Daniel Kahneman and Amos Tversky, "Prospect Theory: An Analysis of Decision Making Under Risk," *Econometrica* 47, 1985, pp. 263–291.

but it has enabled the broad middle class to cling to its status. Even a risky status quo may look better than massive policy changes that bring a leap into the unknown. This may be particularly true today when the public has little trust in the federal government.

Electoral Accountability

Given that we have accused the Republican Party of buying into a set of wrong ideas to justify an unsustainable governing path, we might simply suggest replacing the Republicans with the Democrats as the governing party. The recipe that many political scientists often suggest is that the "out" party must convince the people to replace the "in" party. The governing party would have full control of the machinery of the bureaucracy through "responsive competence" to carry out a program of rectification. That would make sense from a perspective of electoral accountability, but it would not necessarily help in correcting the institutional failures that have contributed to the policy failures.

A standard topic in the first lecture in political science classes following an election is why electoral mandates don't exist. There are several reasons that no election can be seen as an unambiguous signal in support of a particular policy initiative. First, any president has to face the facts that more people didn't vote for him than did—if we count the non–voters. Second, people vote for lots of reasons—because they identify with a party, because they like the candidate, because they favor some of the programs offered. The "mandate fallacy" accumulates these reasons and leaps to the conclusion that all these diverse sources of votes supported one policy.

The 2006 mid-term elections are almost uniformly being seen as a signal for a change in U.S. policies in Iraq, and few commentators have mentioned the fiscal policies we've discussed in this book. So even if the 2006 election could be viewed as a mandate, it is not a mandate for changing the course of fiscal policy. Perhaps the divided government of 2007–2009 will produce saner fiscal policies, but it will not be because of "electoral accountability."

Even more problematic is the fact that much of what needs to be done in restoring fiscal sanity to the federal government is abstract and far from the sloganeering and posturing of electoral politics. It is unlikely that majorities can be assembled around the concepts of sound numbers, honest analysis, and reason deliberations. Electoral accountability is much too blunt an instrument to enforce good governance.

Moreover, fiscally responsible Republicans, endangered rarity as that animal might be, could be better at restoring fiscal sanity than Democrats. Two Republicans, Peter Peterson and Warren Rudman, and a Democrat, Paul Tsongas, founded the Concord Coalition, a nonprofit group whose mission is to encourage prudent financial management in government.[9] Conservatives such as William Niskanen and Bruce Bartlett have kept their focus on the goal of limited government, and they think Republican tax policies do not contribute to that goal.[10] They want spending limitations to go with tax limitations to keep the general system in balance. As critical as Democrats are today of the unsound finances of the Republicans, and as sound a system as the Clinton administration

---

[9]See Peter G. Peterson, *Running On Empty*. New York: Farrar, Strauss, and Giroux, 2004.
[10]See Bruce Bartlett, "Tax Cuts Don't Pay for Themselves," *Real Clear Politics*, March 28, 2006.

ran, it is clear that many Democrats would like bigger government and would not mind a little "speculative augmentation"[11] in health care and other social programs. If Democrats add programs without a reasonable financing scheme to cost them out, the fiscal health of the nation seems likely to continue its decline along the path comptroller general Walker and his Fiscal Wake-Up Tour panel indicated.

This is not to say that the Democrats would run a worse fiscal system than the Republicans; that hardly seems possible. We are arguing something else: the nation needs a commitment to materially strengthening the information-processing capacity of government, and this capacity must be institutionalized in a manner that requires politicians, in as much as that can be done, to pay attention to sound information.

In a word, restoring the healthy respect for sound finances and honest numbers in both parties and among think tanks, political activists, and the general public is critical to rebuilding a sound policymaking system. That would require three important and apparently difficult steps. First, political propaganda of the type used by the Bush administration that spews out disinformation must be reigned in. Second, we need to restore the institutional framework for sound financing, by both the inclusion of targets and triggers that apply to new spending and to revenue reductions, as well as the exclusion of budget earmarking. Third, politicians, as well as key groups including business and the media, must make the restoration of a respect for honest

---

[11]The term is Charles Jones'. See *The Politics of Air Pollution*. Pittsburgh: University of Pittsburgh Press, 1975.

numbers and sound analysis in government a salient public issue. This surely includes a strong input from Republican fiscal conservatives, whose voices were shouted down during the period of Big Government Republicanism.

THE POLITICIANS AND
THE EXPERTS

Political scientists have engaged in a long-running debate about the general role of bureaucracies in the process of policymaking and implementation. The debate is complex, but it has centered on two competing perspectives: pluralism and overhead democratic accountability. On the one hand, the *pluralists* have defended the role of neutral experts using the best evidence and analysis available in the policymaking process. On the other hand, the proponents of overhead democracy stress the need for duly elected political leaders to control the bureaucratic agencies, including the experts, in order to implement faithfully the policies they pursue.

In the ideal world of the pluralists, policy experts would follow the norms of neutral competence. They would provide the best information possible but would not take partisan sides. Experts in one field would defer to experts in another in a kind of system of mutual noninterference. This allows expert advice to filter upward where necessary, but to stay at a lower level of decision making where appropriate. Presidents and cabinet-level political appointees have the role of reviewing and questioning the experts, making the call where policy actions have both positive and negative consequences, and make the value decisions necessary.

The critical issue in the debate is the relative balance between the elected politicians and their political appointees and the career experts in the executive branch. The pluralist model can lead to excessive power in the hands of the experts. Democratic accountability is undermined if expert policymaking removes the executive function from the hands of elected officials and puts it in the hands of the trained specialists. The latter might capitulate to special interest groups that try to capture an agency and have it do their will. Expert decision making invariably leads to subsystem-style politics that attracts mostly those with interests in the matter, and many times those interests are financial. Policy experts can come to identify with the interest groups that try to influence them, and oftentimes experts move back and forth from administrative agency to interest group. Moreover, the experts may look out for themselves. Bureaucrats have self-interest, and policy experts may work mostly on behalf of that interest. Or the experts might believe their objectives and values are superior to those of the public that elected the government and act to incorporate their views rather than those of the elected politicians chosen by the voters. If so, they end up denying democratic control under the cover of neutral competence.

Whatever the potential danger of such transgressions by the experts, efforts to enforce political accountability have gone much too far, leading to excessive power by the president and his political appointees. Substituting political responsiveness for neutral competence in the development and analysis of policy information raises two fundamental questions:

1. How can the political leaders have any chance to make good policy decisions if they do not have the needed sound data and reasoned analyses available and instead use flawed numbers and biased interpretations they want to hear?
2. How can there be democratic accountability if honest numbers are not produced and made available to citizens at election time?

The key lies in establishing and maintaining a workable balance between the politicians and the civil servants so that there is political responsiveness to meet the needs of the elected leaders and neutral competence that follows professional standards and provides hard policy data and analyses.

Principals and Agents

The proponents of democratic accountability see this issue as a principal-agent problem, in which a chief executive (the principal) delegates to experts (the agents) some duties. But the executive finds the agents using their superior information to cheat or impose their values instead of the chief executive's. This class of problems is sometimes known as the *moral hazard,* because the principal runs the hazard of being duped by the agents.

A third position on the issue standing between pluralism and overhead democratic accountability sees policymaking as mostly made by experts, but with occasional intervention by the political branches of government—that is, the president and Congress—

when major changes are necessary.[12] This approach is known as the punctuated equilibrium model, because expert policymaking is at equilibrium but occasionally punctuated by major democratic policy changes.[13] This requires less of the principal and yet still allows the intervention by democratically elected officials when necessary. This model may be realistic, but it really finesses the issue of democratic accountability as a normative standard.

In corporations, a chief executive may be both a chief executive, delegating to others, but he is also an agent of the shareholders. The shareholders risk a moral hazard if the corporation's leadership lies, cheats, and steals. Similarly, in government the president may act corruptly or in the interest of himself and his financial backers rather than the citizens that elected him. Citizens run a moral hazard. If the president asks his cabinet members and agency heads to follow his policies, but his policies are themselves corrupt or wrongheaded, then democratic accountability is thwarted and would be better served if the president's agents refused to act according to his wishes.[14]

In the corporate world there are three methods for trying to ensure conformity of the interests of the corporate leadership and the shareholders. These are *transparency*, where government regulators require that honest numbers about the status of the corporation are reported to the shareholders; *governance rules*, where certain rules of procedure must be followed by management; and

---

[12]Emmette Redford, *Democracy in the Administrative State*. New York: Oxford University Press, 1969; Charles O. Jones, *Clean Air*. Pittsburgh: University of Pittsburgh Press, 1974.
[13]Frank Baumgartner and Bryan D. Jones, *Agendas and Instability in American Politics*. Chicago: University of Chicago Press, 1993.
[14]Gary Miller, "The Political Evolution of Principal Agent Models,"*Annual Review of Political Science*, 8, 2005, pp. 203–225.

professional ethics, where accountants, auditors, and other professionals owe a higher allegiance to their professional creeds than to the corporation for which they work. If these mechanisms break down, then we get the Bernie Ebbers problem, whose financial manipulations caused the collapse of WorldCom and huge losses for shareholders. Invariably in these situations financial officers are in on the deal, and auditors and accountants look the other way.

In government similar rules are at play. Government cannot be held accountable if honest numbers are not produced, if the professional standards of analysts and auditors are ignored. This has become a particular problem at OMB.

The Problem at OMB

One major consequence of the clash between neutral and responsive competence has emerged at OMB. Though the career budget office staff still produces honest numbers, the agency director has not always told the public the truth about them. Honest numbers are published in massive budget documents, but they are not mentioned by the OMB director or his or her political staff. Indeed, they have been ignored and distorted to provide misleading indicators of presidential success.

The Office of Management and Budget came out of the older Bureau of the Budget (BoB), established in the Budget and Accounting Act of 1921. That act gave the president the responsibility of preparing an executive budget, and BoB was the instrument for this. President Nixon's reorganization of the bureau into the OMB was based on the argument that he needed both budget and management control over the bureaucracy to establish proper democratic accountability.

How responsive should the bureaucracy be to the president's wishes? OMB is at the center of this debate. Proponents of neutral competence hold to the notion that political leaders ought to set policy through a clash of political values, and professional nonpartisan bureaucrats ought to implement it. Though presidents and members of Congress must be political, bureaucrats should adhere to a norm of neutral competence. But as we have noted, bureaucrats not only have their own interests, they can overly sympathize with those they are empowered to regulate through delegation. The argument by academics such as Terry Moe is that presidents must gain control of the vast federal bureaucracy to implement programs in a manner true to the intent of the political branches; they need political responsiveness from professional bureaucrats.[15]

When Nixon reorganized the BoB into the OMB, clearly he had in mind bringing order to the vast bureaucracy. However, the result at times has been the feared politicization not just of the management and control function, but also the analytic capacity of the budget bureau. Today's OMB is far more politicized, and if it is not less capable of producing quality analysis, it is less likely to do so because of political domination. As we noted in Chapter 10, many students of public administration have justified such political responsiveness in terms of top-down control of the bureaucracy. But to do so brings up a fundamental problem: Whether Republican or Democratic, liberal or conservative, no president ought to be free to corrupt the facts in

---

[15] Terry Moe, "The Politicized Presidency", in John Chubb and Paul E. Peterson (ed.), *New Directions in American Politics*. Washington DC: Brookings, 1985.

a push to centralize decision making around his agenda. To do so undermines the institutional capacity of the presidency. Political responsiveness can generate demands from the top that agency personnel color the facts, generate happy budget projections, and "fix" intelligence to conform to the ideological and policy commitments of political leaders.

The story at OMB in the Bush administration is one of increased politicization. The career of Joshua Bolten exemplifies the problem. As the classic political appointee, he came from the White House staff to run OMB, and he returned there as chief of staff in March 2006. He was educated as a lawyer, not a budget expert, and except for his stint at OMB, he never had direct experience with budget analysis. Though his role may have been appropriate regarding the "Management" part of OMB, his behavior regarding the "Budget" part was irresponsible.

One option that might be used in treating the problem of politicizing the OMB analytic function would be to separate the agency into two parts. There would be a budget director to serve a long term, whose appointment must be ratified by the Senate and who cannot be fired by the president. The model here roughly corresponds to the Federal Reserve chair, or perhaps the comptroller general, who is the head of the Congressional Accountability Office. The management director could continue to serve at the pleasure of the president. This option would recognize the need for both neutral competence and political responsiveness in the executive branch. Establishing a nonpartisan budget director would make it more difficult for presidents to conduct a Bush-style fiscal propaganda campaign, but it cannot be expected to solve the nation's fiscal problems.

A FISCAL REGIME IN CONGRESS

Democrats have vowed to restore the pay-go rules that structured budget choices in the 1990s but were allowed to expire after Bush was elected. They have done so in the House of Representatives by using chamber rules. These rules require a tabulation of where money for new expenditure is to come from, and what expenditures are to be cut if taxes are cut. Republicans contend that pay-go rules should apply only to expenditures, claiming that tax cuts "pay for themselves." But as we have shown, their arguments are invalid. To work, pay-go rules must apply to both sides of the budgetary equation: revenues and taxes.

The pay-go rules of the GHW Bush and Clinton years were mandated by law. A restoration of that fiscal regime will require both houses of Congress to pass such a bill, and for the president to sign it. Bush refused to support fiscal prudence because of his belief that the pay-go rules should apply only to expenditures. He repeated as usual the "tax-cuts-pay-for-themselves" myth. Bad ideas in the Bush presidency, like cats, have nine lives.

Of course the rules alone cannot ensure compliance. In the fiscally responsible 1990s, exceeding budgetary targets was met with required budgetary sequesters. The Budget Enforcement Act (BEA) of 1997, which extended the Budget Enforcement Act of 1990, required that discretionary expenditures be automatically cut if targets were not met. The Office of Management and Budget was responsible for reporting the numbers. The expiration of the BEA in 2002 enabled Congressional Republicans to drop the pay-go rules that Congress had adopted to enforce the act in the legislative budget process.

We showed in Chapters 3–6 that different fiscal eras, with different institutional and political components, have characterized the federal government since the Second World War. These eras are supported by fiscal cultures characterized by more or less fiscal responsibility. Today we are in an era of high irresponsibility, and it is unreasonable to assume that simple congressional spending rules will restore the system. In the past, only extended debate between Congress and the president established responsible fiscal systems. We expect that something similar will be necessary this time as well.

SOME POLITICAL OPTIONS

Can political coalitions be forged that press politicians into more responsible fiscal behavior?

It is possible that a reform movement will emerge within the Republican Party demanding a return to the tenets of limited government and balanced budgets. This will be difficult, however, because tax cuts remain a central tenet of modern Republicanism, perhaps the only notion holding the coalition together. As a consequence, reformers will need to look outside of the party to find allies.

There seem to be but three viable options. The first is replacement of Republican governance with Democratic governance. Democrats have certainly advocated sounder finances, but this stance could be only a campaign tactic. Democratic activists have moved toward greater advocacy of positive government to solve problems—from the ills of the health care system to the need to attend to basic physical infrastructure. Democrats could pursue finances similar to those that Republicans pursued in the Medicare drug benefit entitlement—lowballing future financial obligations to get the program started.

Liberal *New York Times* columnist Paul Krugman asks what Democrats should do if they free up money from rescinding the Bush tax cuts or ending the Iraq War. Should they "use the reclaimed revenue to reduce the deficit, or spend it on other things? The answer . . . is to spend the money . . . and let the deficit be. . . . Deficit reduction . . . might just end up playing into the hands of the next irresponsible president."[16] The experience of 12 years of responsible financing in the GHW Bush and Clinton administrations being recklessly discarded by GW Bush makes Democrats wary of reestablishing the "Rubinomics" that underpinned fiscal prudence in the 1990s.

A second often-lauded solution from conservatives and occasionally liberals is divided government. The idea seems to have taken hold that divided government is responsible government because the worst tendencies of each party are checked by the other one. But that may have been a quirk of the Clinton presidency. We showed in Chapter 4 that cultures of restrained spending in Washington are associated neither with divided government nor with unified ones. It may be that divided governments are better at control, but it is more likely that both divided and unified governments can be responsible under the proper combination of rules governing taxing and spending, and an elite consensus about the desirability of sound financing.

---

[16]Paul Krugman, "The Democrats and the Deficit," *New York Times,* December 22, 2006, p. A31.

Solutions based on simple electoral logic offer scant solace. We have shown in this book that institutional structures reinforced by sensible political calculations can enforce a regime of sound public financing with competent policy analysis as its underpinning. For most of the postwar years, this system was in place, limiting the excesses of politicians through a general respect for the norms of prudent financial management. When the system got out of balance, the issue was addressed, often when one party, a faction within a party, or a third-party challenge such as that raised by Ross Perot in 1992, embarrassed the offender.

This system did not emerge out of immediate electoral logic, but from the decisions of reformers and politicians that the country would be better governed if some basic rules of good government were observed. Beginning in the Progressive Era, good government principles structured American governments at all levels. Some principles of governance were held to be above partisan politics, and these included merit personnel systems, sensible and transparent financing, and contracts based on performance and cost rather than partisan connections. These principles were instituted in the federal government as the New Deal agencies proliferated, and they became a central tenet of government following World War II.

Because these premises have been under assault since the Reagan administration—and have been completely dismissed in the GW Bush administration—they cannot be restored overnight. On the other hand, in Congress and in many executive agencies, sound analysis is alive and well, corrupted at the top but not destroyed through and through. Can this base be reinforced?

The Progressive movement was nurtured by an alliance between business leaders, good government citizens' leagues, and academics, and spurred by politicians committed to the cause. It is unfortunate that academics have not developed a commitment to the ideals of policy analysis that they harbored in an earlier era. At one time political scientists were best represented on the issue by University of Chicago's Robert Merriam. In the 1930s he stood for honest government and was a thorn in the side of the Chicago Democratic machine. Universities began public administration programs to professionalize public service, and a commitment to neutral competence was unquestioned.

If there is a prevailing academic opinion today, it appears to be a naïve faith in responsive competence, in which bureaucracies compliantly follow the wishes of the president, no matter how destructive. If mistakes are made, it is hoped that electoral accountability will cure all. The "new public management" preaches managerial discretion and customer satisfaction, leading perhaps to more responsiveness but less professionalism and more possibilities for corruption and favoritism. These and other trends have undermined the Progressive ideal of the competently neutral bureaucrat and have allowed the profusion in America of bad government.

For the most part, wealthy businesspeople have turned to apolitical foundations that steer clear of the declining state of American governance. Even when they are political, the wealthy have taken partisan sides rather than attack the governance problem. The models are the apolitical, such as Bill Gates, and the political, such as Richard Mellon Schaife on the right and George Soros on the left, leaving a leadership vacuum on governance issues.

In this void stand only a handful of progressive organizations, perhaps best represented by the Concord Coalition headed by Peterson and Rudman. The Concord Coalition is the beacon of reform in a sea of partisan rancor and avoidance behavior among those who should lead. But they are increasingly isolated in a world in which partisan polarization has swamped considerations of good government.

FACING FACTS

Before such changes can be made, we must understand the full extent of the problems facing the United States, problems directly due to the bad economic and political ideas we have analyzed in this book. Bad economic notions threaten the long-run financial solvency of the federal government and the financial security of working- and middle-class Americans. Bad political ideas are causing severe—possibly irreparable—damage to the institutions of government and their capacities to develop sound information and analytic systems. The shift from reality-based to ideologically driven decision making has undermined effective national governance.

To solve problems, surely we must recognize them. The deleterious impact of bad economic ideas has begun to receive attention, and the particularly poor economic and fiscal performance of the GW Bush administration is coming into focus. However, analysts have not attended nearly enough to the distributional effects of conservative policies that have aided and abetted in the creation of a class of politically powerful super-rich and the associated relative decline of the American middle class.

IT JUST GETS WORSE

Over time as new evidence has come in, the facts of the economic and political failures in the Bush presidency have become increasingly difficult to ignore. In this final chapter, it is useful to consider new data on the superrich and the middle class and the penetrating discussion of governance in two 2007 books that illuminate and extend what we've discussed in this book.

The Cutting of the Economic Pie

In an August 21, 2007 *New York Times* article, David Cay Johnston, who has won the Pulitzer Prize and been a Pulitzer finalist in three other years since 2000, brought together new information and commentary on the impact of the Bush tax cuts. Johnston pointed out that the total income for all Americans rose between 2000 and 2005 but average income in 2005 dropped because of the population increase (more folks sharing the national pie), and observed: "Total income listed on tax returns grew every year after World War II, with a single year exception, until 2001, making the five-year period of lower average incomes and four years of total income a new experience for the majority of Americans born after 1945. . . . The growth in total incomes was concentrated among those making more than a million dollars [in 2005]. . . . [They] reaped almost 47 percent of the total income gain."[17]

---

[17]All data and quotes in this and the next paragraph are in David Cay Johnston, "'05 incomes, on Average, Still below 2000 Peak," *New York Times*, August 28, 2007, C1. For his work on taxation, see David Cay Johnston, *Perfectly Legal,* New York: Portfolio, 2003.

Readers will recall that the 2003 tax cut on taxable dividends and capital gains was a dead-center bull's-eye in targeting the wealthiest of the wealthy. Johnston reported on an analysis by the Center for Tax Justice that showed the unbelievable accuracy of the 2003 Act: "[The Center's] calculations showed that 28 percent of the investment tax cut savings went to just 11,433 of the 134 million taxpayers, those who made $10 million or more [that year], saving them almost $1.9 million each." Average savings from the tax cut on investment income for the 90 percent of those whose incomes were below $100,000 amounted to $318 per person. Robert S. McIntyre, who directs the Center, noted the combination of five years of lower average incomes and tax savings of a tiny handful of the superrich, "shows that trickle down doesn't work." Trickle down is another bad economic idea with great longevity.

Misgovernance in the Bush Presidency

Another bad idea—this time a political one—has been at the core of Reaganism. Antigovernmentism postulates that government is the problem, never the solution. Our view is that government can be the problem or the solution, and what the United States desperately needs is sound governance and that demands competent, responsible political leaders. Responsible presidents will seek to determine the nation's most pressing needs and the means of addressing them, foster bipartisanship on major issues, and inform the citizenry about policies prior to final decisions. And that's not enough—political leaders in Congress need to be competent and responsible too. America must have sound governance if it is to ameliorate the fiscal and financial difficulties facing the nation and its citizens. The biggest problem in moving toward sound governance is the increased damage to the institutions of governance in the Bush administration, particularly the period from 9/11 to January 2007.

The two books published in 2007 that consider governance in the Bush administration are *The Assault on Reason* by Al Gore and *Unchecked and Unbalanced: Presidential Power in a Time of Terror* by Frederick A. O. Schwarz Jr., a distinguished lawyer who is now Senior Counsel for New York University's Brennan Center for Justice, and Aziz Z. Huq, who directs the Liberty and National Security Project at the Brennan Center.[18] Both books came to the same conclusion: President Bush saw himself in his role as commander in chief as above the law with both Congress and the courts subservient to him and his actions based on that premise carried his administration far beyond the boundaries established by the Constitution. This conception has undermined the role of sound analysis in the setting of public policy.

Schwarz and Huq wrote: "For the first time in American history, the executive branch claims authority under the Constitution to set aside laws permanently—including prohibition on torture and warrantless eavesdropping on Americans. A frightening idea decisively rejected at America's birth—that a president like a king, can do no wrong—has reemerged to justify torture and indefinite presidential detention."[19] This behavior had been justified by what the authors labeled "the monarchical theory," which argues

[18] Al Gore, *The Assault on Reason*, New York: Penguin Press, 2007; and Frederick A. O. Schwarz Jr. and Aziz Z. Huq, *Unchecked and Unbalanced*, New York: New Press, 2007.
[19] Schwarz and Huq, p.1

that as commander in chief, the president is unchecked. That new theory is "embarrassingly wrong."[20]

Al Gore observed: "The seductive appeal of exercising unconstrained unilateral power led this president to interpret his powers under the Constitution in a way that brought to life the worst nightmare of the Founders. . . . At least we don't have to guess what our Founders would have to say about this bizarre and un-American theory."[21] The ultimate irony is that the president who claimed that his objective in invading and occupying Iraq was to establish democracy engaged in the same kind of authoritarian leadership as King George III that had brought the American Revolution over 200 years ago.

Both of these well-argued and well-documented books make clear that George W. Bush has pushed far beyond the boundaries of presidential behavior the Founders set out in the Constitution. Gore's analysis is particularly apt in terms of the current problems of sound governance. The book's title indicates an assault on scientific inquiry that rests on sound information and reasoned debate based on facts: "[It is Bush's] inflexibility—this willful refusal even to entertain alternative opinions or conflicting evidence poses the most serious danger to our county."[22]

Congress let him get away with this. Gore writes that "The most serious–and most surprising—failure of checks and balances in the last several years has been the abdication by Congress of its role of coequal branch of government."[23] Finally, Gore raised

---

[20]Ibid., p. 7.
[21]Gore, pp. 154, 161.
[22]Ibid., p. 55.
[23]Ibid., p. 235.

a new problem threatening sound governance: "The United States has survived many assaults on its integrity and has endured lengthy periods during which high levels of corruption twisted the nation's goals and distorted the operations of democracy. . . . This is different: the absolute dominance of the politics of wealth today is something new."[24]

These two books shed light on the degree of damage to the institutions of governance during the Bush presidency and the likelihood of restoring sound governance. Checks and balances live again as the Democratic Congress has restored the oversight function. Yet, we fear the damage done during the Bush presidency will prove to be a difficult barrier to restoring sound governance. Congress has been unable or unwilling to attack seriously Bush's monarchial theory and the actions he bases on it. The dominance of the politics of wealth hardly appears to have diminished as money poured into the presidential candidates in record amounts. It may hearten Democrats that their presidential candidates are raising more money than Republicans for the first time since records have been kept, but for us it just highlights the problem.

It is particularly unfortunate that damage to the capacity of the national government and the relationship between the economy and that government have been so poorly perceived by those who study politics and policy. Few in the media and academia strongly criticized the Bush administration until 2005, when much of the public finally became anxious about the administration's gross ineptitude in a number of areas such as Iraq and Katrina. It is particularly disappointed that so many political scientists have

---

[24]Ibid., p. 82.

trusted elections to sort out the horrendously complex issues that have driven our democracy so far off course. Parties and elections alone cannot solve these problems; indeed, the bad ideas are associated with Republicans and their electoral successes. Nor can the Democrats necessarily be trusted to solve the problems either, because once reality-based analysis is abandoned, both parties are freer to ignore the facts. Further, Republicans can be expected to cut taxes regardless of the future well-being of the country, whereas Democrats will likely promise programs that cannot be paid for.

Our schools of public policy are supposed to be professional training academies for modern policy analysts and administrators. But professors in policy schools and programs of public administration too often address policies and administrative procedures as if the two exist in separate worlds. They may not link public administration to the dynamics of public policy or investigate the extent to which poor public administration invariably leads to poor public policies. Even worse, the word *politics* is often scorned by faculty members in the prestigious schools of public policy as contaminating the objectivity of their research. However, politics got us into this, and only politics can get us out—and not necessarily party politics. Surely it is not too much to ask that schools of public policy stand for something other than microeconomic analysis and technical competence.

We recommend that those who are training the next generation of public policy managers and policy analysts support more self-consciously the values of neutral competence and telling the truth to their political leaders. National organizations representing faculties in schools and departments teaching public policy and administration should speak out against the nation's leaders when they use flawed data and deceptive interpretations to mislead the public. For example, the Association of Public Policy Analysis and Management (APPAM) should have criticized the Bush administration, not for its policies, but for its abandonment of sound policy information and analysis as a factor in decision making. This anti-analytic stance in effect rejects the basic premise of policy analysis. But APPAM leaders chose to avoid politics rather than defend the profession.

In all fairness, criticizing the Bush administration in its first term was nasty business. Early critics were ignored or derided, not just by the administration and its supporters in think tanks and the media, but by the establishment pundits who saw the critiques as going too far in claiming that the administration used misinformation and deception in selling its policies. After 9/11 and the invasion of Iraq, many with severe reservations about the course of public affairs chose to play it safe because of the vitriolic right wing attacks on their patriotism in criticizing a wartime president while troops were fighting in Iraq. Fox News analysts blithely linked *liberal* and *traitor*, and Ann Coulter—Chief Inquisitor on Fox, and still a star on the Republican circuit—wrote a book making this link historically. When one of us asked the head of the Young Republicans at the University of Washington why their national conference would invite such an individual to be their major speaker, he commented that "the troops need red meat." (Would "blue meat" have been more appropriate?)[25] The media, even the most prestigious newspapers, pulled their punches lest they be stigmatized as part of the liberal press that

---

[25]It is worth mentioning that this young man changed parties in 2006 and joined the military.

the conservatives claimed, with no evidence, treated them in a biased manner. Criticism was dead in war, as usual in America, but why in departments of economics? And why in schools of public policy and administration?

It is critical for America to come to grips with John Maynard Keynes' great insight about bad economic and political ideas. The greatest economist of the 20th century pointed out that such bad ideas are as likely as good ones to be entertained. These bad economic and political ideas thrive on bad information. They can be cast aside before they do irreparable damage only if the concepts driving public policy are subjected to sound factual analysis.

We have done so in this book for a very important set of ideas. But more is necessary. The government itself must re-establish the capacity to do the analysis, and leaders must themselves be governed by empirical evidence and reason, not ideological dogma. Only a consensus among political elites can restore the necessary respect for the facts, a consensus sorely missing in America today.

CONCLUDING COMMENTS

In politics, attention is the coin of the realm.[26] Politicians hawk ideas to attract attention to policy proposals. Bad ideas in politics—those that have been disproved by the facts—survive because they have utility for a sizable segment of the polity. They attract attention. In America, nothing attracts attention so much as a "get rich quick" scheme, and the tax cut proposals and their justifying ideologies have all the characteristics of such a scheme in a market

---

[26]Bryan D. Jones and Frank R. Baumgartner, *The Politics of Attention*. Chicago: University of Chicago Press, 2005.

bubble. In market bubbles, there are always analysts, the Warren Buffets of the financial world, who stick to long-range programs of sound valuation. But too many lose their bearings. Finally the bubble ends, and only the lucky and the Buffets survive unscathed.

Bad ideas can last even longer in democratic polities than in investment markets. Elections are blunt instruments that evaluate governing performance over a panoply of issues, and they occur at infrequent intervals. Moreover, the massive borrowing capacity of the United States and other national governments may allow politicians to postpone the consequences of bad policies for many years. Though investors are in the market for only one reason—to make money—participants in politics are there for many reasons, and one of these is to make the world better. They are often too easily convinced that an appealing but wrong idea can lead to this better world, and they identify so strongly with the idea that it becomes almost part of their identities. The investment in bad economic and political ideas, as a consequence, is far more intensely felt than a bad market investment. That is, selling a bad common stock that previously looked like a good investment does not compare with abandoning a bad idea that had become a fundamental belief.

If the Republican tax cut programs were exposed to fact-based competition in the marketplace of ideas, we would confidently predict the coming end of the "boom." Republicans have thrown up justifications that have become increasingly far-fetched, and though they may not have "cooked" the books, they have been less than truthful about the facts. But democratic politics are even less efficient than markets, so it will not be easy to end the tax-cut frenzy, and it will be even more difficult to re-establish sound public finances.

What can bring the politicians to their senses? A key ingredient must be honest numbers, made readily available. James Madison wrote in 1822, more than three decades after he participated in the constitutional convention, "A popular Government without popular information or the means of acquiring it is a Prologue to a Farce or Tragedy."[27] Going on two centuries later, it is clearly a tragedy, well beyond the prologue, as the elected leaders of the first great democracy chose to turn information into a weapon to sell and defend their ideological policies rather than use it as the basis for reasoned decision making.

Are sound policy numbers really so important to governance? "Those of us who emphasize the crucial place of information and analysis in the American political system may be naïve or myopic in stressing the importance of mere numbers in the political equation."[28] We think not. Surely, this study of George W. Bush's fiscal policy could not be clearer on the critical role of information in governing America and the dangers of misusing it. Of course sound numbers alone cannot solve the nation's problems. But without sound numbers, democratic accountability can not be forged. Without them, political leaders will invariably be deceived into enacting and implementing bad policies with their unavoidable bad policy outcomes. Even in an era of profound partisan and class divisions, citizens must demand that policy choices be made using sound analyses based on honest numbers. It is a starting point to more sensible politics and policies.

---

[27]Gaillard Hunt (ed.), *The Writings of James Madison.* New York: Putnam's Sons, 1910, Vol 9, p. 103.
[28]Walter Williams, *Reaganism and the Death of Representative Democracy,* Washington: Georgetown University Press, 2003, p. 43.

Finally, we re-emphasize that good numbers are not the magic solution, and policy analysts are not necessarily the folks in white hats. Strong democracy in America requires that policy analysts must be subordinates of the politicians chosen by the people to represent them. Democratic accountability is possible only if the elected representatives of the voters make the key policy choices. That's Government 101. But the corollary is that sensible policy decisions in our complex world must be fueled by honest numbers. That was Madison's basic message in 1822. We simply reaffirm it today after offering evidence that shows the dangers to the nation and its people in not heeding that message.

APPENDIX

More Detailed Analyses of Results Presented in Chapter 3

For the more technically inclined, we present in this appendix some statistical analyses of the data presented in Chapter 3. Our analyses are rudimentary from the standpoint of modern statistical theory as it has developed in social science, but they will suffice to give confidence that our arguments are on the right track, and perhaps suggest a path for future research for those interested in pursuing these matters.

The analyses sometimes use top marginal tax rate for families and sometimes a sum of the top marginal rate for families and the effective rate on capital. We have generally used the former when dealing with public opinion (which should be more sensitive to individual rates) and the latter when dealing with government revenues.

TAX RATES AND REVENUES

Table 1 presents an ordinary least squares regression analysis of U.S. government revenues in constant (2000) billion dollars. The independent variables are a variable labeled Total Tax Rate Change,

All tables in this Appendix were calculated from Truth and Politics.org and Tax Facts: Washington, DC: Urban Institute-Brookings Tax Policy Center; Revenues from the U. S. Office of Management and Budget, Budget of the United States Government, Fiscal Year 2008, Historical Tables. Public mood measure in Table 3 updated from James A. Stimson, Public Opinion in America, from Professor Stimson's website [http://www.unc.edu/~jstimson/].

TABLE 1
Regression Analysis of Inflation-Adjusted Revenues: 1948–2004

VARIABLE	COEFFICIENT	STANDARD ERROR	t-VALUE
Constant	3.901	0.865	4.5
Total Tax Rate Change	0.152	0.073	2.1
Recession	−4.638	1.929	−2.4

$R^2 = 0.199$; Adj $R^2 = 0.165$

$F = 5.40$; df = 49

DW = 2.16

which is a simple sum of the annual change in the top marginal individual tax rate and the effective tax rate on capital. This is a very rough estimate of the tax burden on both income and wealth. A lag for the previous year's revenue was statistically insignificant. The variable labeled Recession is a dummy assessing whether the economy had reached the depth of the recession that year.

It is possible that businesses and individuals find ways to reduce their tax burdens by exploiting (or getting enacted) various provisions in the tax codes. Or over time they might reduce effort, as the supply-siders claim. All we claim here is that tax rate cuts do reduce revenues, even though these reductions can be partially offset by long-term economic growth.

TAX RATES AND THE DEFICIT

It is reasonably clear that tax rate cuts are associated with increases in the size of the deficit, as can be seen from Table 2, but the

TABLE 2
Regression Analysis of the Federal Surplus in Constant (2000) Billion $: 1970–2004

VARIABLE	COEFFICIENT	STANDARD ERROR	t-VALUE
Constant	–3.093	20.257	–0.15
Total Tax Rate Change	2.358	1.407	1.68
Lag Surplus	0.865	0.090	9.6
Recession	–101.293	31.714	–3.19

$R^2 = 0.779$; Adj $R^2 = 0.757$

$F = 35.23$; $df = 33$

$DW = 1.41$

relationship barely reaches statistical significance. (This is the case even though we study only the period from 1970 to 2004, the era of greatest tax cuts.) Clearly, however, the one-tailed test that tax rate cuts are associated with decreases in the deficit can be rejected.

A regression with lags for tax rate changes does not reach significance, nor does the variable for recessions. Previous cuts are carried forward via the lag surplus variable. Nor does entering the current tax rates (for individuals or capital) affect the surplus; lower levels of taxation do not lead to lower deficits.

TAX RATES AND PUBLIC OPINION

Table 3 presents a more complete model of the relationship between public mood and tax rates. The dependent variable in the analysis

TABLE 3
Regression Analysis of Change in Public Mood, 1970–2004

VARIABLE	COEFFICIENT	STANDARD ERROR	t-VALUE
Constant	0.852	0.300	2.8
Tax Rate Change	–0.124	0.052	–2.3
Revenue Percentage Change	–0.172	0.051	–3.4
Surplus Percentage Change	–0.123	0.133	–0.9
Recession	–1.400	0.611	–2.4

$R^2 = 0.393$; Adj $R^2 = 0.312$

$F = 4.86$; df = 34

DW = 2.3

is year-to-year change in public mood, which provides a good test of the starve-the-beast claim that tax rates will generate voter revulsion at government. Moreover, it is necessary for technical reasons (to correct for autocorrelation).

Tax rates and the revenues collected by government are both negatively related to liberalism on the public mood measure, as is the "recession" variable, which is simply a dummy variable for whether the economy was in recession. It may surprise some that recessions are associated with conservatism, but that may reflect successes of the Republican rhetoric about the failure of liberalism. The size of the deficit was not related significantly to mood, either in absolute or relative terms. In any case, the coefficient is in the wrong direction—larger surpluses are associated with more conservative public opinion.

It is theoretically possible that the effects of tax rate cuts take a while to work themselves through the system, but various lags of both the variables and changes in the variables failed to improve the model.

TAX RATES AND THE SIZE OF GOVERNMENT

Table 4 is an analysis of the effects of changes in public mood on public expenditure relative to the size of the economy. Though the relationship is assessed here after 1970, it holds for the entire 1953–2004 period (the period for which we have data on the generic public mood). The t-value for Change in Public Mood is 1.57 for the full period, not statistically significant.

TABLE 4
Regression Analysis of Public Mood and the Size of Government, 1971–2004

VARIABLE	COEFFICIENT	STANDARD ERROR	t-VALUE
Constant	1.354	1.579	0.86
Change in Public Mood	0.130	0.066	1.97
Recession	1.137	0.282	4.03

$R^2 = 0.840$; Adj $R^2 = 0.824$

$F = 52.62$; df = 33

DW = 2.5

Index

Note: A page number followed by a"n" refers to a footnote.

Kingdon, John, 3n
Kirschten, Dick, 244, 245n
Knowledge memory, 254
Knowledge Networks, 304n
Kogan, Richard, 7n
Krugman, Paul, 215n, 221n, 252n, 257n, 349n; growth, analysis, 220–221
K Street Project. See Delay
Kurtz, Howard, 263n

Labor unions, Democratic ally, 323
Laffer, Arthur, 33; argument, 41–42; citation, 40n; curve, 185, example, 41f, government policy, placement, 42–43; emergence, 181
Lawmaking; intensity, 107–108; topics, 110
Lazear, Edward P., 37n, 51n
Lazowska, Edward, 190
Legislation, topic classification, 111f
Legislative appropriations procedures, number (increase), 316–317
Legislative branch; information suppression, 292; Republican control, 294
Lelyveld, Joseph, 142n
Levy, Frank, 163n
Liberalism; decline, 175–177; tax reductions, impact, 74–75
Lindsey, Lawrence, 191–193; false claims, 193
Lobbying, honeypot theory. See Honeypot theory of lobbying
Lobbyists, impact, 308–310
Long, Russell, 299
Losses, dread (psychological tendency), 336
Lott, Trent, 179
Lowi, Theodore, 49, 49n
Lublin, Joann S., 221n
Lynn, Jr., Lawrence E., 242n

Macroeconomics; mathematical equations, 185–186; study, 33
Madison, James, 270n, 362; Federalist Papers, 267
Mallaby, Sebastian, 303n
Mandatory expenditures, 143–144
Mandatory spending programs, 148–151
Mankiw, N. Gregory, 286n, 308n
Mann, Thomas E., 24, 261n; citation, 24n–26n, 265n, 270n, 313n; pessimism, 25–26
Marginal rate, capture, 56–57
Marginal tax rate, public mood; relationship, 74f; scatterplot, 75f
Market booms, 330
Mass transportation/transit, spending, 116–117

McCarty, Nolan T., 264n, 265n, 320n
McGovern, George, 123
McIntyre, Robert S., 354
McMurtry, Virginia A., 124n
McNamara, Robert, 240
Means, identification, 325
Median family income (1947-2000), 218–219
Median subfunction, value, 99–100
Medicare; classification, 97–98; coverage, eligibility, 207; expenses, 149; growth, 149; mandatory expenditure, 143; mandatory programs, 129; Part D, 150–151, 204–205; Parts A/B, 204; prescription drug, bill, 291–292, costs, 203–205, 291
Medicare Hospital Insurance (HI), 149
Medicare Reform Act of 2004, 317
Meese, Edwin, 244
Meyerson, Harold, 198n
Middle class, status, 197, 198–199
Middleton, Roger, 36n
Mid-term elections (2006), signal, 338
Miller, Gary, 343n
Milligan, Susan, 268n
Mishel, Lawrence, 171n
Moe, Terry M., 16n, 248n, 275n, 345n; presidential image, 282
Monthly Budget Review, OMB posting, 274
Moore, Kevin B., 10n, 220n
Moore, Stephen, 46n
Mortgages, importance, 225–226
Municipal machines, benefits, 314
Murphy, Kevin M., 37n, 51n

National balance sheet, imbalance (blame), 308–309
National debt, 198–199
National Defense Education Act, 106
National government, capacity (damage), 357–358
National Opinion Research Center, 302
Net national debt, 215
Neutral competence, 234–236; attack, 238–240; CBO adherence, 237–238; emphasis, 15; impact, 294; value, 16–17; virtues, 280
New Deal, 147; coalition, politics, 174–175; egalitarianism, 32; legislation, 108–109
New Economy (Clinton argument), 170–171
New Public Management; discretion/satisfaction, 351; proponents, 316–317
Niskanen, William, 27–28, 338; citation, 27n, 46n, 79n, 81n; federal revenue study, 63, 63n

374